Vision Into Reality

Art Gallery of Greater Victoria Early Years, 1951–1973

Mary Jo Hughes • Michael Morris • Barry Till

Art Gallery of Greater Victoria

Library and Archives Canada Cataloguing in Publication

Hughes, Mary Jo
Vision into reality : Art Gallery of Greater Victoria early years, 1951-1973 / written by Mary Jo Hughes, Michael Morris, Barry Till ; edited by Joan Padgett.

Includes bibliographical references.
ISBN 978-0-88885-357-8

1. Art Gallery of Greater Victoria—History. 2. Art Gallery of Greater Victoria—Exhibitions. I. Morris, Michael, 1942- II. Till, Barry III. Padgett, Joan IV. Art Gallery of Greater Victoria V. Title.

N910.V52H84 2009 708.11'128 C2009-903001-

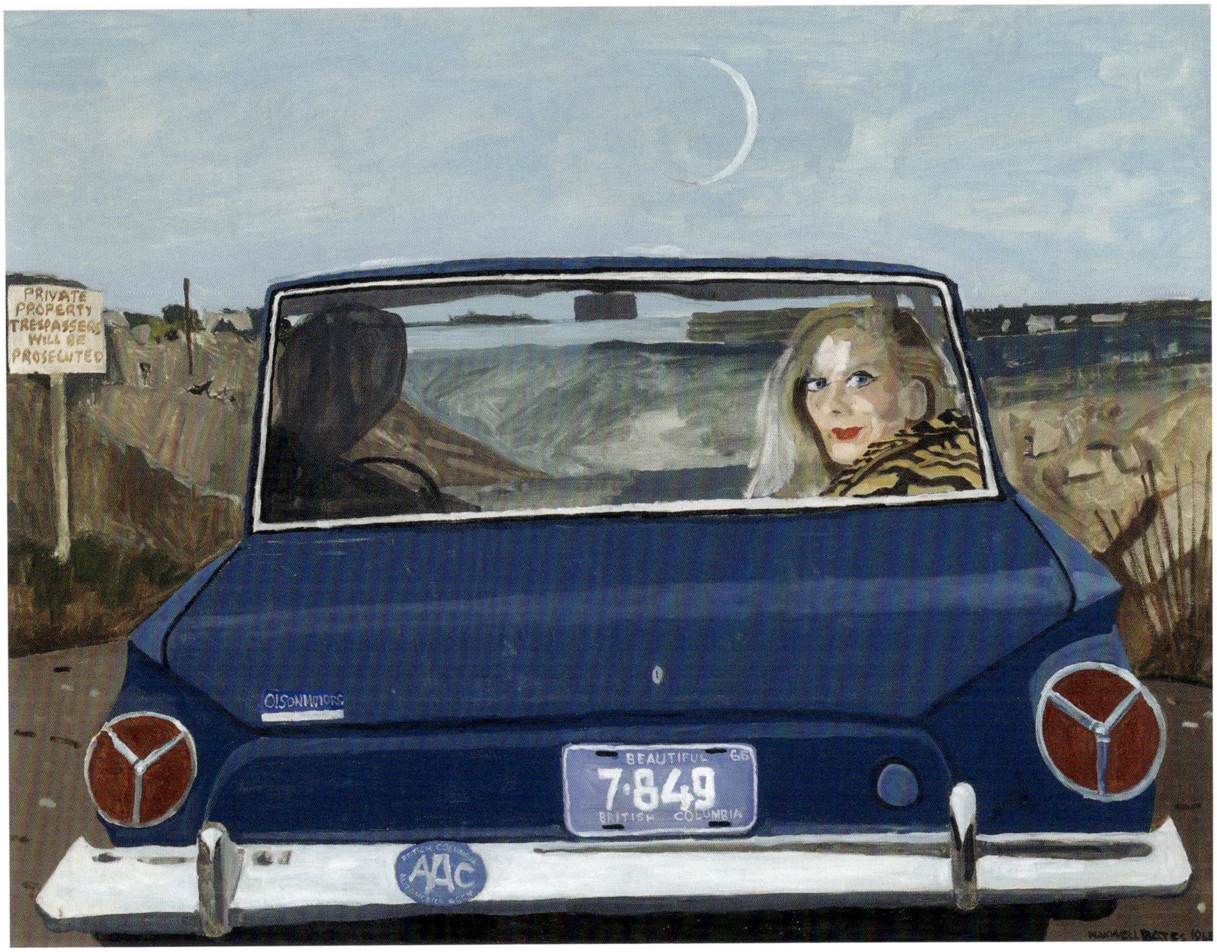

Maxwell Bates 1906-1980, Canadian, *Beautiful* B.C., 1966, oil on canvas

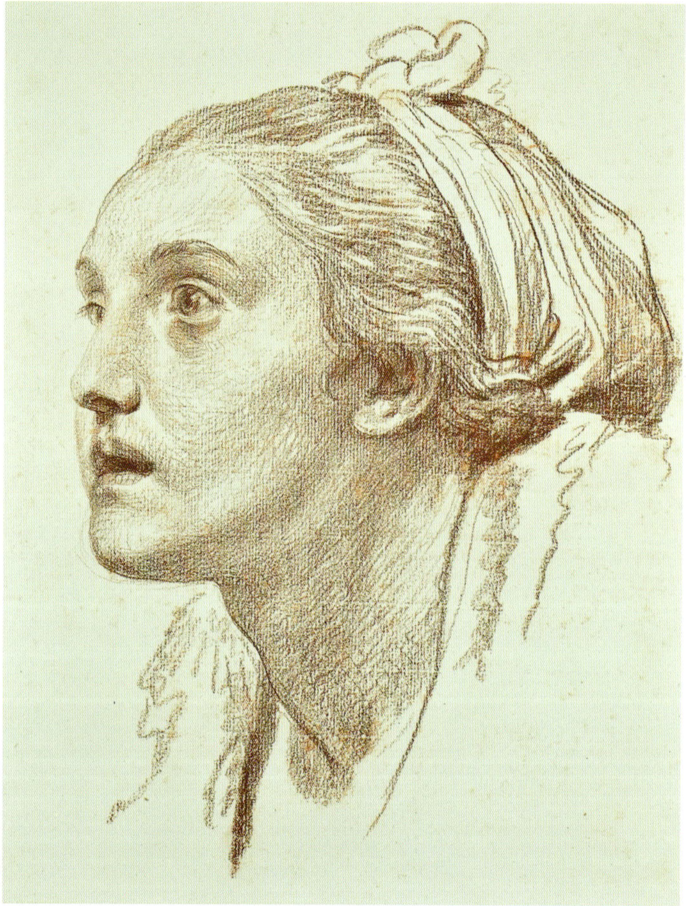

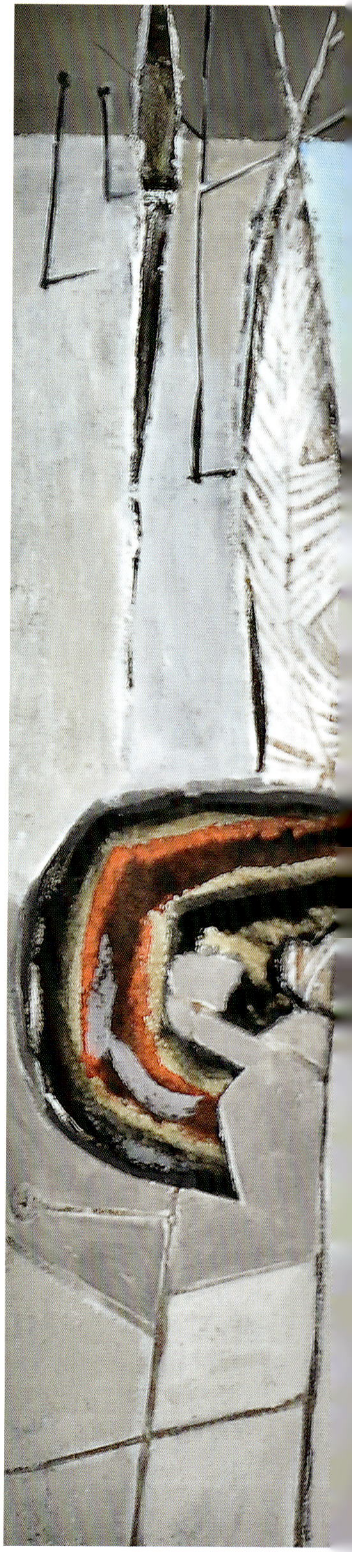

Jean Baptiste Greuze 1725-1805, French, *Head of a Girl*, c.1778, red chalk on laid paper

Jack Shadbolt 1909-1998, Canadian, *Winter Pods*, 1951, watercolour on paper

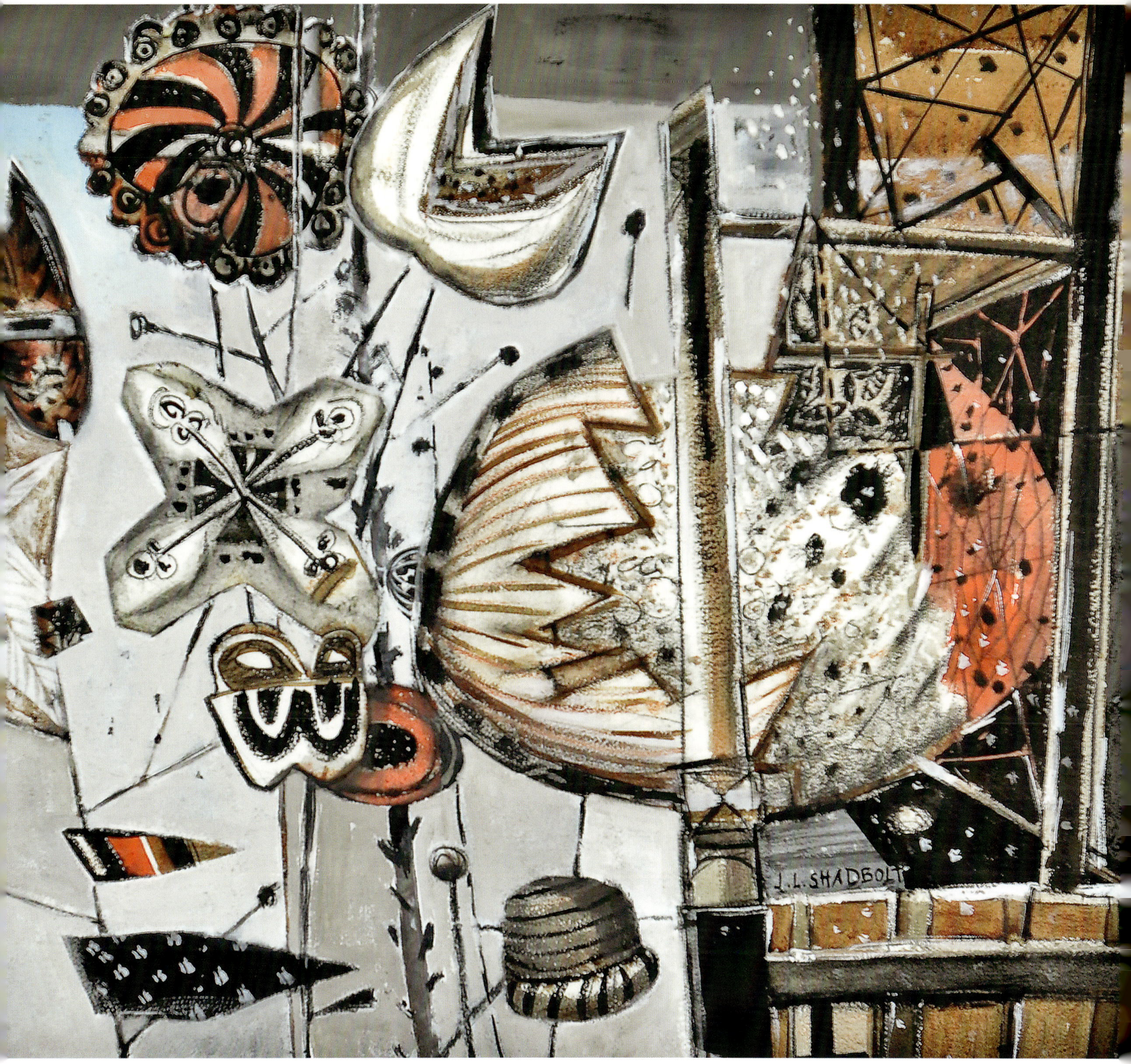
J.L. SHADBOLT

Sponsor's Message

In 1952, the Volunteer Committee of the Art Gallery of Greater Victoria was formed to foster interest in and support the Gallery. The committee has done this mainly through fundraising events, as well as through the development of a number of programmes and by providing dedicated volunteer service. The funds have enabled the Gallery to purchase works of art, sponsor exhibitions, and develop education and public programs. Over the years these events have helped promote public awareness of the important role the Gallery plays in Victoria. The Volunteer Committee continues to raise funds and support programs for the benefit of the Gallery, and in this way contributes to the community through the arts.

In the early 1950s Colin Graham, Founding Director of the Gallery, began acquiring works of art using funds provided by the Volunteer Committee. Since then, more than 700 works of art have been purchased, significantly contributing to the establishment of the core strengths of the permanent collection.

This year we are very proud to be the presenting sponsor for this important series of exhibitions and the publication *Vision into Reality: Art Gallery of Greater Victoria Early Years, 1951–1973*. We believe it is important to honour Colin Graham and all those dedicated supporters including Volunteer Committee members who in the past worked diligently together to establish and grow this fine institution into what it is today.

Jennie Hurley, President
Volunteer Committee
2008–2009

THE VOLUNTEER COMMITTEE
ART GALLERY
OF GREATER VICTORIA

Kitagawa Utamaro 1754–1806, Japanese, *Mother with children*, nd, woodblock print

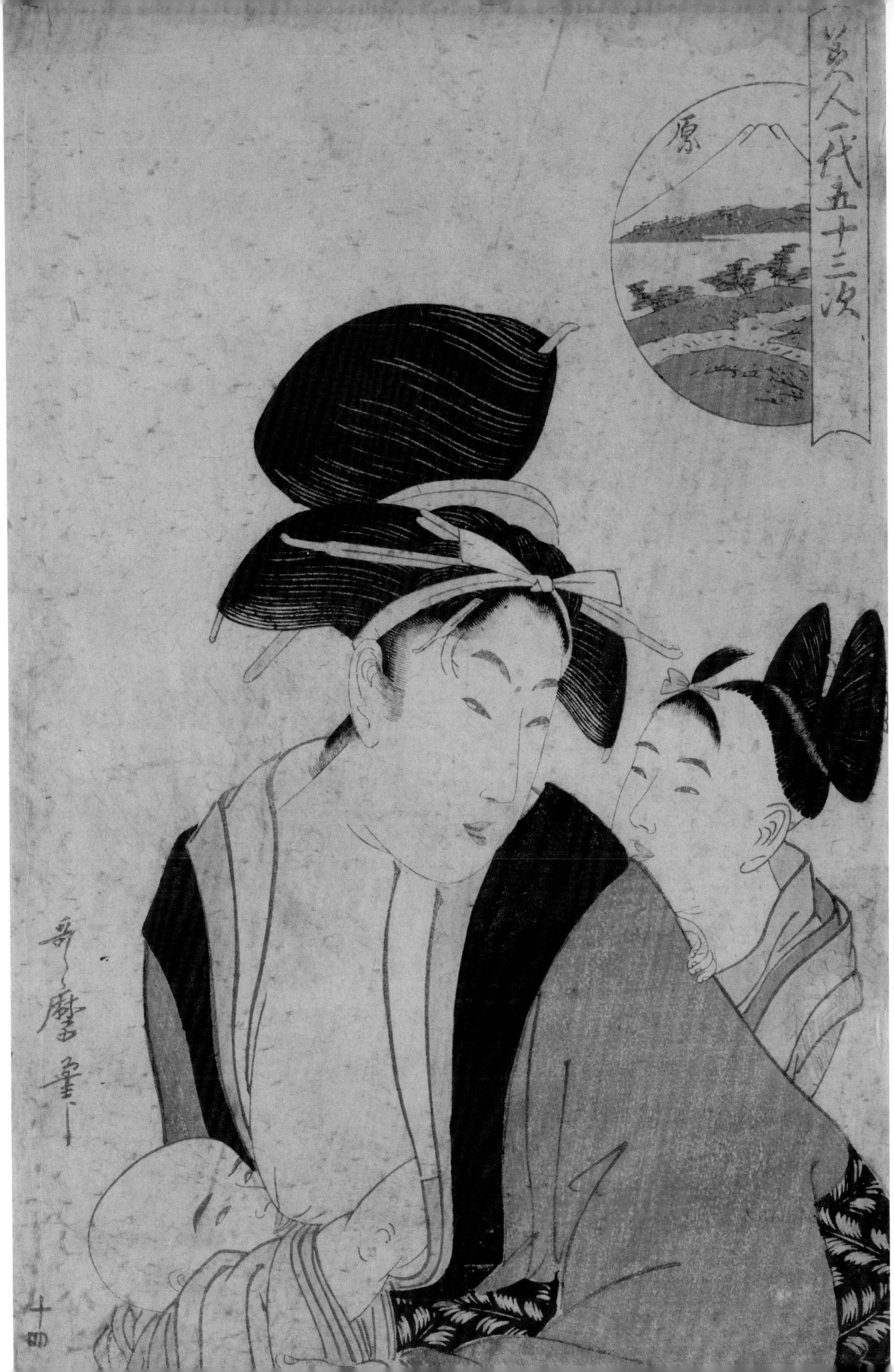

美人一代五十三次
原
哥麿筆
十四

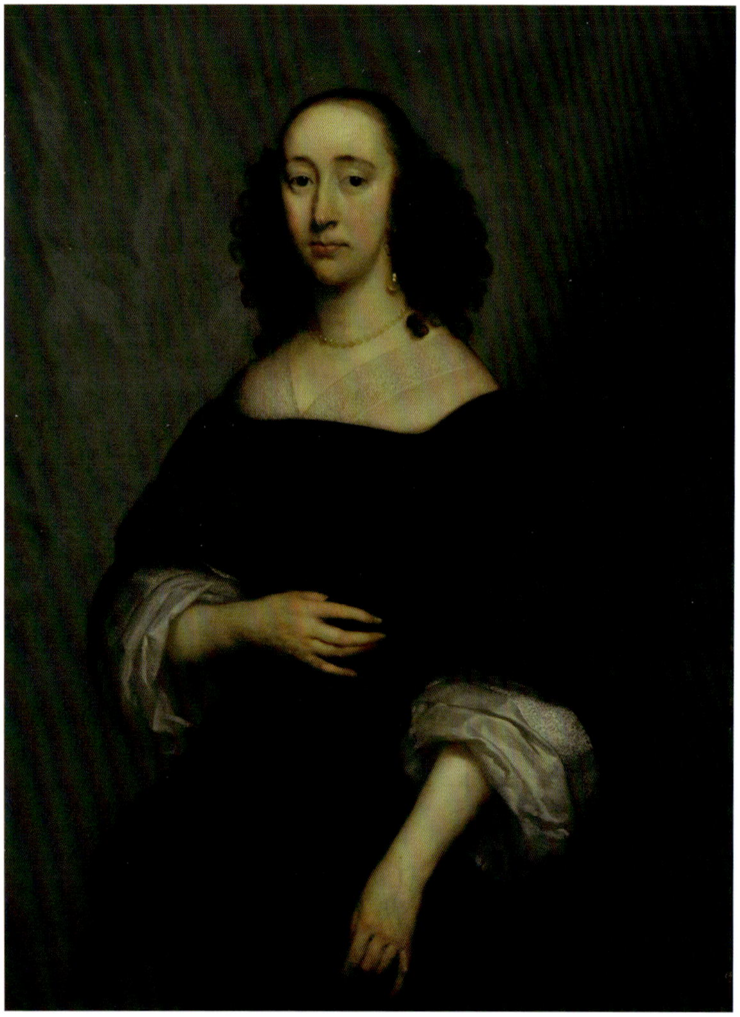

Cornelis Janssens Van Ceulen 1593-1664, Dutch, *Portrait of a Lady in Black*, 1658, oil on canvas

Matthijs Maris 1839-1917, Dutch, *The Flower Arrangement* 1873, oil on canvas

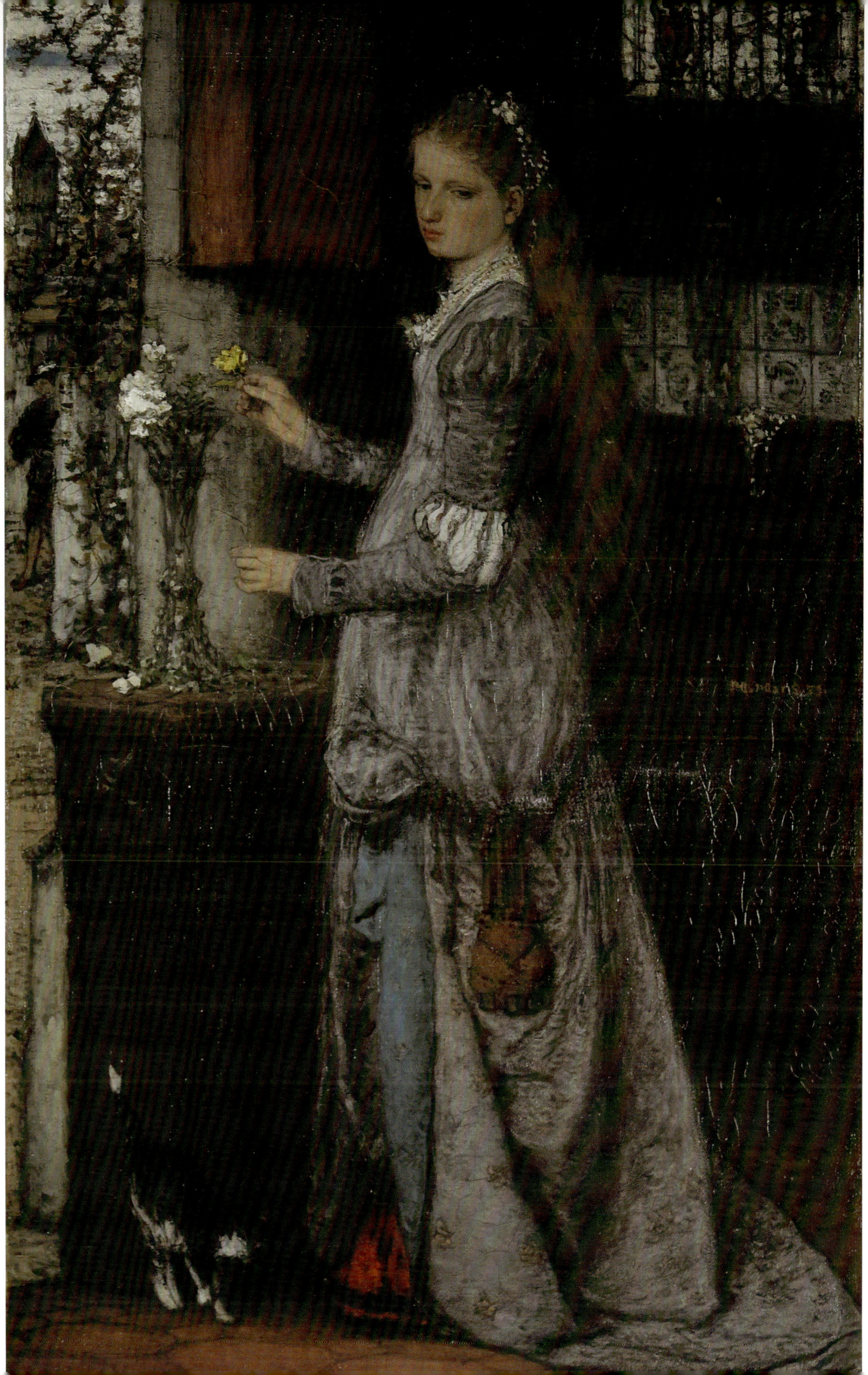

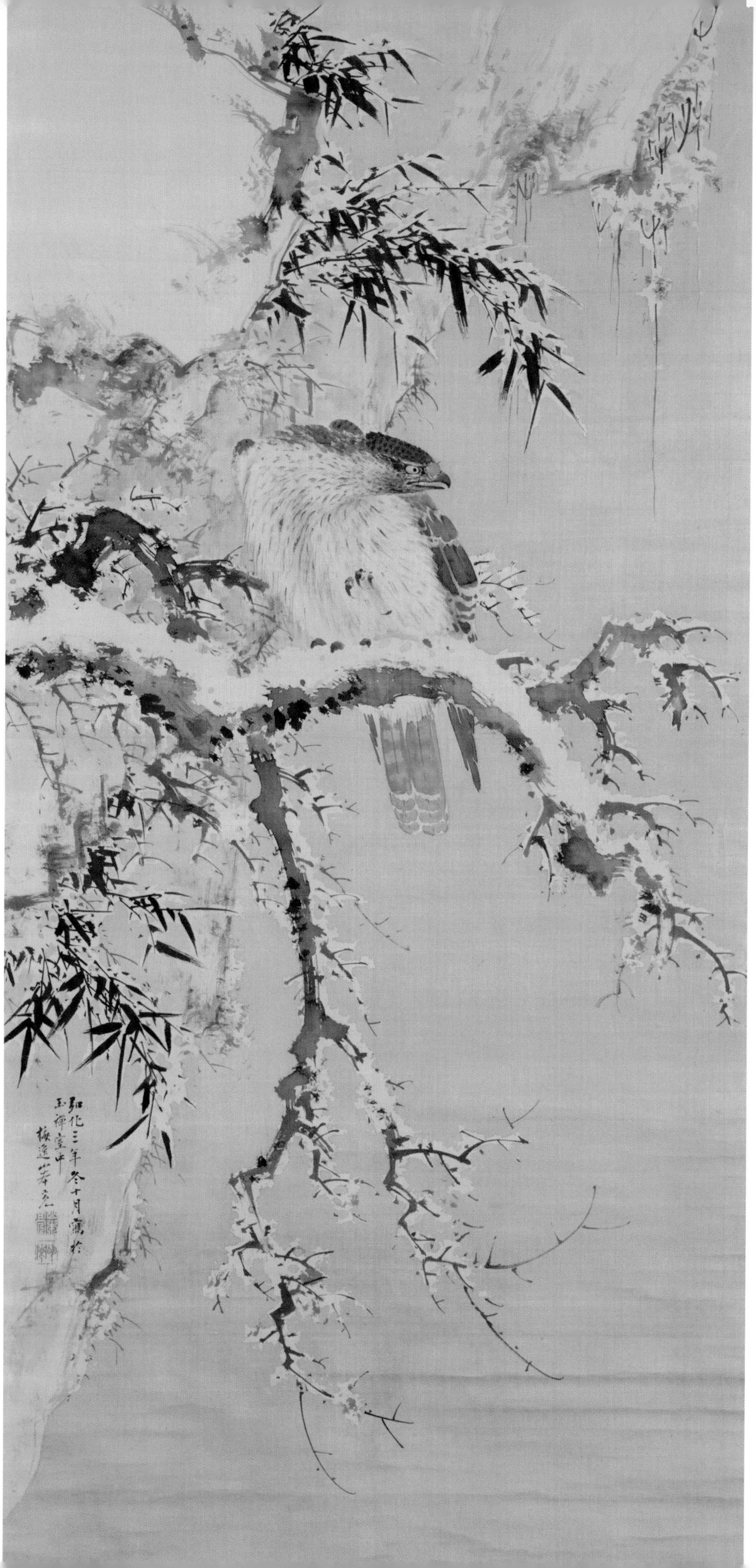
弘化三年冬十月寫於
玉禅室中

contents

Yamamoto Baiitsu 1783-1856, Japanese, *Hawk in Snow*, hanging scroll, ink on silk

Director's Foreword

This publication maps the early history of the Art Gallery of Greater Victoria. In many ways it charts a familiar course, mirroring what has taken place in cities across Canada. It begins with the dream of a few people who wish to see their community engage with the global circulation of art, culture, and ideas. They struggle with a climate that seems to go beyond indifference to outright hostility. Ever so slowly the landscape changes: audiences grow, support is established, and a level of professional sophistication is attained. From the darkness light emerges, and it begins with one or two people who go on to make the community proud of its cultural achievements.

Central to the development of the Gallery in Victoria was Colin Graham who coalesced a group of artists and volunteers that was instrumental in introducing modern art to the city. Graham was the Gallery's first Director, and his commitment to new ideas and new art inspired an entire generation. Providing modernism with a place to grow in a city that seemed to be nostalgically looking at the past must have taken great courage. The material evidence of that courage is apparent in the permanent collection of the Gallery, as it contains significant examples of the global art movements of the past 50 years. The seeds of the Asian collection were sown in those early years, a commitment to distinction and excellence that has made it such a strong component of the Gallery.

Made clear in the essays is the fact that many of the problems and issues the Gallery faced in the early years are still with us. The building, both its location and its physical attributes, was then and still is a hindrance to growth. Finding the appropriate level of resources to keep the Gallery afloat was a struggle in the early years and remains so. But beyond these many problems, the Gallery continues to provide the community with fresh art and new ideas bringing the world to the Island. In doing so it is building on that significant legacy of Colin Graham and his circle.

On behalf of the curators (Mary Jo Hughes, Michael Morris, and Barry Till) I would like to thank the following people for their assistance in various ways with this project: Grant Arnold, Russell Baker, Jordan Beggs, Eric Charman, Ted Clarke, Allan Collier, Brian Dedora, Shushan Egoyan, William Everett Family, John Feigl, Dr. Hans and Ruth Heimlich, Gunter Henrich, Vicky Husband, Michael and Donna Kanovsky, Bob Matheson, Pat Martin Bates, Anne Mayhew, Trevor Moat, Joan Padgett, Frank Reimer, Caroline Riedel, Naomi Sawda, Martin Segger, Paddy Stewart, Terri Sudeyko, Kim Svendsen, Andy Sylvester, Ian Thom, and Scott Watson. For their significant financial support of the project I express gratitude to the Volunteer Committee, a group of dedicated volunteers who, since 1952, have made possible much of what we do. I also sincerely thank all the Gallery staff who brought this project to fruition through their hard work and dedication to the concept of honouring the history of the institution. Furthermore, I acknowledge with gratitude the toil and significant achievements of the AGGV directors who built upon the foundation set by Colin Graham and who have brought us to where we are today: Richard Simmins, Roger Boulet, Patricia Bovey, Pierre Arpin, and Shirley Madill. Above all I wish to express my appreciation to Colin and Sylvia Graham for their contributions to the Gallery, which have inspired us for more than fifty years.

Jon Tupper
Director

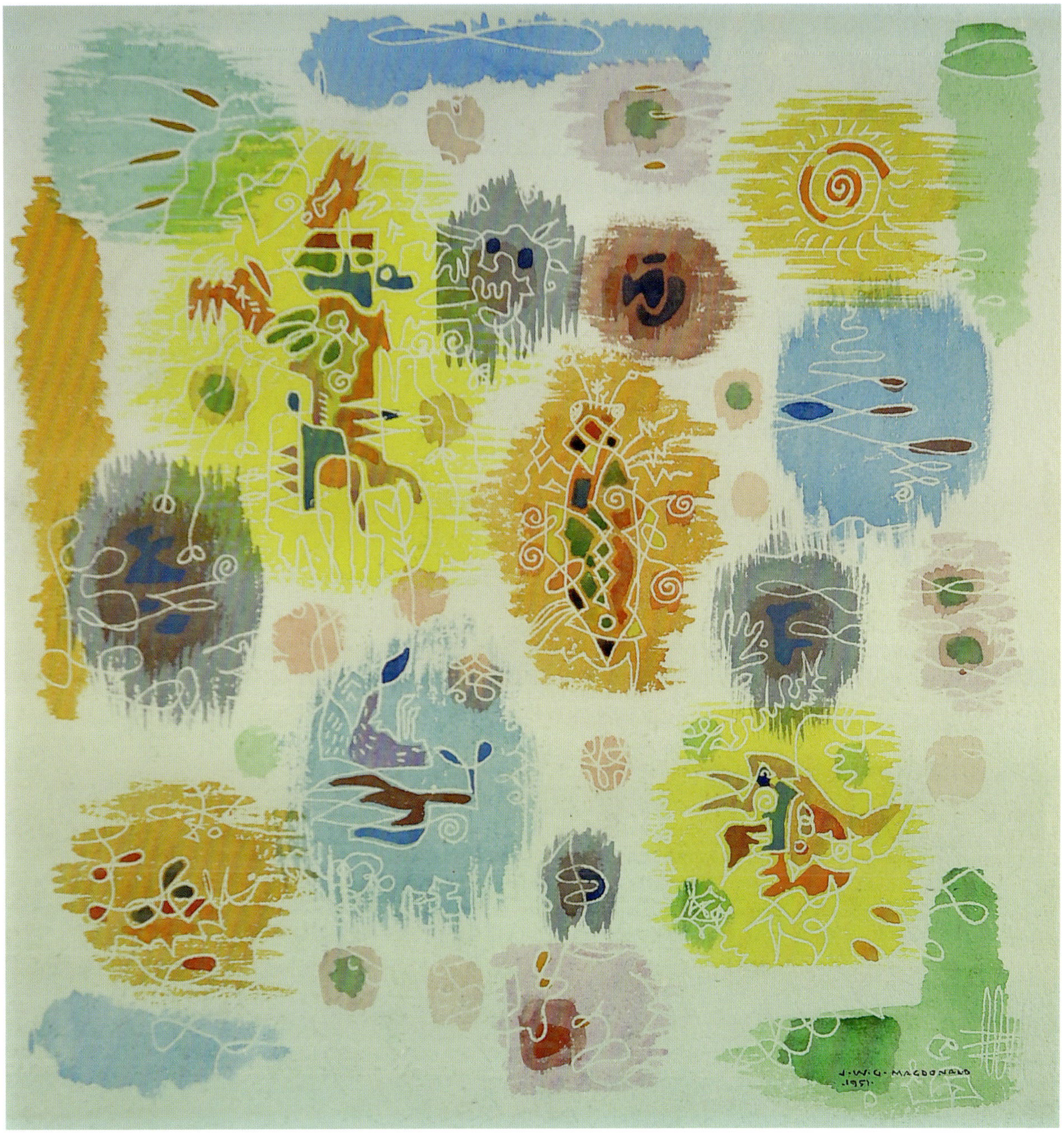

Jock Macdonald 1897-1960, Canadian, *Forms Evolved*, 1951, watercolour, scraffito on wove paper

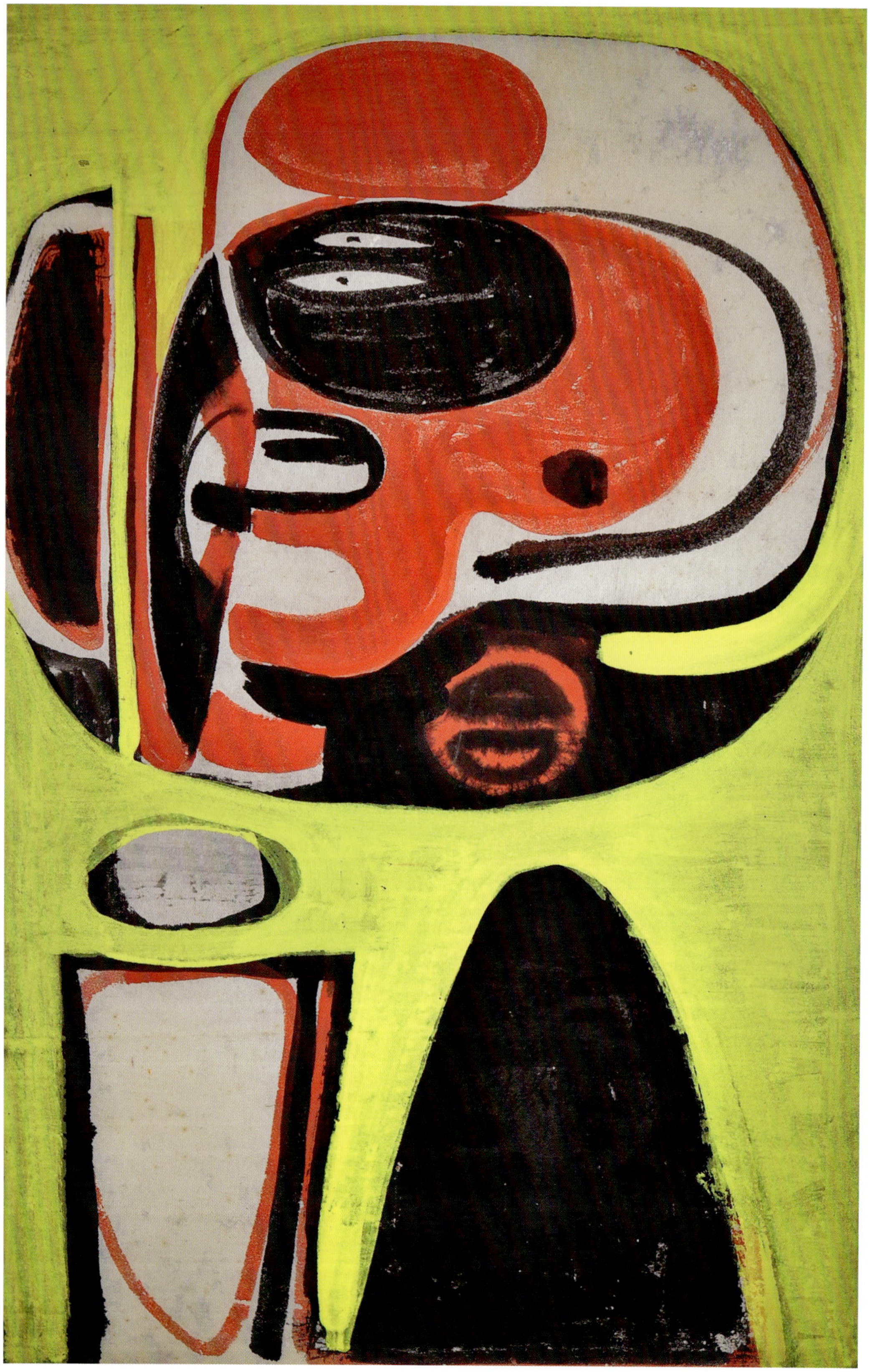

Colin Graham and the Birth of an Art Gallery in Victoria

MARY JO HUGHES

I can think of no individual in Canadian art who has fulfilled more [of] his obligations to artists and audience than Colin Graham. Moreover, he has done so with humility and wisdom, kindness and concern.
– Donald Harvey [1]

Early History of the Gallery

The Art Gallery of Greater Victoria did not spring forth fully formed. Its emergence was slow and, at times, painful, guided by the tireless labour of many dedicated artists, volunteers, and supporters of the arts who wished to see their city shine, not just economically, but culturally as well. The most significant hurdle was that the city did not yet fully appreciate the value of an art gallery to a community. Nonetheless, the Gallery flourished and matured between 1951 and 1973 under the direction of Colin Graham, its first Curator and Director (figure 1). Graham enthusiastically took the reigns and established a vision for an art gallery worthy of British Columbia's capital city, playing a critical role in exposing Victoria's citizens to modern art. His vision centered on establishing a place where people could come to experience, learn about, and celebrate art from all regions of the world and from all periods, with a special focus on the work of contemporary artists from their own community—a community that was slowly awakening to, and developing an appreciation for, the ideas and ideals of the modern period.

Indeed, as a capital city, Victoria was slow to establish its own cultural presence in the form of a gallery. Manitoba's Winnipeg Art Gallery opened in 1912; the Edmonton Art Gallery was established in 1926. Of the western provinces, only Saskatchewan was slower in gaining a capital city art gallery, founding the Norman MacKenzie Art Gallery in Regina in 1953. The idea of establishing an art gallery in Victoria had been desirable for decades. As early as 1887, visiting artists Charles and Georgina De L'Aubinière appealed to the local government to establish an art gallery and art school to encourage the growth of culture in what was then a frontier city. The problem was getting the municipality

Margaret Peterson
1902-1997, Canadian,
The splitting of Tiamat, nd,
watercolour, tempera
on Japanese paper

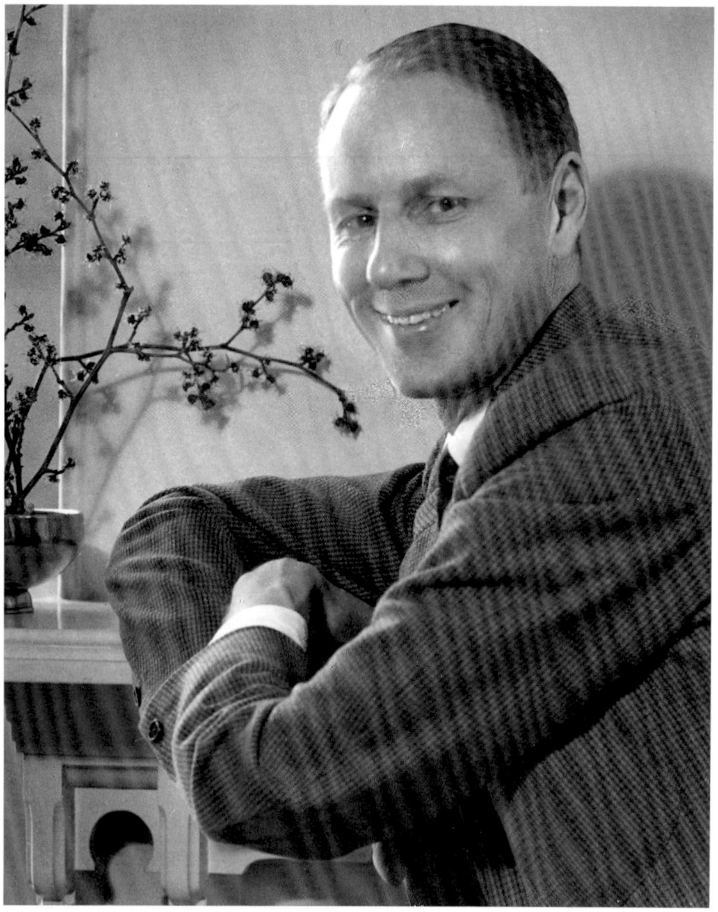

1. Colin Graham, c. 1953.
Photo: Ken McAllister.

and local residents to recognize the important role art plays in developing a vital community. For many years, Victoria's exposure to art remained relegated to picture exhibitions that were part of agricultural fairs, temporary exhibits around town, and, beginning in 1909, the Island Arts and Crafts Society, which held annual exhibitions of its members' works.

In 1938 a serious attempt to found a public gallery was presented to the city by prominent artist and citizen Katharine Maltwood, who proposed that she and her husband, John Maltwood, give their impressive art collection to the city and build a small hall downtown to house it if the city would pay the operating budget. Reluctant to assume any fiscal responsibility linked to this project, the city ignored their repeated offers, forcing the Maltwoods instead to donate their collection and lend their financial support elsewhere. Decades later, their initiative found a home as the Maltwood Museum and Art Gallery at the University of Victoria.[2]

A few years before the Maltwood offer, another significant proposal was turned down by the city—a proposal that, if it had been supported and allowed to grow, could have prevented the loss of the Emily Carr collection from Victoria to Vancouver. In 1932 Emily Carr presented her vision of what a civic art gallery should be by offering her own house as a public gallery. Now recognized as one of

Canada's most significant artists of the twentieth century, Victoria's own Emily Carr was consistently frustrated with the city's lack of sustained interest in art. Years earlier she had bemoaned the reaction of the community to her art following her return to Victoria in 1911 after studying modern art movements in France, calling the city "an impossible field for my work."[3] The only venue available to show her work was the Island Arts and Crafts Society exhibitions, which she found far too conservative and exclusive.[4] Carr's vision was to establish a People's Gallery, a place open to "all classes, all nationalities, all colours," with displays changing regularly. Carr went so far as to renovate her boarding house to allow two empty flats to serve as four exhibition rooms, one space dedicated to her painting—which was by far the most progressively modern work available in Victoria at that time—and the remaining spaces to the art of other painters. In December 1932 she installed the first exhibition and opened her home for people to hear her speak about her idea.[5] The initial reactions of all who attended were enthusiastic; however, despite her appeals to the mayor, councillors, prominent citizens, and the lieutenant-governor, she was unable to establish enough interest to secure the financial support necessary to keep her venture running.[6] The People's Gallery idea faded away, and Carr reconverted the galleries to their original use: rental suites.

This experience served only to further entrench in Carr the belief that her native city was backward in its approach to culture and modernity.[7] In the last years of her life when she was planning her estate, she again regretted the fact that there was no gallery in her home town:

> Did you know I presented 80 canvases to the Nation, that is to British Columbia, ...45 will be kept for a permanent collection, housed in Vancouver... It is called the Emily Carr Trust and should have come to Victoria only Victoria is too hopeless. She could never have bothered to arrange or house, all her top men are ossified.[8]

This is why, in the end, her executors Lawren Harris and Ira Dilworth arranged for the best of Carr's work to be given in trust to the Vancouver Art Gallery, founded in 1931. It is the cruelest of ironies that if only the People's Gallery or the Maltwood proposal had established the roots for a civic art gallery, the bulk of Carr's work likely would have remained in Victoria rather than in Vancouver.[9]

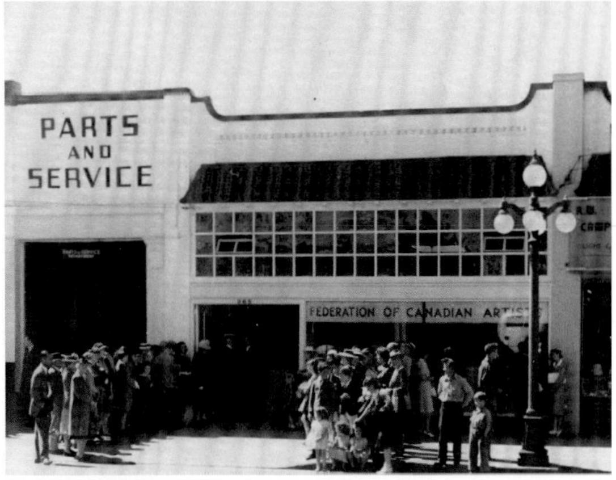

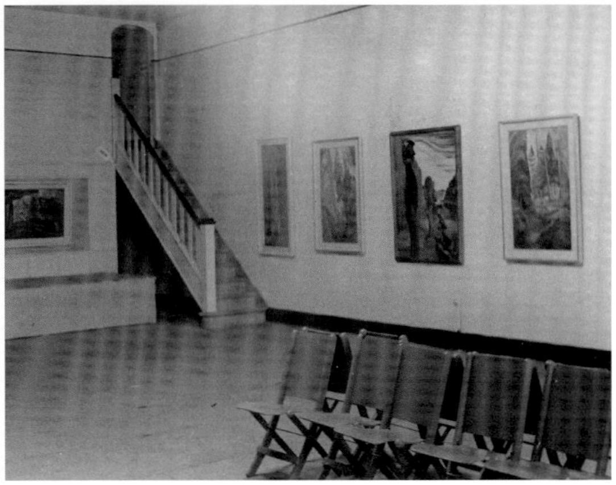

2. Opening of The Little Centre on Yates Street, Victoria, 1945. Photo: Ken McAllister.

3. Emily Carr exhibition at The Little Centre June 1946. Unknown photographer.

While Victoria was not ready to embrace a civic art gallery when Emily Carr was alive, the spirit with which she longed for one did not die; in fact, Carr's passion was the core motivation for the group that eventually founded The Little Centre which eventually would be renamed the Art Gallery of Greater Victoria (for the purposes of this essay I will refer to it as the Gallery).[10] Many in this group who championed the cause for a gallery in the 1940s, such as artist Ina Uhthoff, had known Carr and shared not only her desire to see a place where art would have a permanent home in the city, but also her aim for a gallery to be a place where people would see new art, art that reflected their era. At its very core, the founding group believed the gallery's mission was to educate the people of Victoria about modernism, allowing the city to take part in the living culture of its time rather than merely revering its past. This indeed became a central aim of the Gallery, particularly under the leadership of Colin Graham.

Before Colin Graham was hired, the active movement for a gallery had been in the works for about seven years. Mark Kearley, the son of a viscount, who had been living in Switzerland, arrived in Victoria in 1944 and was shocked that such a fine city lacked a cultural centre. He took it upon himself to form a committee of passionate volunteers to discuss how to establish a gallery.[11] They started by joining the Federation of Canadian Artists,[12] a national organization through which they could secure travelling exhibitions. In 1946 they opened up The Little Center in temporary quarters on Yates Street in an automobile dealership (figure 2). With Mark Kearley as their first Board President, this group's vision was not just to show visual art in a vacuum, but rather in the context of all arts including music and theatre. It is not insignificant that their first exhibition in 1946 featured the work of Emily Carr (figure 3).

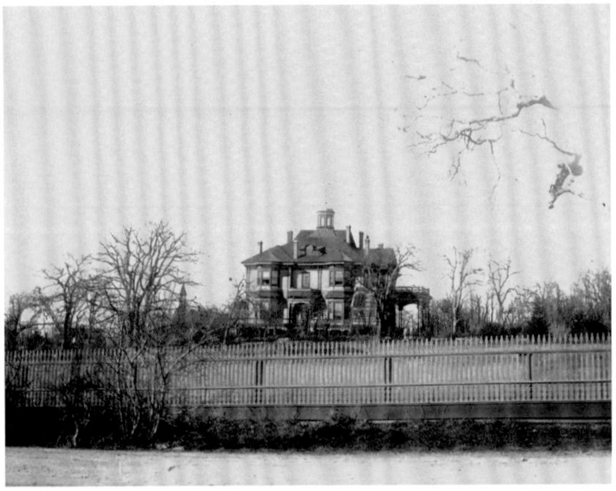

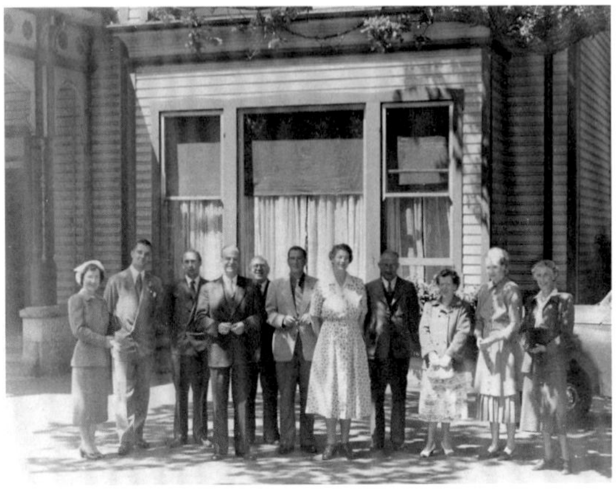

By 1947, however, auto sales were increasing, and the Gallery was nudged out of the dealership and was homeless until 1949 when it moved to a rented shop at 832 Broughton Street. The enthusiasm of the volunteers running the place was vital; during those two years on Broughton, the Gallery managed to hold numerous exhibitions on various themes featuring the works of local, national, and international artists, as well as musical events, lectures, and films. Colin Graham believes that the true impetus for this movement toward founding a gallery rests with "[Mark] Kearley's European experience and artist Ina Uhthoff's open-minded acceptance of anything new and vital."[13]

However, without a professional staff[14] and no permanent space, the Gallery struggled to make a significant cultural impact; it was not practical to engage in serious collection building, and opportunities to receive significant travelling exhibitions were limited by the lack of space. Kearley returned to Switzerland after two years of tireless work, and it was left to the rest of the group to lead the cause. What was essential throughout this time, and even during the two-year hiatus when the Gallery did not have a physical presence, was that there were determined supporters who publicly called for the city to establish a civic gallery.[15] A breakthrough occurred when they were offered a permanent home on Moss Street. Finally, the possibility of establishing roots for the institution to grow to a level more suitable to British Columbia's capital city was becoming more tangible.

4. Future home of the Art Gallery of Greater Victoria. "Gyppeswyck" the residence of Alexander Green at Moss Street as seen from Belcher Avenue which would later be renamed Rockland Avenue, n.d. Image #85738 courtesy of Royal BC Museum, BC Archives.

5. Board of Directors of the Arts Centre of Greater Victoria, Late summer 1951. Left to Right: Unknown, Ronald Grand, John Wade, Major Cuthbert Holmes, Walter Jeune, Commander, D. F. Fairfull, Hildegard Wyllie (President), unknown, Gwen Scott, Sara Spencer, Ina Uhthoff. Unknown photographer.

In 1951, one of the Gallery's strongest supporters and Board members, Sara Spencer, offered her home to the city for an art gallery.[16] Designed by W. Ridgeway Wilson, the Moss Street mansion was built in 1889 for Alexander A. Green, a Victoria banker. This lovely late Queen Anne-style house was named *Gyppeswyck* (figure 4) and stayed in the Green family until 1899, after which it served as temporary residence for the lieutenant-governor when Government House burned down later that year. In 1903 David Spencer, a Welsh immigrant and entrepreneur who founded Victoria's first department store, purchased the house for his family of thirteen children. By the 1930s only the unmarried Spencer daughters, Sara and Mary, lived in the home. When Mary died in early 1951, Sara decided she no longer needed a mansion, and she offered it as a home for an art gallery and made plans to move to a smaller residence in Cadboro Bay. With this firm proposal in hand, the dream of a permanent civic art gallery was so palpable that the Board continued with plans to make the mansion a gallery despite the lack of any financial commitment from the city (figure 5).[17]

The mansion, however, was not ideal as an art gallery and everyone knew it.[18] While it had large, well-proportioned rooms with high ceilings that were somewhat serviceable as exhibition

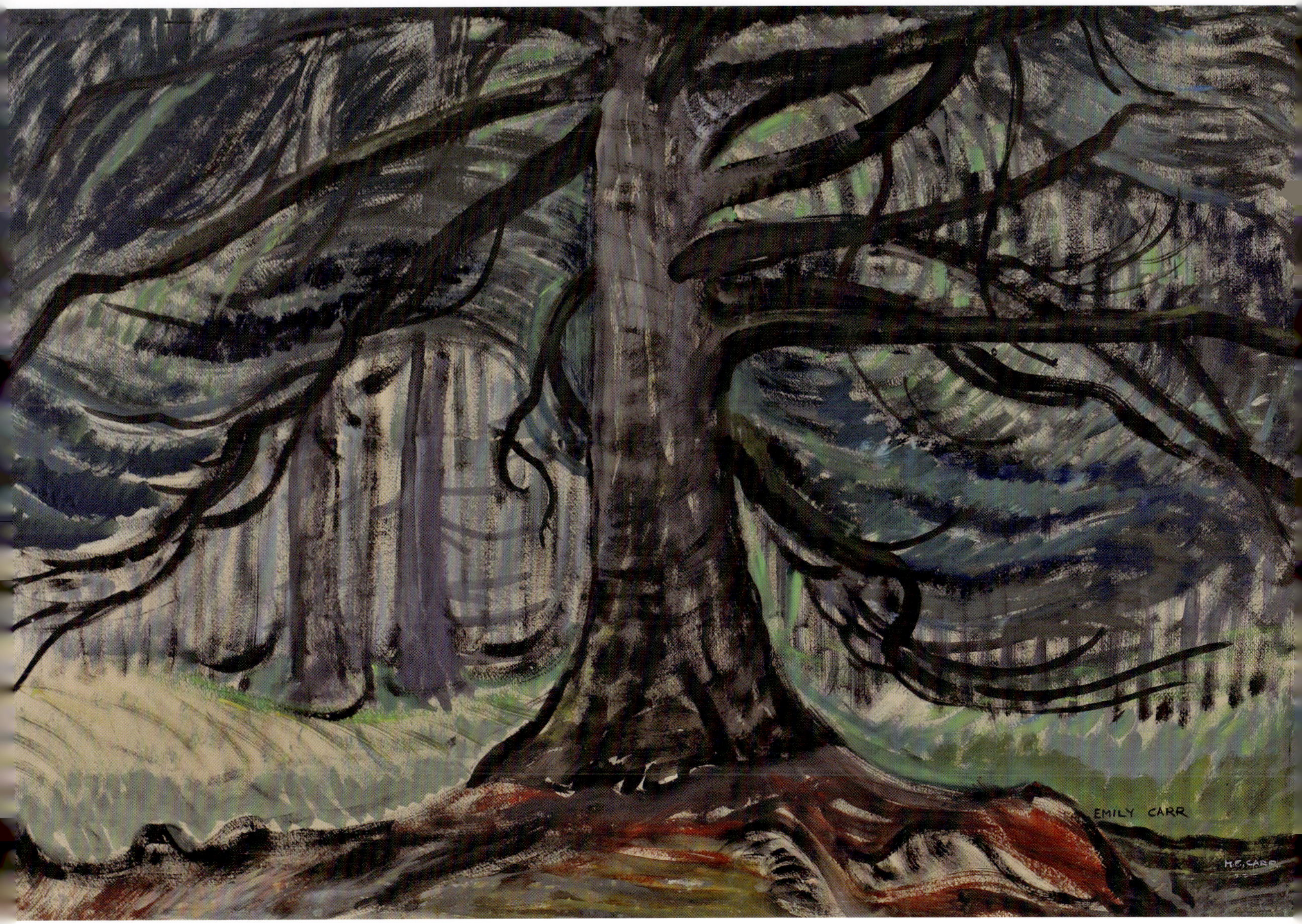

Emily Carr 1871-1945, Canadian, *Dancing Tree*, c.1938, oil on paper spaces, it was seen as an embryo from which a new vision would be built on its large property. Board President Hildegard Wyllie was interviewed by the *Victoria Daily Times* when the gift of the house was announced:

> Miss Spencer's offer is an important milestone in the permanent and continuous growth of the cultural life of the city. Our hope is the citizens will participate actively in the expansion which lies ahead and help us make this project worthy of the capital city of B.C.[19]

Former Board President Harry Hickman also commented: "This splendid gesture indicates that Victorians are ready to take their places with other leading cultural centres in development of the arts."[20] Their next step was to secure a professional curator to run it.

Hiring Colin Graham

With the physical location secured, the Board now had enough leverage to begin wooing their desired candidate, Colin Graham. Graham, a Canadian originally from Vancouver, was thirty-six, married to Sylvia Graham, and working as the Head of Education at the Legion of Honor, San Francisco's civic art museum. He held a BA from Cambridge University and an MA from Berkeley. He had experience lecturing at the California College of Arts and Crafts in Oakland, and had taught courses in art education at the California School of Fine Arts where Emily Carr had once studied. In San Francisco he regularly saw the works of foremost American modernists such as Mark Tobey, Arshile Gorky, Jackson Pollack, and Robert Motherwell, among others.[21] He was, however, extremely eager to return to Canada since his parents were living in Victoria. He had written to Ina Uhthoff in spring 1951 to see if she was aware of any teaching positions available in the city. Uhthoff, who was the Convener of the Exhibition Committee for the Gallery, wrote a letter in reply on June 22, 1951, informing Graham that there were no teaching positions. Instead, she encouraged him to apply for the position of curator at the new gallery:

> The Curator's job would be quite varied. He would be in control of the Gallery as far as Exhibitions, Lectures etc. … We want someone who is trusted enough to build up the Gallery & make it a really live concern. There is a beautiful suite of rooms available on the ground floor with its own bathroom. This would go with the job!
>
> Of course the house is not by any means ideal for a picture Gallery, no house is, but if we could accept its limitation and make the art activities as important as the exhibitions we could make a start. Later on we would hope to build a fireproof gallery on to the present building….So much depends upon whether we have a good Curator or not.[22]

Graham had absolutely no curatorial training and disclosed that he did not know the workings of a gallery. His position in San Francisco had been primarily as lecturer. Because of this he answered her frankly:

> There are many things about the possible curatorship that I find stimulating and exciting. For lone (sic) thing I've long had an urge to contribute what such as I could to raising the

quality esthetic feeling in B.C., and there certainly could be no more challenging ground than in Victoria.

> ...while I am capable of organising things, I know myself well enough to know that I am fundamentally a lecturer and a teacher of painting. Administration does not come easily to me, or particularly congenially.[23]

He further explained that he wanted to be free to accept a teaching job if one came up:

> If they do not mind having someone willing to put in a year or so of work getting the thing going, well and good. But if they want someone who would be permanent and anxious to make a career of the thing, I would like to give them a chance to decline my services.[24]

By August of 1951 Graham had started to find the idea more appealing and wrote again to Uhthoff about how he would like to see the Gallery become a vital place with an imaginative educational focus to "...make the museum less a staid repository of art objects and more a vital participating element in community life. It would be interesting to see if we could make the Gallery something of a leader among Canadian museums in this respect."[25] In September he accepted the position, which came with the remuneration of $200 per month, plus the suite in the mansion.[26]

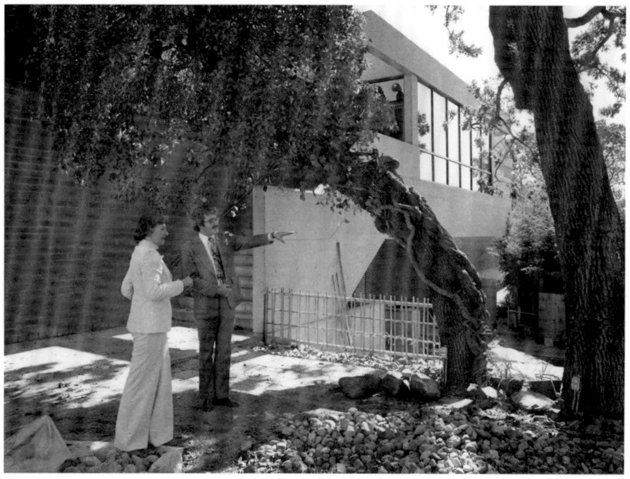

The honesty that Colin Graham revealed in this initial correspondence demonstrated he was a man of integrity, a quality that drew people to him throughout his career. At that moment this quality won over the board of the Gallery. Somewhere along the way he changed his mind about making "a career of the thing." Instead of a year or two, he was Curator (a title he preferred) and then Director from 1951 until 1973, after which he was named Director Emeritus in which capacity he volunteered his services for many more years. Furthermore, his wife Sylvia Graham (figure 6) worked tirelessly as a volunteer throughout Colin's tenure and beyond.[27]

6. Sylvia Graham with Gallery Director Roger Boulet in the Japanese Garden, c. 1979. Unknown photographer.

It is clear from his words to Uhthoff that even before he arrived in Victoria, Graham was under no misconception that the biggest challenge ahead of him was developing a sympathetic climate for the arts in Victoria. There was very little art available to the public, very little enthusiasm amongst city officials for it, and even less interest in new forms of art related to modernism. One of the Board members, Ken McAllister, wrote to Graham in September before he arrived on site: "Victoria is a virgin field for an Arts Centre. It does not vary seriously from any other Canadian City except that there are not very many people who have learned to appreciate the new forms of the arts."[28] Graham and the Board understood that they had to cultivate public support in order to win over the city and secure the government funding necessary for the Gallery to flourish and grow. They recognized their best strategy was to concentrate on the essential value in educating the public on all forms of art, so that Victoria's art gallery would be current, welcoming, and vital. Graham knew that if the Gallery only presented traditional art that appealed to the vocal few, the audience would not grow and it would not rank highly along with other galleries in Canada as a leader championing and exhibiting art of its time.

To this end, the Gallery opened in the Spencer mansion on November 20, 1951, with the exhibition *Québec Painters*, which included numerous modern artists such as Jean-Paul Riopelle, Jean-Paul Mousseau, and Paul-Emile Borduas. Graham referred to this exhibition, which was on the books before his arrival, as a real shocker that elicited many letters to the editor.[29] It was, however, paired with a more traditional exhibition entitled *Old Masters* to soften the blow and please the vast majority of people with the financial means to support the fledgling gallery and who were certainly much more comfortable with traditional art. Graham would continue to formulate exhibition programming that met the dual needs of making its supporters feel comfortable while at the same time challenging them and bringing them slowly forward toward acceptance of less familiar, more contemporary art. His approach was all about balance and education.

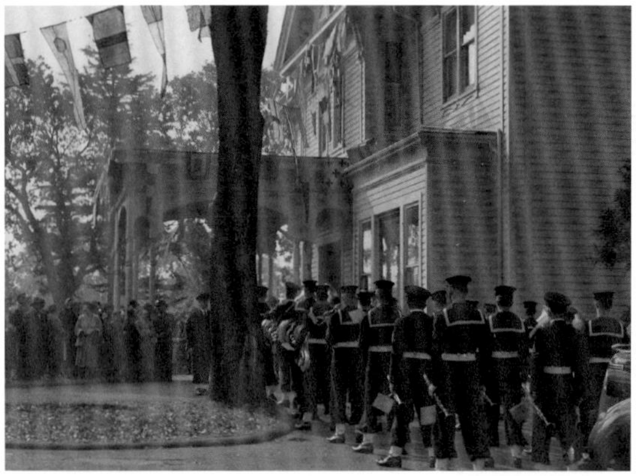

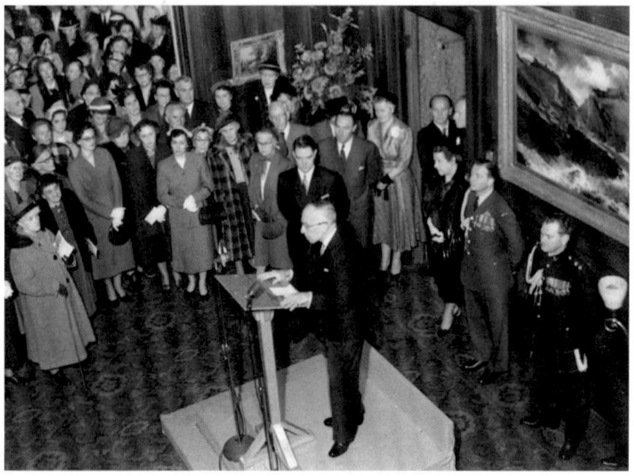

7. Official opening ceremonies at the Art Centre of Greater Victoria, October 15, 1952. Photo: Ken McAllister.

8. Official opening ceremonies with Governor-General Vincent Massey addressing the crowd inside the mansion. Photo: Ken McAllister.

When the Gallery opened on Moss Street (figures 7 and 8),[30] Victoria was struggling to emerge fully as a community with a modern cultural sensibility. It had long held the dubious distinction of being "more English than the English."[31] Many of its most prominent and outspoken citizens were of British ancestry and had for decades preferred to see Victoria stay nostalgically frozen in time. However, in the post-war boom, the city grew exponentially with people arriving from various parts of Canada and abroad. As in Vancouver, new ideas about architecture and design, as well as an optimistic outlook borne out of the period's economic prosperity began ever so slowly to permeate Victoria's collective consciousness. Colin Graham, fresh from San Francisco where he had studied with modernist artists such as Clyfford Still and Mark Rothko, was enthusiastic about the new era and the various opportunities to invigorate the cultural life of the community in Victoria. Having arrived from another West Coast city, Graham brought with him the concept that the Canadian West Coast was part of the Pacific Rim. Graham believed that although Victoria had long been considered by many as merely a British colonial outpost, its citizens were ready to embrace this broader concept. The Gallery, in its infancy, seemed like a blank slate upon which Graham could introduce both a modern and a pan-Pacific mandate. But first Graham had to break through the cultural situation in Victoria which he, like Emily Carr, found to be fixated on a definition of art that excluded all but the most conservative artists, preferably those belonging to the Royal Academy. Recently Graham remarked on how this attitude prevailed over the first few years of his tenure, though it did not deter him:

> I was impressed but oddly enough not dismayed by the number of people who came up to me at various functions and said in effect, "You don't know Victoria, – this won't last."[32]

A Beehive of Activity: Building the Exhibition and Education Programs

Graham's reaction was to put together his own strategy to gently educate and expose the community to the vital modern art of the day. He was an educator and sought to reach people through art education. One of his first plans was a lecture series on modern art that he was sure would illuminate the value of new artistic movements and bring more people into the Gallery. Arrangements were made to conduct these lectures as part of the night courses offered by the provincial government. Although the course was advertised widely, not one person showed up on the first night.[33] It was then that Graham realized that he had a lot more work to do than he had ever considered. Not only was there no modern art being shown in Victoria and no knowledge of it, there was also no desire to learn about it.

In response, Graham took a step back and considered how he could first gain the trust and interest of the public through the Gallery's exhibitions and related education programs, while also introducing these new ideas. He offered tours of the exhibitions every Friday afternoon to satisfy his desire to teach and to initiate his strategic community education program. He kept this up until 1959 when the docent program was established, with volunteers providing tours to adults and school children.[34]

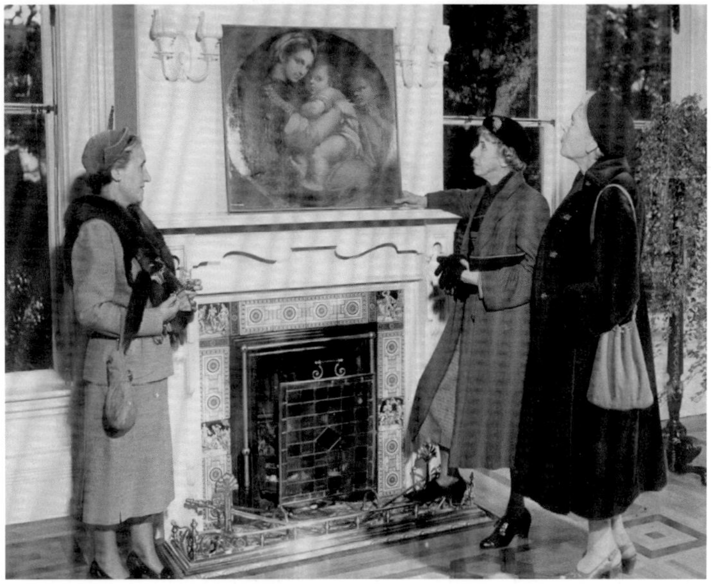

9. Volunteers admiring a reproduction in the Spencer Gallery in the mansion, c. 1950s. Photo: Ken McAllister.

In an era when travel was not as accessible as today, most citizens never left Vancouver Island. Graham therefore felt it was the Gallery's responsibility to provide this cultural experience. He developed a fast-paced exhibition schedule that changed every two weeks to expose people to the widest variety of art possible and encourage return visits. For example, in 1957 there were a total of 54 exhibitions over the course of the year. Graham's vision was to cover the entire visual arts spectrum, exposing Victoria's citizens to various world cultures. Exhibitions were brought in from the permanent collections of the Vancouver Art Gallery and the National Gallery of Canada. Graham also tapped into the Western Canadian Art Circuit, a group of galleries that shared exhibitions, as well as an equivalent organization which circulated exhibitions from the west coast of the United States. Access to art by living Canadian artists was sourced through exhibitions organized by artist societies, such as the Canadian Group of Painters and the Royal Canadian Academy.

Because of the sheer number of exhibitions held, they varied in quality; some included only reproductions of masterworks, such as the 1954 exhibition *Leonardo Da Vinci Drawings: 100 Facsimile Reproductions*. While such an exhibition would not be received well today, at the time it was completely acceptable since it was so difficult to transport original artwork over the Rockies.[35] Further, since people had little exposure to masterworks they welcomed the opportunity to see and learn from high quality framed reproductions (figure 9). There were exhibitions of prints, drawings, paintings, photographs, and crafts. One exhibition in 1952, entitled *Fakes*, presented an array of forgeries.[36] Another interesting one was *Framing, Right and Wrong* in 1961 which instructed people on how to effectively frame their own artwork. Each year there were also exhibitions of architectural, industrial, and theatre design because Graham felt it was important not to limit the range of visual experience that he was offering to his audience. Each exhibition broadened the visual vocabulary he was teaching to the community as a whole.

In addition to borrowed exhibitions, Graham curated several monumental projects. His most ambitious project in the international realm was *3,000 Years of Chinese Art* in 1963. In curating this huge and impressive undertaking, Graham secured loans from the collections of the Royal Ontario Museum, the Cleveland Art Museum, and the Seattle Art Museum, among others. For an earlier project, *From the Age of Elegance* in 1961, Graham brought in eighteenth century master works for

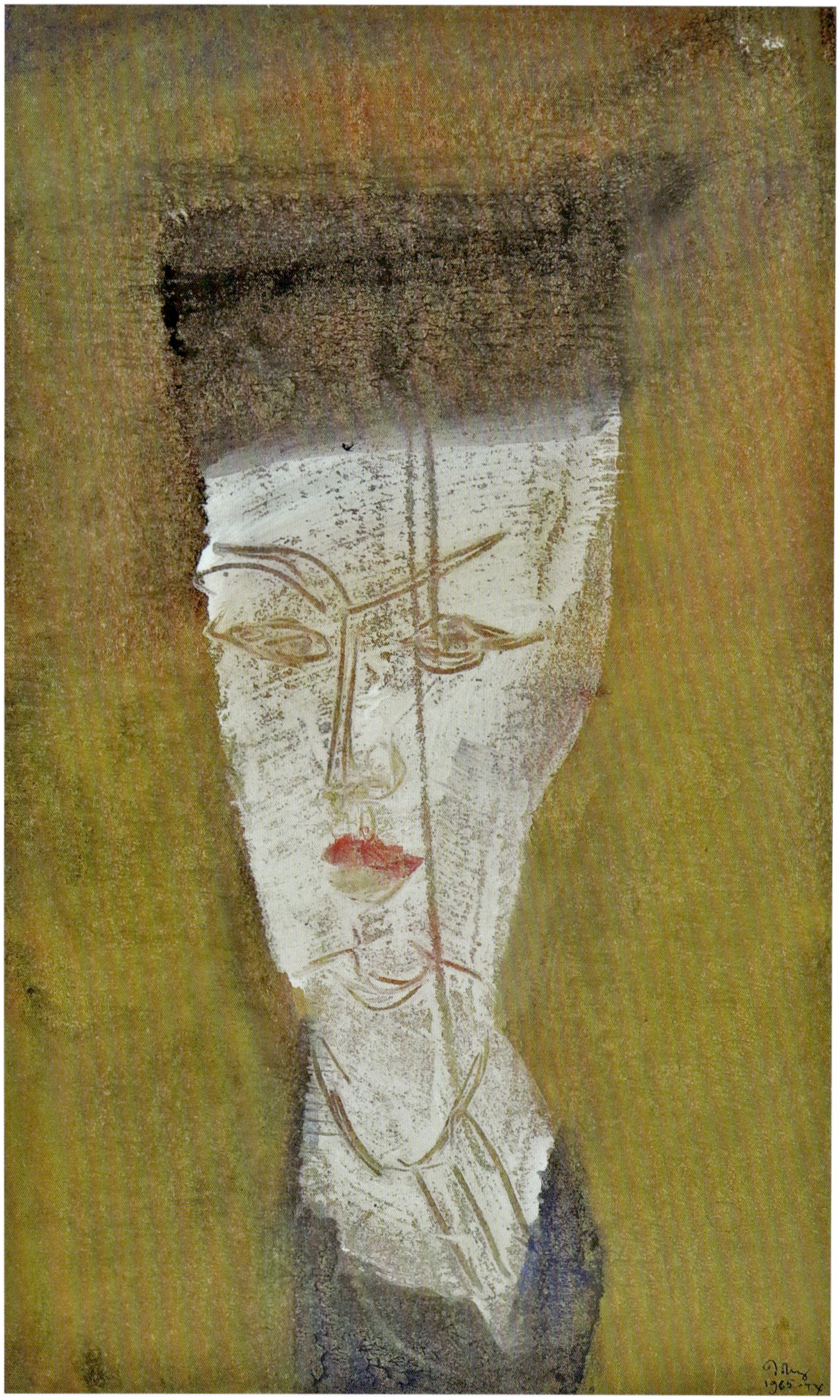

Mark Tobey 1890-1976, American, *Woman in Hat*, 1965, tempera on paper the community to experience. In 1967 he organized a Japanese exhibition, *Kamukura to Edo*, that included over 200 loans from around the world. To be able to lead tours and speak with authority on the panoply of subject matter that the ever-changing exhibitions presented, Graham spent the rest of his waking hours studying.

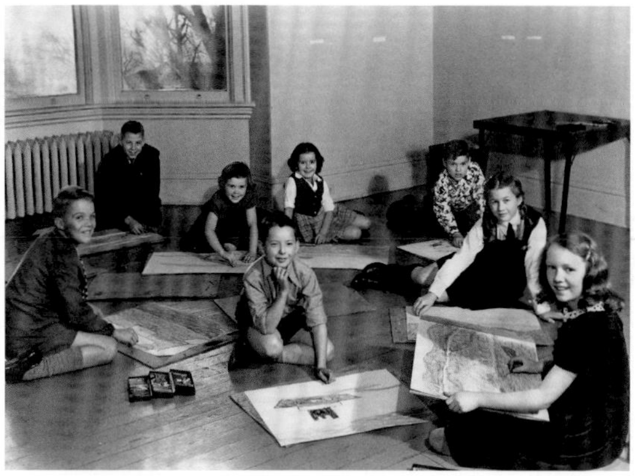

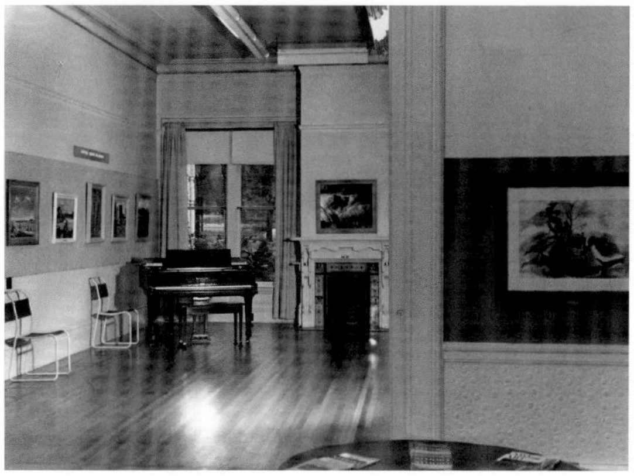

Other popular exhibitions presented works by students taking art classes at the Gallery. Graham instituted these classes immediately upon his arrival in 1951. That there was a pent-up need for art classes was borne out by the line-up outside the door of the mansion on registration day. The classes took place upstairs in one of the large Spencer bedrooms. For the first while, students in the children's classes had to work on the floor until furniture could be purchased (figure 10). Reputable contemporary artists were hired to teach, including local artists such as Ina Uhthoff and Jan Zach. Vancouver artist Jack Shadbolt and former Vancouver artist (then living in Toronto) Jock MacDonald taught summer sessions. By exhibiting the students' work, Graham brought into the Gallery not only the students themselves but also their friends and family. The exhibitions were concrete proof of the value of the art classes, and encouraged budding artists to continue their explorations of art. Indeed, there are numerous examples of students who started in classes at the Gallery at this time who went on to become well-known professional artists, such as Anne Kipling and Michael Morris.

Other types of exhibitions that attracted throngs of supporters were juried shows presenting the work of local artists and amateurs. Graham put out an annual call for submissions and appointed a jury to choose works to exhibit. It soon became apparent that this process was backfiring, creating ill will toward the institution as artists whose work was not selected year after year became resentful. In their place, Graham established non-juried exhibitions allowing all submissions to show in the Gallery. In this one example he may have compromised exhibition quality in favour of developing broader audience support.

As the permanent collection began to grow, Graham was able to curate exhibitions from its modest holdings. At first these were simply titled *Permanent Collection* and included an assortment of pieces with no particular theme or curatorial thesis. Within a few years and through the diligent development of the collection, Graham was able to devise more succinct exhibitions such as *Dutch Graphics* and *British Drawings and Paintings*. By exhibiting recent donations, Graham pleased the donors and encouraged further giving. This was the strategy behind exhibitions that honoured specific donors, such as the exhibition *F. Maud Brown Collection* in 1955, and in 1957, *Pictures Presented by H. Mortimer-Lamb*.[37] Others, such as *Canadian Art in Victorian Collections* in 1956 and *Collectors' Favourites* in 1961, not only demonstrated the wealth of art held in the city, but encouraged donations to the new gallery. With little or no purchase funds, Graham realized the primary way to build the collection was through donations, and this occurred as a result of sensitive cultivation of collectors through relationship building. Graham, with his charming and unassuming personality, was very skilled at this aspect of his job.

10. Children's art classes upstairs in the mansion, 1951. Photo: Ken McAllister.

11. Looking from the Kearley Gallery into the Spencer Gallery in the mansion, early 1950s. Photo: Ken McAllister.

Alongside these tamer exhibitions, Graham scheduled shows of modern art that strategically broadened the audiences' tastes. These too were varied, from borrowed exhibitions such as *Contemporary U.S. Trends* in 1955 to *The 1958 Winnipeg Show* that introduced some of the most daring abstract art being produced in Canada.

However, fully believing in the Gallery's role to cultivate its own arts community, Graham gave priority in his exhibition programming to British Columbia artists. These exhibitions were mainly one- or two-person projects that included more traditional artists such as Sophie Pemberton, as well as others in the more modernist vein such as Sybil Andrews, Molly Privett, Elsa Mayhew, Donald Harvey, Jack Shadbolt, Gordon Smith, members of the Limners group including Maxwell Bates, and international artists who had moved to Victoria such as Jan Zach, Herbert Siebner, Margaret Peterson, and Richard Ciccimarra.[38] As the years passed Graham kept up to date on art trends, conscious of introducing to the Victoria audience new art approaches as they developed. Examples include the feminist work of Joyce Wieland, the innovative light boxes of Pat Martin Bates in 1971, and the conceptual works of Michael Morris, Iain Baxter, and Eric Metcalfe, among many others.

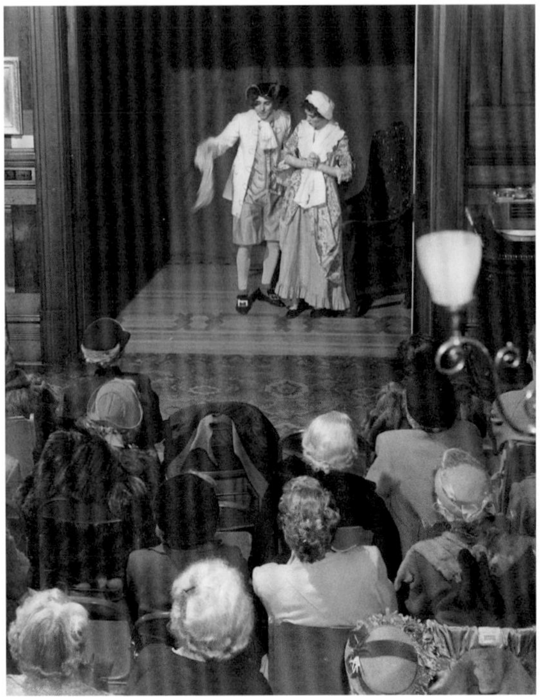

12. Drama performance in mansion lobby, c. 1950s. Photo: Ken McAllister.

Until 1958, when the first of the gallery expansions was built, all of these various exhibitions were shown exclusively in the mansion. Upon taking over the Spencer home, Colin Graham and the volunteers stripped the rooms of Edwardian ornament and wallpaper in preparation for developing more suitable exhibition spaces. The Kearley, Massey, and Spencer galleries were painted white and fitted with burlap covered panels that protected the plaster and made for easier picture-hanging, with little need to touch up wall surfaces between exhibitions (figure 11). Fluorescent fixtures were mounted on the ceiling, providing an even (albeit stark) light across the walls. In accordance with the taste of the day, Graham installed the exhibitions with a minimalist look, the flow of the paintings interrupted only by the most simple wall labels. Unlike today, there were no curatorial statements or expansive label text to help visitors understand the art. Instead, Graham relied on the media, including CBC radio and the newspapers, to help him educate the public before they visited the exhibitions. Of particular support was Stuart Keate of the *Victoria Daily Times*, its publisher from 1951 to 1964. The paper printed regular stories on the activities at the Gallery. These articles, based on interviews with Colin Graham, introduced the public to the content and the concepts of each exhibition. People arrived at the gallery with a basic understanding of what they were about to see. If they wanted more information, they could attend one of Graham's tours or an artist's talk.

Hand in hand with his diverse and ever-changing exhibition programming, the second part of Graham's strategy to vitalize the Gallery and grow its audience was to make it a "beehive of activity":

> Our situation was obviously precarious, but still there was a simple way of solving this problem without compromising our principles, and that was to have so many things going on at Moss Street that if things reached a crisis point financially there would be too many people involved to let it crash.[39]

He orchestrated as many lectures and performances as possible and, by the end of Graham's first year, the Board President reported that there had been more than six hundred functions at the Gallery including events such as drama discussions, plays, dances, musical recitals, and gramophone concerts (figure 12). Graham asserted: "It all proved that while Victoria had seemed culturally somnolent, underneath things were becoming effervescent."[40] In 1958, when the Board was trying to rally support for their new wing, a promotional brochure enthusiastically claimed that the Gallery had more than 30,000 visitors each year ("One of the highest per capita attendances in

Canada" it stated), more than 40 exhibitions, and more than 750 functions including lectures, concerts, creative writing classes, choral singing, film evenings, and an anthology series.[41] These events, along with the hugely popular studio classes for children and adults, established a great loyalty in the community. One particular example of this loyalty was demonstrated in 1953 when the Victoria Parent-Teacher Association rose up in support of the Gallery after Mayor Harrison had denied the Gallery a grant from the city's charitable budget. Graham was providing studio classes for the schools at a significantly reduced rate—the regular price being beyond what the PTA could afford—and they felt for this reason alone that the Gallery deserved funding.[42]

All this activity was accomplished in these early years with Colin Graham as the only full-time staff member, a part-time secretary, eventually a live-in caretaker, and myriad volunteers. Given this pace, it is not surprising that Graham was exhausted by 1966 and took a year off.[43] That same year the Board agreed to hire another curator, Will Hoare, recognizing that the institution had grown well beyond the scale of a one-man show. By the time Graham took his recuperative break, not only had he created his beehive of activity, he had overseen and raised money for two major building expansions.

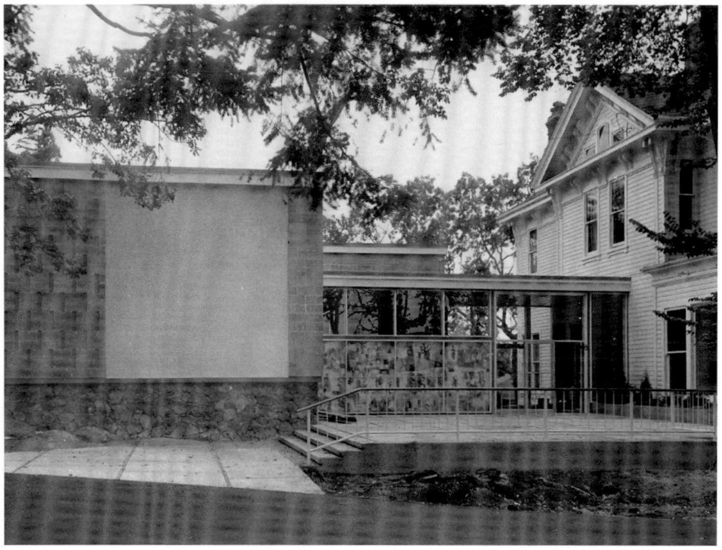

13. New addition to the Gallery, 1958. Photo: Ken McAllister.

Building Expansions

From the beginning, the vision for an expansion of the Gallery was on the minds of the Board and Colin Graham. Without a fireproof wing they could not be granted Class A status, a requirement for eligibility to receive higher-end exhibitions. Furthermore, the art was in constant peril given that the wooden framed mansion was a veritable tinderbox. Security and the fire risks of the mansion made it necessary for someone to be on site at all times. When the Grahams lived in the mansion from October 1951 until early in 1953, the year their first child was born, both of them could not be out of the house at the same time. If they were invited to dinner, for example, one would go for a couple of hours, return to the mansion, and then the other would go to the last half of the party. When a caretaker couple was hired in 1953, the Grahams were relieved of such duties. Nonetheless, if there was a particularly valuable exhibition on display, Colin Graham would sleep in the Gallery cloakroom.

In 1958, thanks to a $30,000 provincial centennial year grant from the four Victoria municipalities,[44] the first Gallery expansion was given life (figure 13). Graham raised the rest of the funds with a campaign entitled "Bring Emily Home" which referenced the fact that the Emily Carr estate did not reside in Victoria because it needed a fireproof home. The modern addition allowed the Gallery to borrow Emily Carr paintings from the Vancouver Art Gallery, an opportunity they promptly seized for the second exhibition in the new wing.[45] This first addition, called the Centennial wing, was built in front of the mansion edifice, with a walkway from the original front door leading to two new exhibition spaces (figure 14).[46] Below the galleries were installed a fireproof vault, a workshop, and registry spaces. Almost immediately the second phase of expansion began with the construction of a long, narrow gallery on the east side of the first addition.[47] The Ker Gallery, largely funded by prominent citizen and businessman Robert Ker, was created in honour of the centenary of his family's residency in Victoria.[48] The Ker Gallery was dedicated to displays of the growing permanent collection, while the other two spaces were reserved for travelling exhibitions.

In 1969 Graham began lobbying the Board for a third expansion to address issues of collection growth and the need for even more gallery space. Again, Robert Ker came to the Gallery's aid, donating $10,000 towards the cause and offering to help with the remainder of the fundraising. Having set the example, he approached nine of his friends to match his gift. Through this undertaking they raised $100,000. The remainder of the funds was raised by selling a painting that Kenneth Drury, a retired newspaper publisher, had bought for the Gallery collection years before in memory of his brother and sister. Since he had always disliked the painting, Drury was quite happy to see it sold with the funds going toward an exhibition space named after his family.[49] It was in this way that Graham built the Founders and Drury Galleries, which opened in 1970 (figure 15).[50]

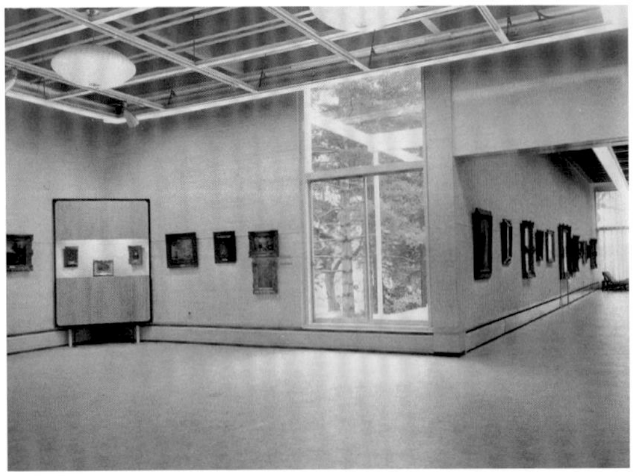

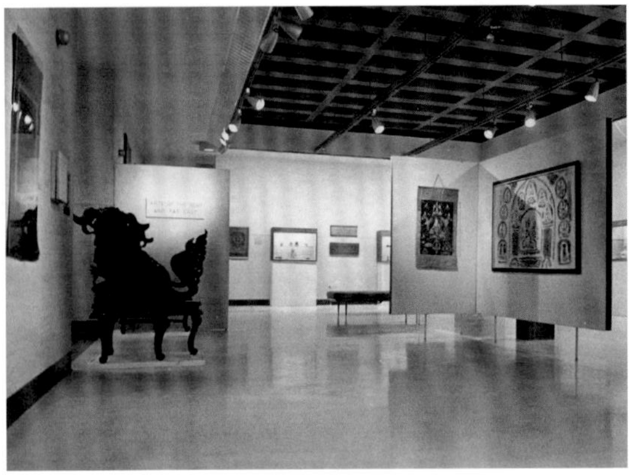

14. Interior of Centennial Gallery addition, c. 1958. Photo: Rogers, Victoria.

15. Interior of the Founders Gallery looking toward the Drury Gallery, 1965. Photo: Barry Casson.

Birth of the Collection

Along with Colin Graham's success in bringing a strong exhibition program to the community, building the facilities, and ensuring broader financial support, was the tremendous work he did in establishing a strong foundation for the permanent collection. Today the Art Gallery of Greater Victoria has the largest collection of any other public gallery in the province. Similar to his exhibition strategy, and working with a nearly blank slate, Graham envisioned a collection culled from every corner of the world. He wanted to "give Victoria the whole gamut of ethnic cultures."[51] He went about collecting by building relationships with Victorians who had art in their homes, and he appealed to them to help establish and build the collection through donation. Many people responded well to Graham's passion to see a collection held in public trust for the citizens of British Columbia.

The main growth of the collection was through consistent and respectful relationship building. Some important relationships included Graham's friendship with Vancouver artist and collector Harold Mortimer-Lamb, who added such gems to the collection as several Fred Varley paintings, a significant A.Y Jackson painting, and prints by Millet, Whistler, and other masters. Following his death, the Gallery received half the proceeds of Mortimer-Lamb's estate which, over the years, have purchased more than 200 significant historical, Asian, contemporary, and decorative art pieces.[52]

Another significant donor was Dr. Gustav Schilder and his wife Marie (also from Vancouver) who, as avid print collectors, made more than 300 donations including old master prints and drawings. Their gifts were particularly focused on Dutch prints including those by such important artists as Adriaen Van Ostade, Jan Lievens, and Rembrandt Van Rijn, as well as German artist Albrecht Dürer. Because, at the time, the Vancouver Art Gallery was not interested in acquiring prints, Schilder began donating to Victoria, thereby establishing the core of what is now a superb international historic print collection.[53] A local resident who also collected historical drawings and prints was Hans Klaverwyden. Retired and living nearby, he loved to visit the Gallery and talk about art with Graham.[54] Some of the significant objects he donated to the collection include a stunning painting by Dutch artist Matthijs Maris, snuff bottles and other Asian gems, and an intriguing eighteenth century sketchbook whose source remains a mystery to this day (figure 16).[55]

The decorative arts collection also grew as a result of Graham's countless visits to the homes of people in the community, finding out what they owned and encouraging them to donate. Graham also became friends with Anne Pearson who was a major dealer of decorative arts in Victoria. Over the years Graham developed a rapport with her and held an exhibition of her collection in 1964. As a result of this respectful treatment, Mrs. Pearson bequeathed her entire collection of superb figurines and tableware to the Gallery in 1979.

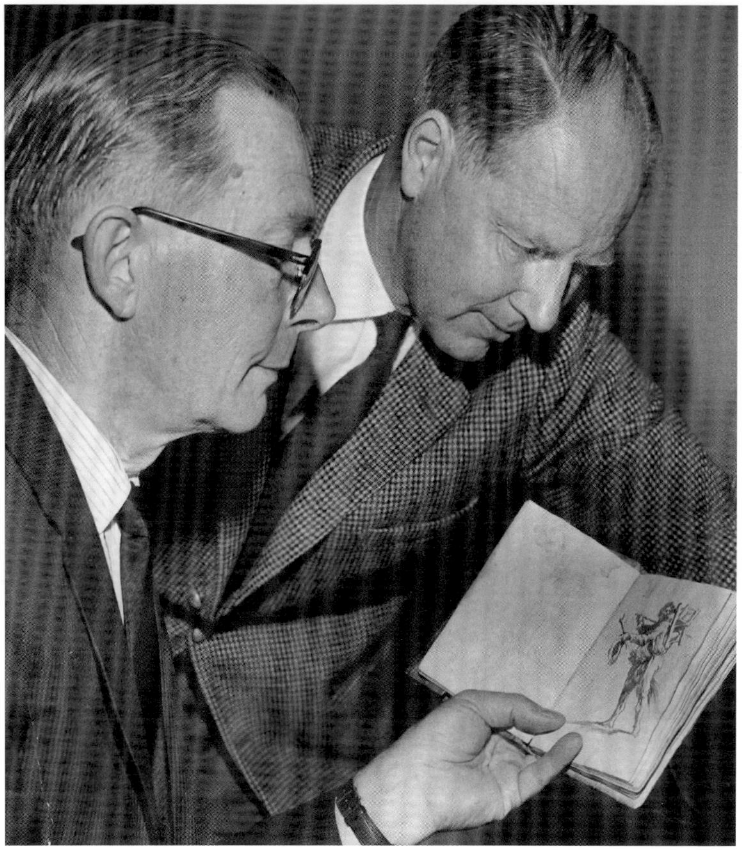

16. Colin Graham and Board President George Maycock examining the unidentified Klaverwyden sketchbook in 1966. Photo: Robin Clarke.

The Asian collection also grew extremely well as a result of close contacts Graham developed with people like Elizabeth Pollard and Syd Hoare. (See Barry Till's essay for information on the development and growth of the Asian collection.) The contemporary collection grew as a result of the great respect artists had for what Graham was doing to support artists both nationally and locally. Consequently, the Gallery received numerous noteworthy gifts from artists such as Herbert Siebner, A. Y. Jackson, Jack Shadbolt, Myfanwy Pavelic, Mark Tobey, and Arthur Lismer. Others who contributed significantly to this great public collection came from many walks of life and had varying interests. Some gave one piece, others whole collections or on-going gifts. Some were involved in the Gallery as volunteers or Board members, notably Hildegard Wylie. Others were merely casual members or visitors. Many who gave did so anonymously, believing whole-heartedly in the value of the collection, but requiring no recognition.

Purchases were rarer than donations due to lack of funding, as is the case today. When buying contemporary work, Graham purchased mostly from various contemporary exhibitions held at the Gallery itself. In those days commercial art galleries did not exist, and artists sold their works through exhibitions held in public galleries, a practice that is no longer acceptable. Graham did not have a travel budget, so he also relied on visiting vendors who occasionally came through Victoria to sell prints. Both Colin and Sylvia Graham fondly recall the Ferdinand Roten Galleries from Baltimore, Maryland arriving on several occasions in the late 1960s with a truck full of art. They would set up tables in the Gallery and offer international prints for sale, allowing Graham first crack. It was in this way that many modernist works entered the collection, such as the Kollwitz and Rouault prints.[56]

The funds for purchases were not large, but over the years Graham managed to build relationships with individuals and organizations that could help in this regard. Occasionally a prominent citizen would provide money to buy works for the collection, such as Massey Goolden, Graham's aunt. Myfanwy Pavelic, the niece of Sara Spencer, who of course had a special relationship with the Gallery, also helped. Graham held an exhibition of her work, and she donated the proceeds from sales towards a fund for collection purchases. Many works have been acquired from this fund such as pieces by Henry Moore, Pablo Picasso, as well as Goya prints. The Leon and Thea Koerner Foundation, founded in 1955 and which provided grants to cultural organizations, also helped Graham to purchase important acquisitions ranging from a sixteenth century illuminated manuscript page to a contemporary work by Gordon Smith. Also assisting in the purchase of contemporary pieces was the newly founded Canada Council for the Arts that, beginning in 1957, provided matching grants to galleries across the country to assist in purchasing the work of living Canadian artists. In this way, and usually along with funds from the Women's Committee, Graham was able to secure works by important national figures such as Bruno Bobak, Oscar Cahen, Margaret Peterson, and Tony Urquhart.[57]

The most consistent source of funds for the collection, however, came from the Women's Committee (later renamed the Volunteer Committee), which was founded in 1952 under the direction of Mrs. Diana Culver. This invaluable group, which is still a driving force today, had the dual mandates of raising money to support the needs of the Gallery and to promote an understanding and appreciation of its role in the community. Each year the Committee would not only provide an army of volunteers for the myriad duties needed at the Gallery, but also conceive of and run a number of fundraising and promotional events including the film club, dances, a tearoom, auctions, rummage sales, fundraising trips, and the very popular Victoria House Tour. They also founded the Art Rental and Sales service in 1957 (formerly Picture Loan Service) as well as the Gift Shop in the mid 1970s. In the early years the funds they raised were used mainly to purchase administrative necessities such as chairs, a slide projector, and art reference books. Increasingly, more and more of these funds were allocated to exhibitions and the collection. In this way, the Women's Committee was responsible for helping the Director develop various aspects of the collection such as international prints, including works by Paul Cézanne, Erich Heckel, Käthe Kollwitz, Marcel Duchamp, Joan Miró, and George Rouault; decorative arts; First Nations art; significant pieces by local artists such as Maxwell Bates's *Kindergarten* and works by Pat Martin Bates, Donald Harvey, and Richard Ciccimarra; works by artists of national significance such as Arthur Lismer, Paraskeva Clark, Bertram Brooker; and modernist works by Claude Tousignant, Harold Town, Gordon Smith, Jack Bush, among many others.

What Colin Graham managed to accomplish in the two decades of his tenure, in terms of the exhibition and education programs, collection growth, building expansions, and audience development, is more than impressive, especially given his small support staff. It speaks to his incredible energy, tenacity, and vision at that time as well as the dedication of the vast numbers of volunteers, including his wife Sylvia, who were there to assist and encourage him. Many of his undertakings brought to fruition the dreams of earlier cultural advocates including, most prominently, Emily Carr. Further, the work that Colin Graham accomplished set a firm foundation upon which the rest of the history of the Art Gallery of Greater Victoria was formed and continues to grow. Today we look back to honour these early roots and to appreciate Colin Graham's early endeavours to break through stagnant attitudes and shepherd Victoria forward into the modern cultural age.

> *...we were faced at the gallery with a situation where roughly 80% of our income came from membership fees and most members had conservative tastes. In retrospect I find it remarkable that while most of our exhibition program could be described as avant garde, our membership kept growing.*
>
> – Colin Graham, 2007.

ENDNOTES

1. Donald Harvey, "Colin Graham" in *B.C. Artists' Tribute to Colin Graham*, (Victoria: Art Gallery of Greater Victoria) 1974, n.p.

2. See the website The John and Katharine Maltwood Collection for a discussion of the offer to found a municipal gallery (http://www.maltwood.uvic.ca/k_maltwood/history/museum.html). Their collection is now the core of the Maltwood Museum and Art Gallery at the University of Victoria, which officially opened in 1977.

3. Emily Carr, *Growing Pains: An Autobiography of Emily Carr*, (Toronto: Oxford University Press) 1946, p. 305.

4. Carr wrote of the Island Arts and Crafts Society: "The Club held exhibitions, affairs of tinkling teacups, tinkling conversation and little tinkling landscapes weakly executed in water colours. None except their own class went to these exhibitions. Ordinary people would never dream of straying into an "Arts and Crafts" exhibition, would have been made to feel awkward had they done so." Emily Carr, *The House of All Sorts*, (Toronto: Oxford University Press), 1944, p. 129. Despite Carr's animosity toward the Society at that time, it must be recognized that many of the volunteers who eventually brought the AGGV to fruition were actually members of the Island Arts and Crafts Society. Longtime Art Gallery of Greater Victoria (AGGV) supporter and volunteer Gwladys Downes wrote: "…this group provided a nucleus and much-needed backing when a movement finally got under way for the establishment of a permanent gallery with a public mission…" Gwladys Downes, "Art Gallery History," unpublished document (January 1995), AGGV Archives, file: Gallery Info History.

5. Carr held an exhibition in the house: "The exhibition was a varied show and so successful that a few of us got together, working on the idea of starting a People's Art Gallery in these six rooms of mine. It was winter time, there were no Band Concerts in the Park. People walked until they were tired, then went home chilled. To drop in, sit by an open fire, warm, rest themselves and look at pictures, might appeal to the public." Carr, *The House of All Sorts*, pp. 130–131.

6. "But influential Victorians were uninterested, apathetic. Why, they asked, was it not sponsored by the Arts and Crafts Society? It was endowed. Unless Victoria could do something bigger and more flamboyant than Vancouver she would do nothing at all." Ibid., p. 131.

7. Upon hearing the news that the People's Gallery did not fly, National Gallery director Eric Brown wrote Emily Carr a letter stating, "Victoria just is not art minded. Go ahead, paint, don't give way to discouragement. Paint, paint!" Ibid., 133.

8. Letter from Emily Carr to Humphrey Toms, June 15, 1942, as quoted in *Dear Nan: Letters of Emily Carr, Nan Cheney and Humphrey Toms*, edited by Doreen Walker, (Vancouver: UBC Press), 1990, p. 374.

9. Despite this missed opportunity, over the years the AGGV has amassed numerous donations and a few purchases to comprise a fine yet modest collection of Carr's work. The AGGV endeavours to have it on permanent display for public access.

10. Founded in 1946, the Gallery was originally called The Little Centre. When it was incorporated the next year its name was changed to the Art Centre of Greater Victoria. In 1955 the name changed to the Art Gallery of Greater Victoria.

11 See Mark Kearley, "Twentieth Anniversary Address," October 20, 1964, AGGV Archives.

12. The Federation of Canadian Artists was established in 1941 to help address the isolation of artists and arts organizations across the country. It allowed the young Gallery to develop contacts across the country and most significantly, bring a variety of borrowed exhibitions into their isolated community.

13. "When, a year later, Mr. Kearley was forced by indifferent health to go elsewhere, the burdens of the operation fell mainly on Ina Uhthoff's shoulders… There had been moments when the whole project would probably have collapsed had Ina Uhthoff not given her services unstintingly, tirelessly, and constantly regardless of the fact that the fledgling institution's incessant demands ate into her time for painting, teaching and earning a living." Colin Graham, *Ina D.D. Uhthoff, Memorial Exhibition*, AGGV, 1972, n.p.

14. In 1950 all administrative, creative, and physical work was undertaken by volunteers, except for two hours of weekly paid secretarial help.

15. An article entitled "Its Artists Have No Gallery" *Victoria Daily Times* on October 23, 1948, led the rallying cry.

16. Miss Spencer was on the Art Centre Board from 1947 to 1954 and served as Vice-President in 1952.

17. The Board believed the city would at the very least pay the property taxes and provide upkeep of the grounds, up to a maximum of $250 per year, as per a letter from M.F. Hunter, City Clerk to Ronald Grant, 13 September 1951, AGGV Archives, *Correspondence with City of Victoria, 1951–53*. However, within a short time the city changed its mind about the taxes, and it would be several years before the relationship with the city would be settled. In his opening remarks at the 1952 Annual General Meeting, Board President, Ronald Grant, remarked upon the difficult relationship the Gallery had with the city: "It is interesting to note that the evolution of the Victoria Arts Centre is following much the same pattern of development as in other cities of Canada, the only difference being the peculiar slowness or reluctance of Victoria to recognize before this the essential necessity for a large community to have a civic art centre and to give expression to their natural desire for it. It is, I believe, a fact that Victoria is the last of the large cities of Canada to establish a permanent art centre." In 1953 a bill was passed where the City of Victoria agreed to exempt the Gallery of taxes, support maintenance, and enable each of the four municipalities of greater Victoria to provide grants. See *Correspondence with City of Victoria, 1951-53*, AGGV Archives.

18. Prominent early Board member Major Cuthbert Holmes suggested the mansion be used as an art gallery for a maximum of 20 years before a new site would be located. *Moss Street Year: Three Decades of Controversial Hangings*, unpublished manuscript, 1981, p. 16.

19. "Miss Sara Spencer Offers Family Residence to City as Art Gallery." *Victoria Daily Times*, Saturday July 21, 1951.

20. Ibid.

21. Colin D. Graham, *Moss Street Years. Addendum Draft Notes, February 2007*, p. 2.

22. Letter to Colin Graham from Ina Uhthoff, June 22, 1951, AGGV Archives, file: 1951 Curator Application.

23. Letter from Colin Graham, Berkley, California to Ina Uhthoff Victoria, B.C., July 13, 1951.

24. Ibid.

25. Letter to Ina Uhthoff from Colin Graham, August 5, 1951.

26. The Grahams would live in mansion until 1953, when they purchased their own property at the foot of Mount Tolmie and commissioned architect John Di Castri to renovate an old barn into a modernist style house.

27. "In my opinion the Gallery got two for one with Sylvia helping out." Graham interview, October 31, 2007. Sylvia remained a volunteer for the Gallery In The Schools program until 2001.

28. Letter to Colin Graham from Ken McAllister, September 12, 1951.

29. Interview with Colin Graham, April 14, 2009.

30. While the Moss Street site opened to the public in November 1951, they did not hold the gala opening until October 15, 1952 when the Governor-General, Vincent Massey, was available. It was on this day that the three main exhibition spaces in the mansion were officially named the Spencer (after the Spencer family); the

Kearley (after Mark Kearley who had kick-started the serious movement towards forming an art gallery in the 1940s); and the Massey (after Vincent Massey).

31. Emily Carr used this term in discussing her father's attitude toward Victoria in *The Book of Small*, (Toronto: Oxford University Press), 1942, p. 112.

32. Colin Graham, "Early Days on Moss Street." Handwritten notes given to author, November 2007.

33. Ibid.

34. The docent program was initially developed by Irene Conn, Jane Jermain, and Justine Housser who were Women's Committee members. This year the program is celebrating its 50th anniversary, and today its 20 volunteers provide tours to over 5,000 people annually.

35. Colin spoke about the poor quality overland route through the Rockies and the expense of air travel which deterred many lenders from sending art out west. Interview with Colin Graham, September 23, 2008.

36. A listing of the entire history of exhibitions at the AGGV can be found on the AGGV website: (www.aggv.bc.ca).

37. Maud Brown was the widow of first Director of the National Gallery, Eric Brown. Mrs. Brown was also interested in art and travelled across Canada after her husband's death lecturing on the value of art and education. It is in this context that she met Colin and Sylvia Graham and eventually decided to donate some of her collection to the Gallery.

Harold Mortimer-Lamb was a very important connection for Graham. He was the editor of the *Canadian Mining Journal* and a great supporter of the arts. He was not happy with his relationship with the Vancouver Art Gallery and developed a great friendship with Graham. He made numerous donations to the AGGV, introduced Colin to Vancouver artists, and eventually bequeathed the remainder of his collection and half of his estate to the AGGV, which represents a perpetual endowment allowing for purchases for the permanent collection.

38. See Michael Morris's essay "Vision Into Reality: Colin Graham and West Coast Modernism" for further discussion of the importance of Colin Graham's relationship with the contemporary artists of the period 1951–1973.

39. Graham, *Early Days on Moss Street*, p. 2.

40. Ibid.

41. See "A New Wing for the Art Gallery of Greater Victoria" brochure, c. 1957, AGGV Archives.

42. In 1953 the City of Victoria had $25,000 to give to charitable organizations. Mayor Claude Harrison decided to give nothing to either the Victoria Symphony or the Gallery. The PTA presented a brief to City Council shaming them into helping the Gallery with their back taxes and providing a grant of $1,500 each year for the next two years. *Moss Street Years*, pp. 39–41.

43. A decade earlier Colin fell terribly ill in 1956 as a result of viral hepatitis, which no doubt was exacerbated by the hectic work schedule. Board member and President, Anthony Emery, served as Acting Director over the summer while Colin recuperated.

44. Victoria, Oak Bay, Saanich, and Esquimalt.

45. *The Emily Carr Trust Collection* exhibition was on display at the AGGV from September 30, 1958 to October 19, 1958.

46. These exhibition spaces represent the front halves of what are currently the Graham and Centennial galleries (previously the North and South Centennial galleries). This addition was designed by Clack, Clayton and Pickstone, chosen from a Rotary sponsored architectural competition that began in 1955. See "A New Wing for the Gallery."

47. This wing was designed by Robert Siddall.

48. His grandfather emigrated from Scotland and had been the first Auditor General of British Columbia. See *Plans for the Art Gallery of Greater Victoria: Its Growth in the Coming Years – An Invitation to Victoria to Participate in the Development of their Gallery*, AGGV Promotional Brochure, 1962. The width of the Ker gallery was enlarged by 12 feet in 1977.

49. This painting was a Lawren Harris canvas that was purchased for $500 and sold for $28,000. According to Graham, Drury was quite proud that a gallery was named after him with only an initial investment of $500.

50. To raise the money for the Founders Gallery, Robert Ker helped Graham encourage nine people to donate $10,000 each to the project as well as a number of smaller gifts from members. The major founders were: Princess Jennie Chikhmatoff, Mrs. James W. Benning, Mrs. Massy Goolden, Mr. and Mrs. Robert H.B. Ker, Mrs. Charles J. Martin, Mrs. W.F. Pinfold, Mrs. Will Spencer, Lady Stuart Taylor, Mr. H.A. Wallace. The only other expansion occurred in 1977 under Roger Boulet creating the Pollard Gallery and doubling the size of the Ker Gallery.

51. Interview with Colin Graham, October 31, 2007. He quickly decided against collecting North West Coast and other First Nations art because he felt the Royal British Columbia Museum was doing a great job and did no want to have competing mandates. In more recent decades this area of artistic production has become a priority for the Gallery.

52. Harold Mortimer Lamb lived in Victoria at the turn of the century working as an editor. It was when he saw the work of Sophie Pemberton that he became enraptured with art. He was the person who brought Emily Carr to the attention of Eric Brown, director of the National Gallery in the late 1920s. This meeting of Carr and Brown lead to Carr's breakthrough exhibition in Ottawa in 1927. Colin Graham and Lamb met in 1957 in Vancouver where Lamb lived out his retirement. The two men remained great friends until Lamb's death in 1970.

53. Colin Graham was adamant that he never stepped on the toes of the Vancouver Art Gallery by trying to scoop their donors. In this case they obviously had no interest in Schilder's collection and therefore he felt it was fair game to court the mainland collector. Interview, November 7, 2007.

54. Much as he enjoyed his discussions, Graham admits to parking his car far away from the Gallery so that Klaverwyden wouldn't think he was there. When the dear old fellow figured out the trick, Graham once crawled out his office window to escape.

55. When Graham made a casual comment that the artist might be Goya as a young man, Klaverwyden became obsessed with proving it. However several experts have disputed this idea and we have not yet developed a satisfactory attribution. Nonetheless the drawings are lovely, animated images some done in sepia watercolour and others in sanguine. The original showing of this sketchbook was highly publicized due to the Goya attribution. At the last minute, Graham had to cancel the premiere display of it in 1957 when he received a quote from an insurance company for many thousands of dollars per day due to the fact that it would be relatively easy for all 80 bound drawings to be stolen at once.

56. In 1972 Ferdinand Roten gave several important prints to the AGGV including a Renoir and a Magritte in recognition of Graham's ongoing patronage.

57. The Canada Council for the Arts fund and the Volunteer Committee (formerly Women's Committee) are still essential funds regularly utilized by the Gallery to build its contemporary art collection.

The Birth of the Collection

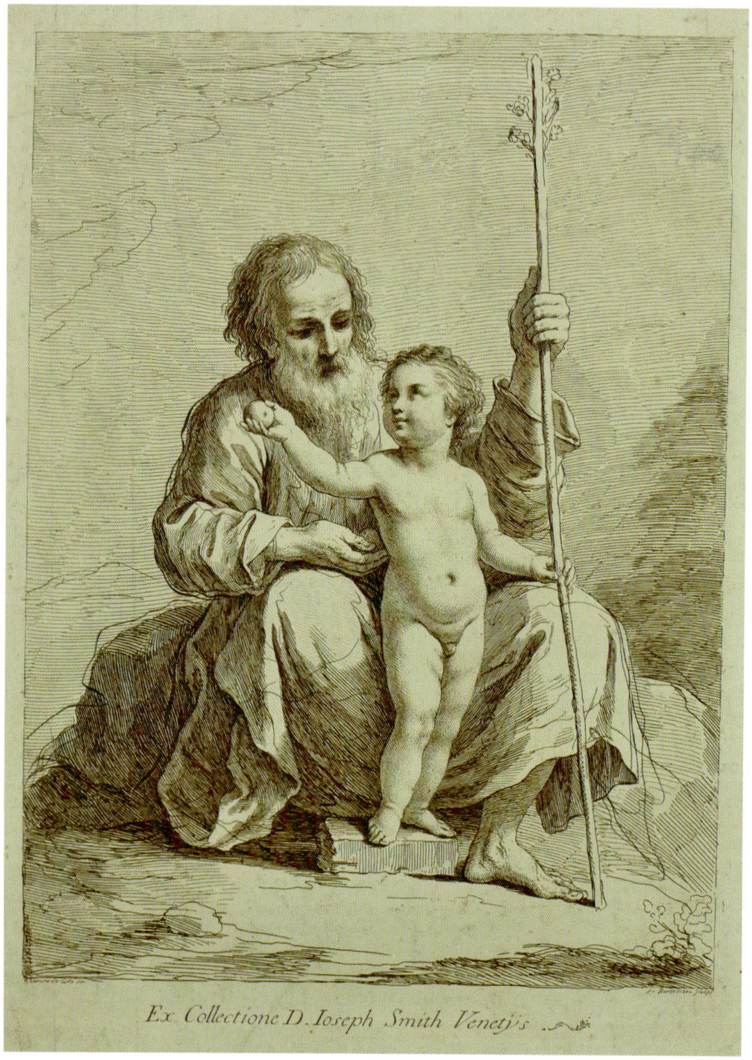

Francesco Bartolozzi 1727-1815, British, *Joseph and Christ Child*, nd, engraving on laid paper

Unknown Artist 18th C, Italian?, *Page from a Sketchbook*, nd, sanguine crayon on laid paper

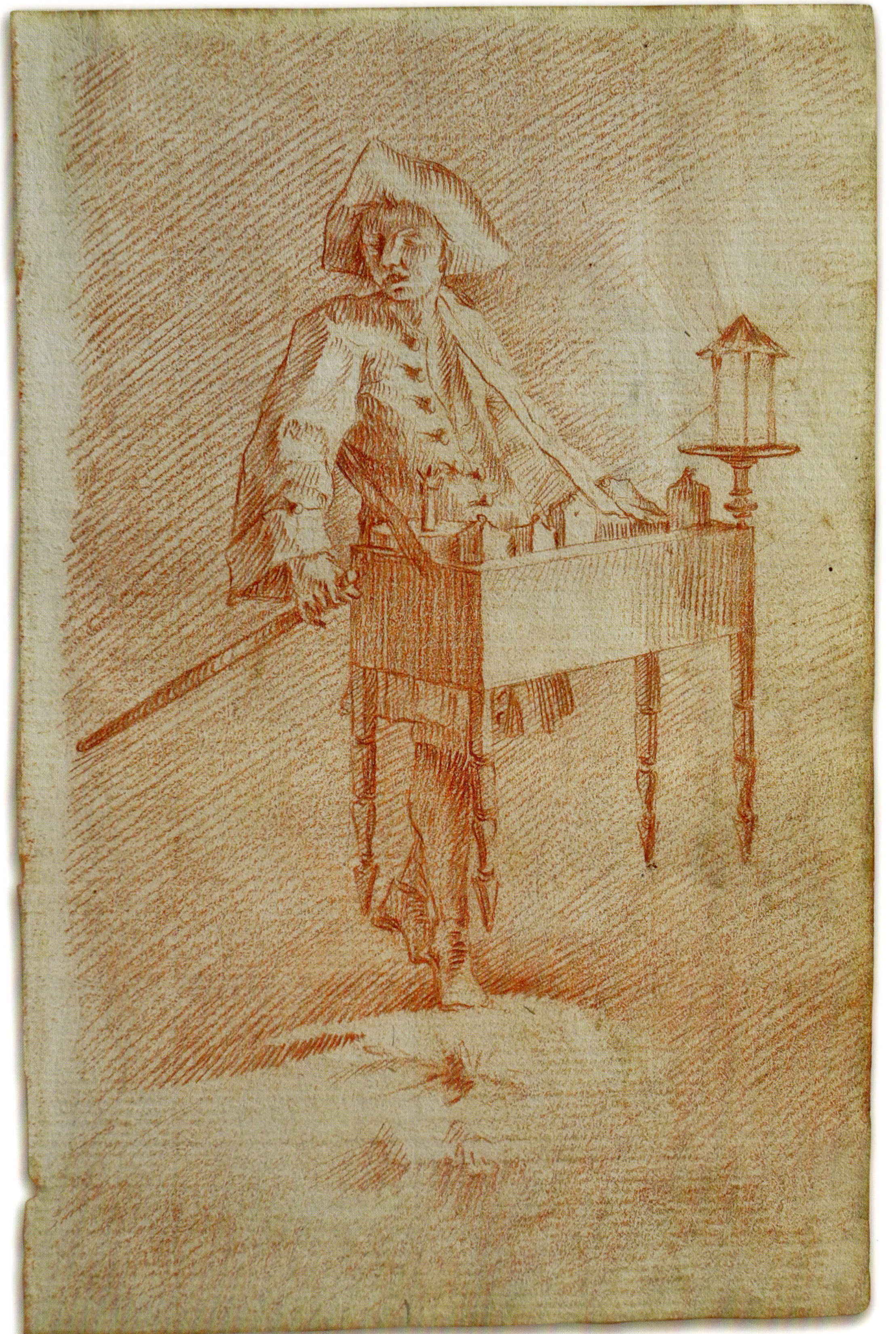

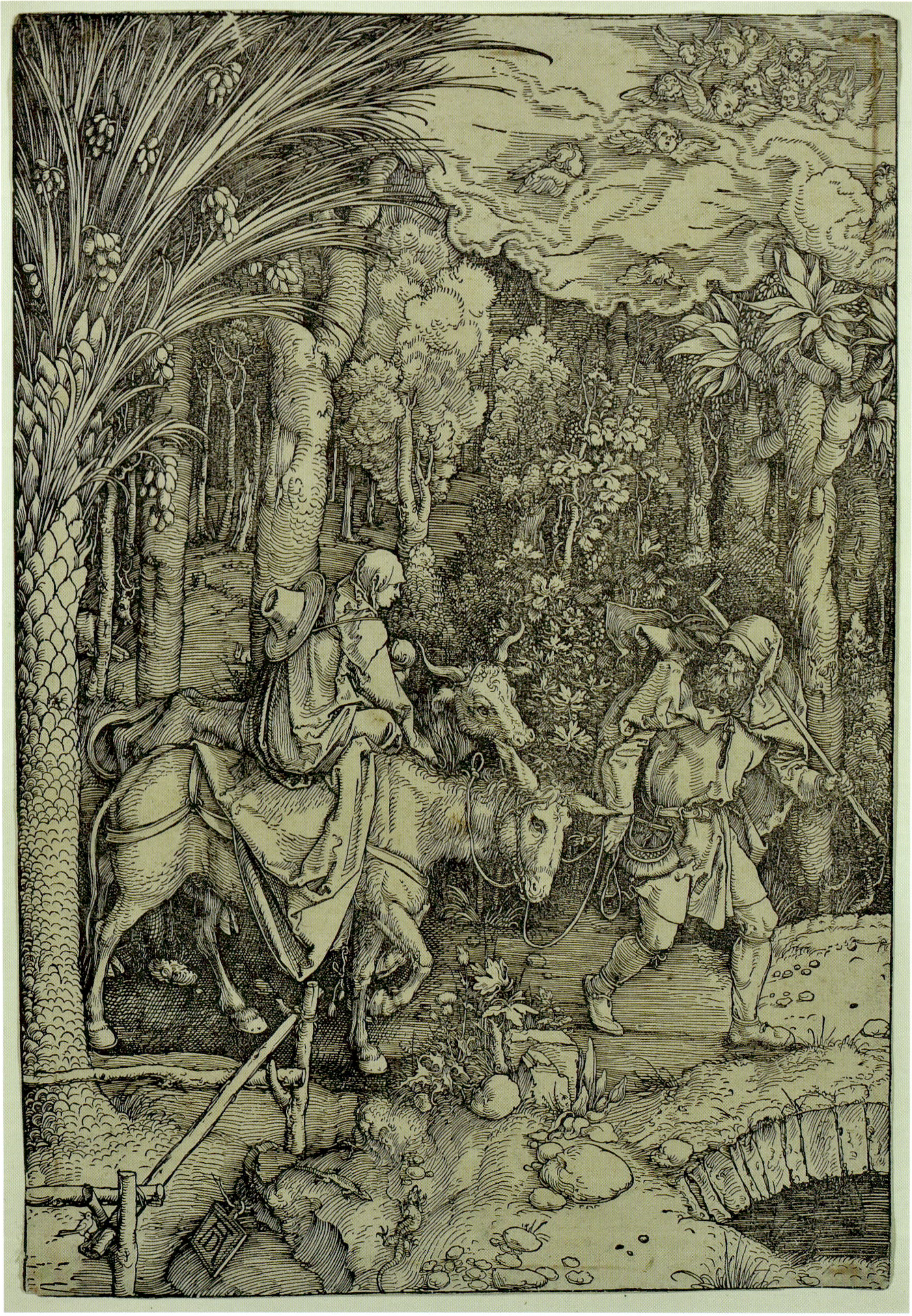

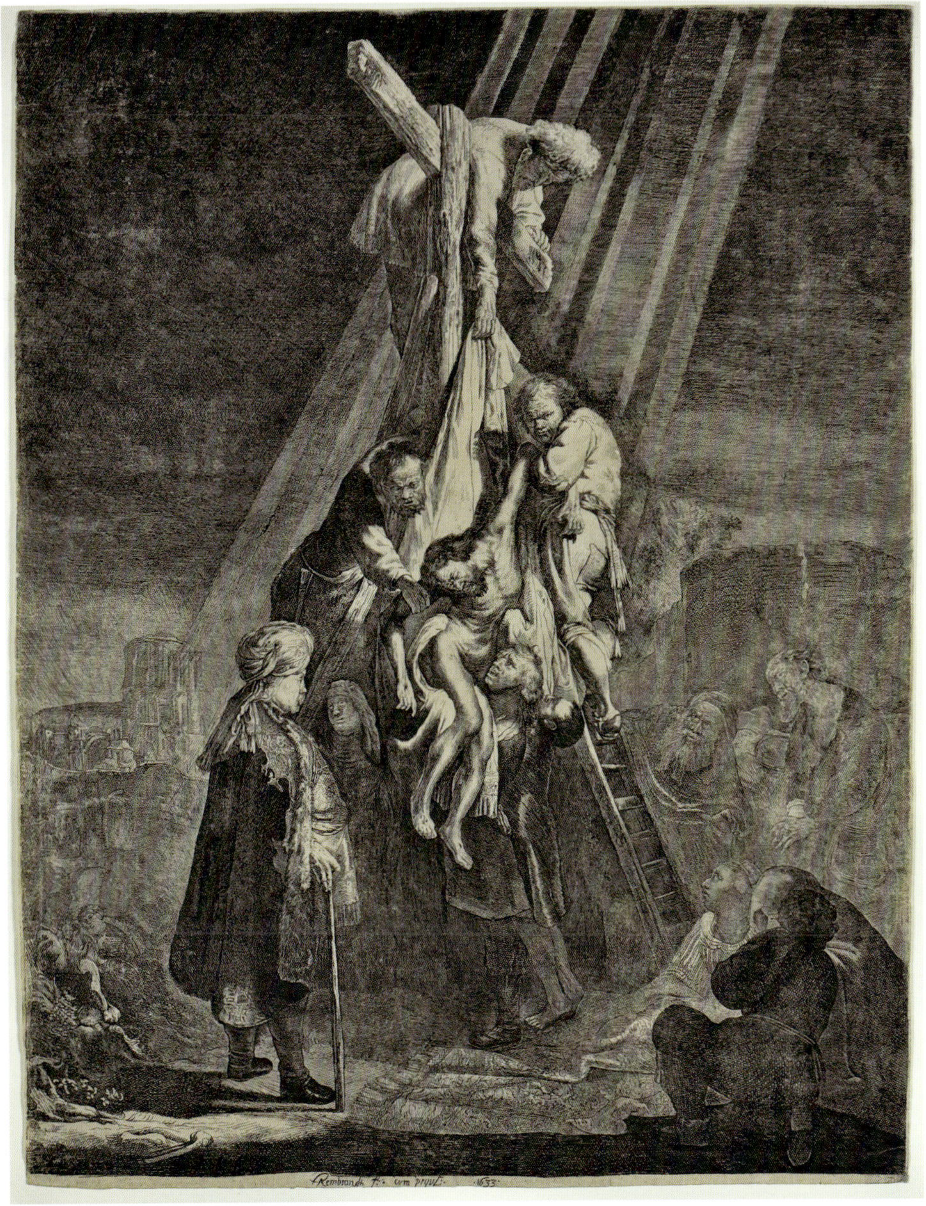

Albrecht Dürer 1471-1528, German, *Flight into Egypt*, c.1504, woodcut on laid paper

Rembrandt Van Rijn 1606-1669, Dutch, *Descent from the Cross*, 1633, etching on cream coloured laid paper

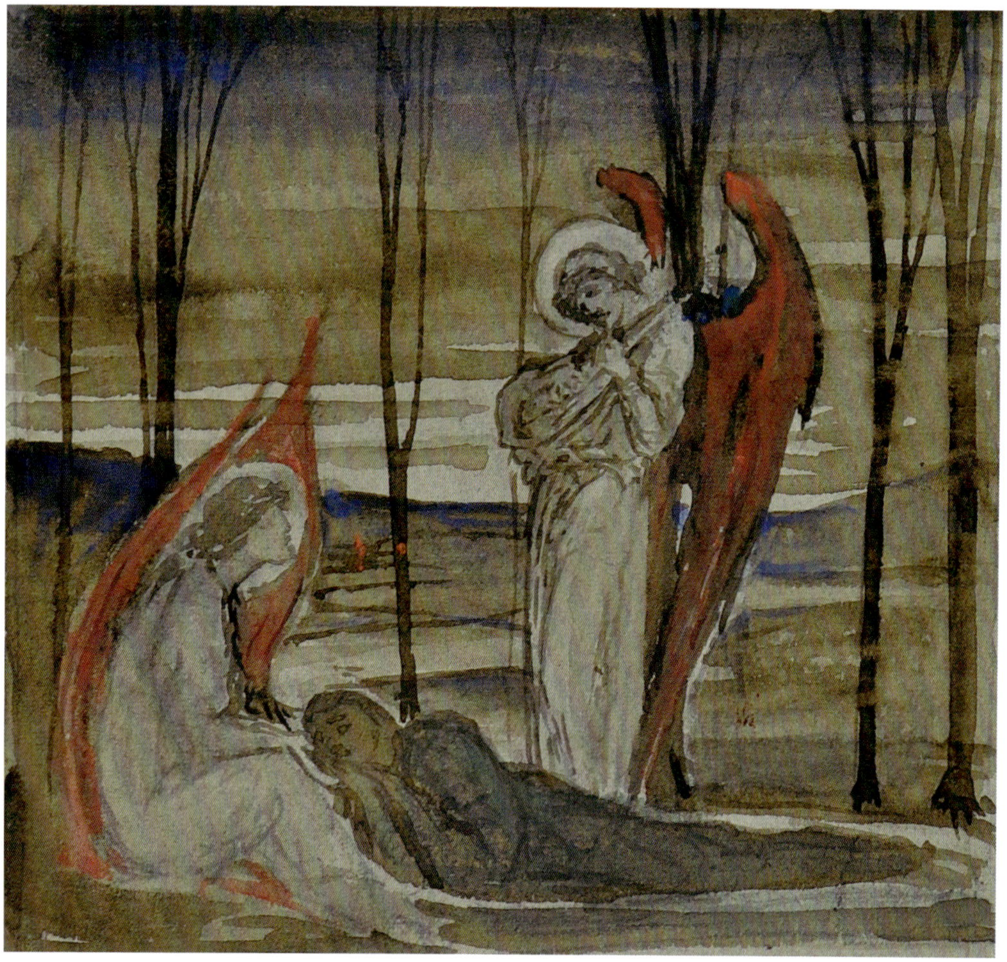

Phoebe Anna Traquair 1852-1936, Irish, *The Saint's Hour*, nd, watercolour, pencil on wove paper

Mary L. Gow 1851-1929, British, *The Young Scholar*, 1897, watercolour on wove paper

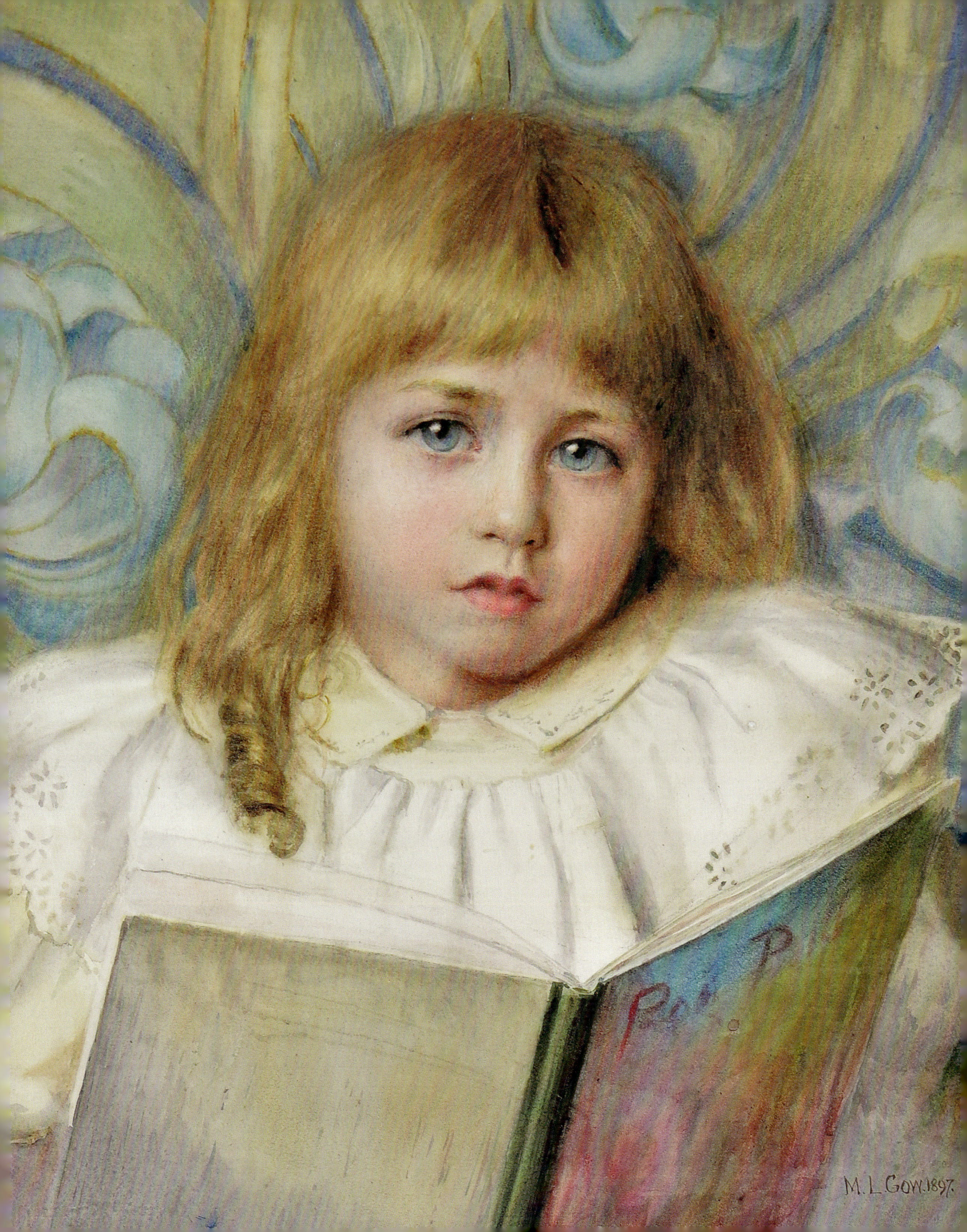
M. L. GOW. 1897.

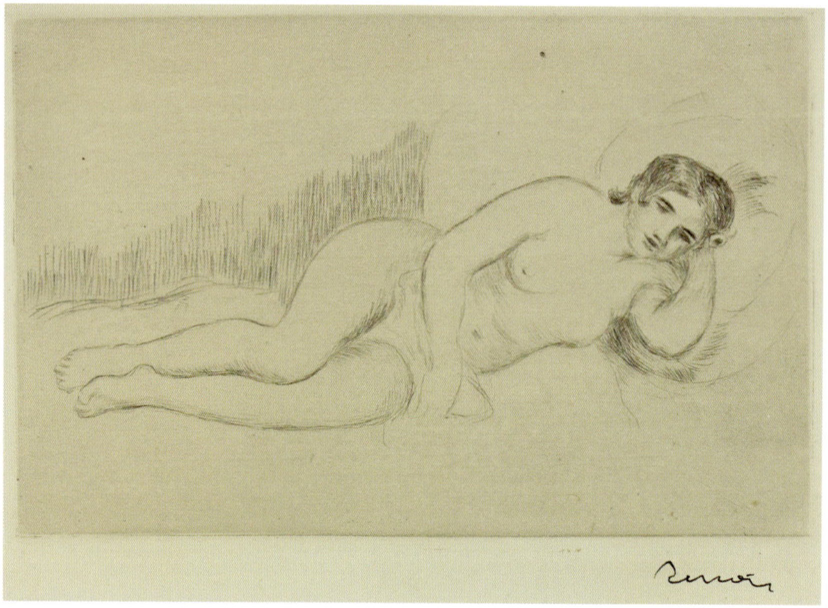

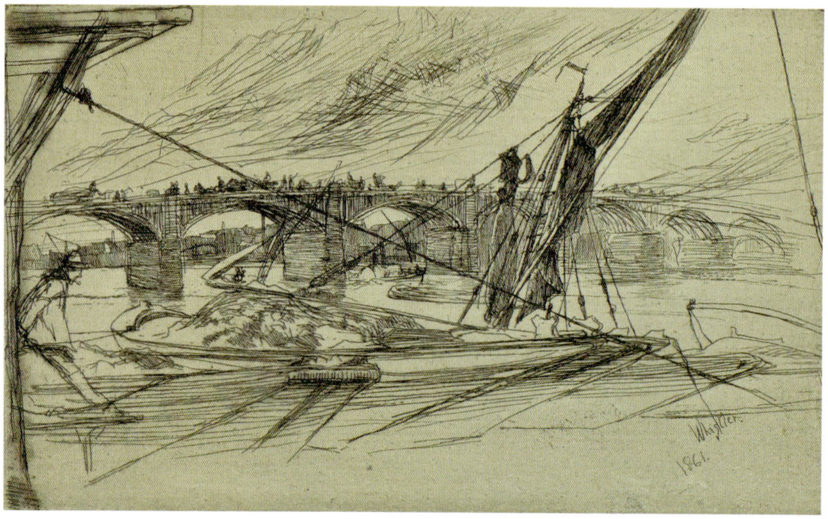

Pierre Auguste Renoir 1841-1919, French, *Femme Nue Couchée*, nd, restrike drypoint on cream coloured wove paper

James MacNeill Whistler 1834-1903, American, *Vauxhall Bridge*, 1861, etching on paper

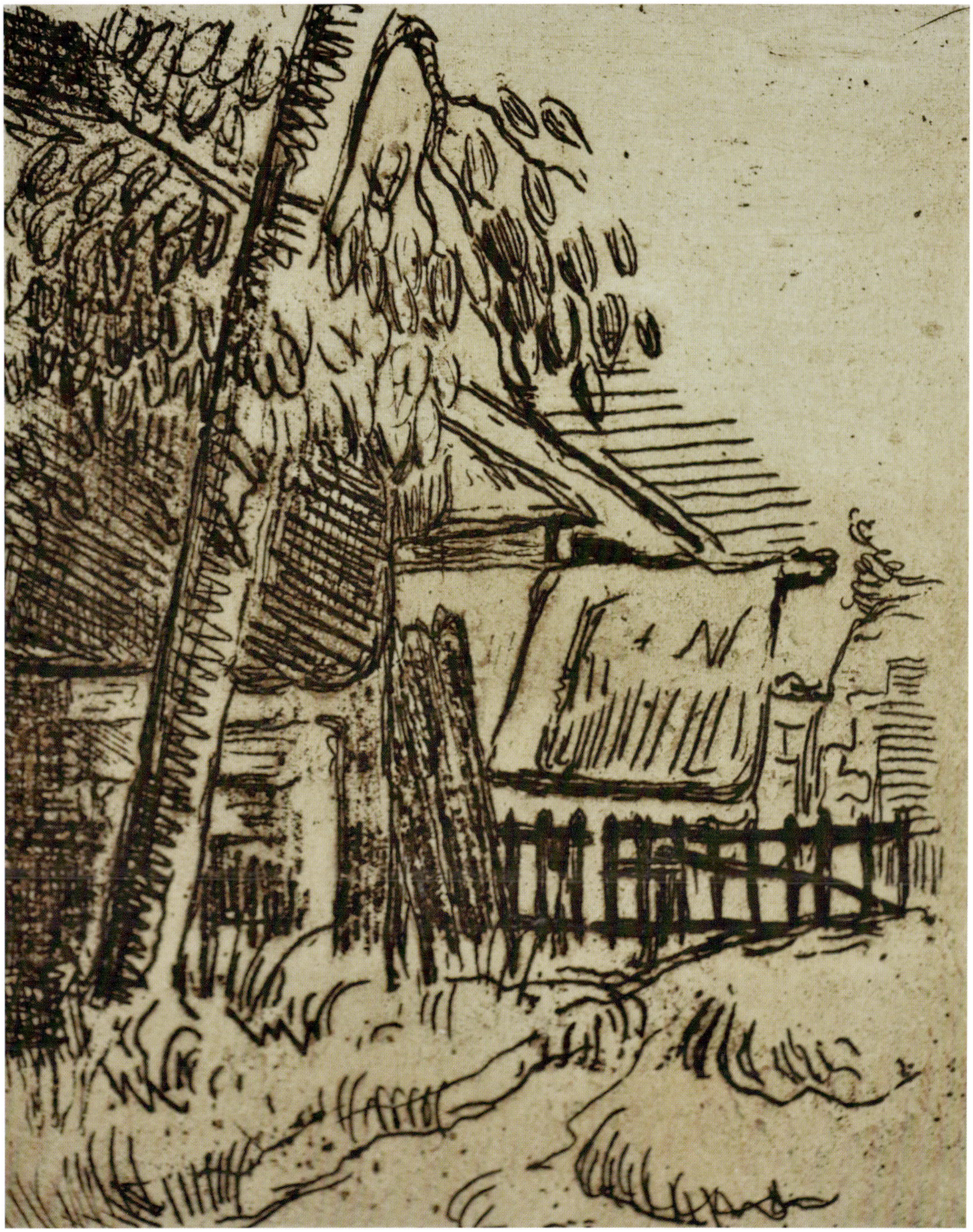

Paul Cézanne 1839-1906, French, *Artist's House at Anvers*, nd, soft ground etching on white wove paper

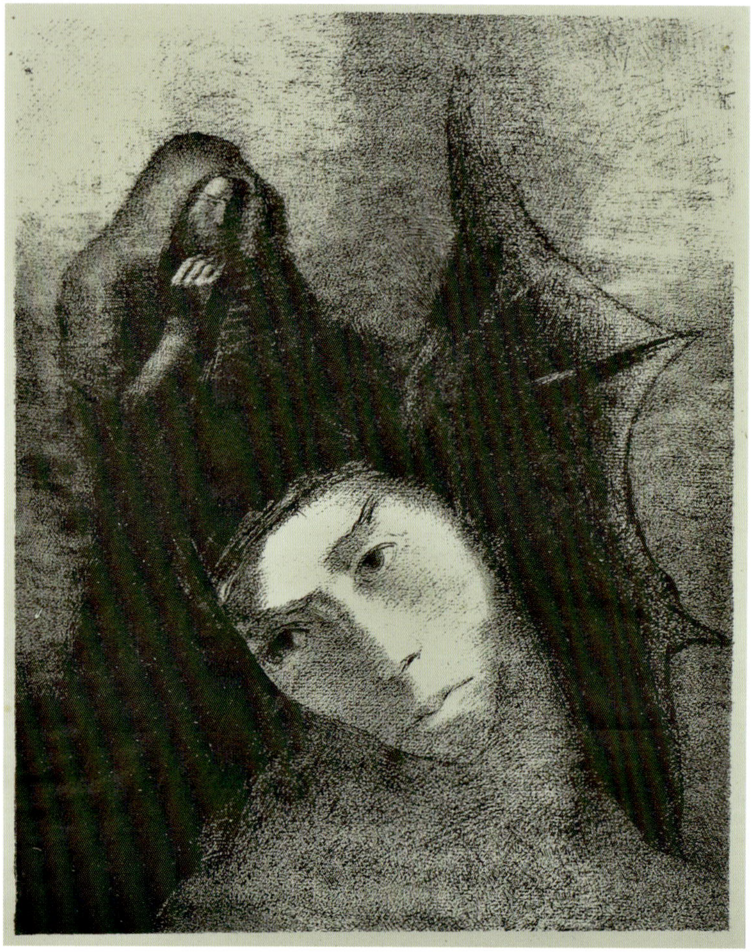

Odilon Redon 1840-1916, French, *Satan, From the Temptation of St. Anthony*, nd, lithograph on toned laid paper

Käthe Kollwitz 1867-1945, German, *Sharpening the Scythe* 1921, etching on cream colour wove paper

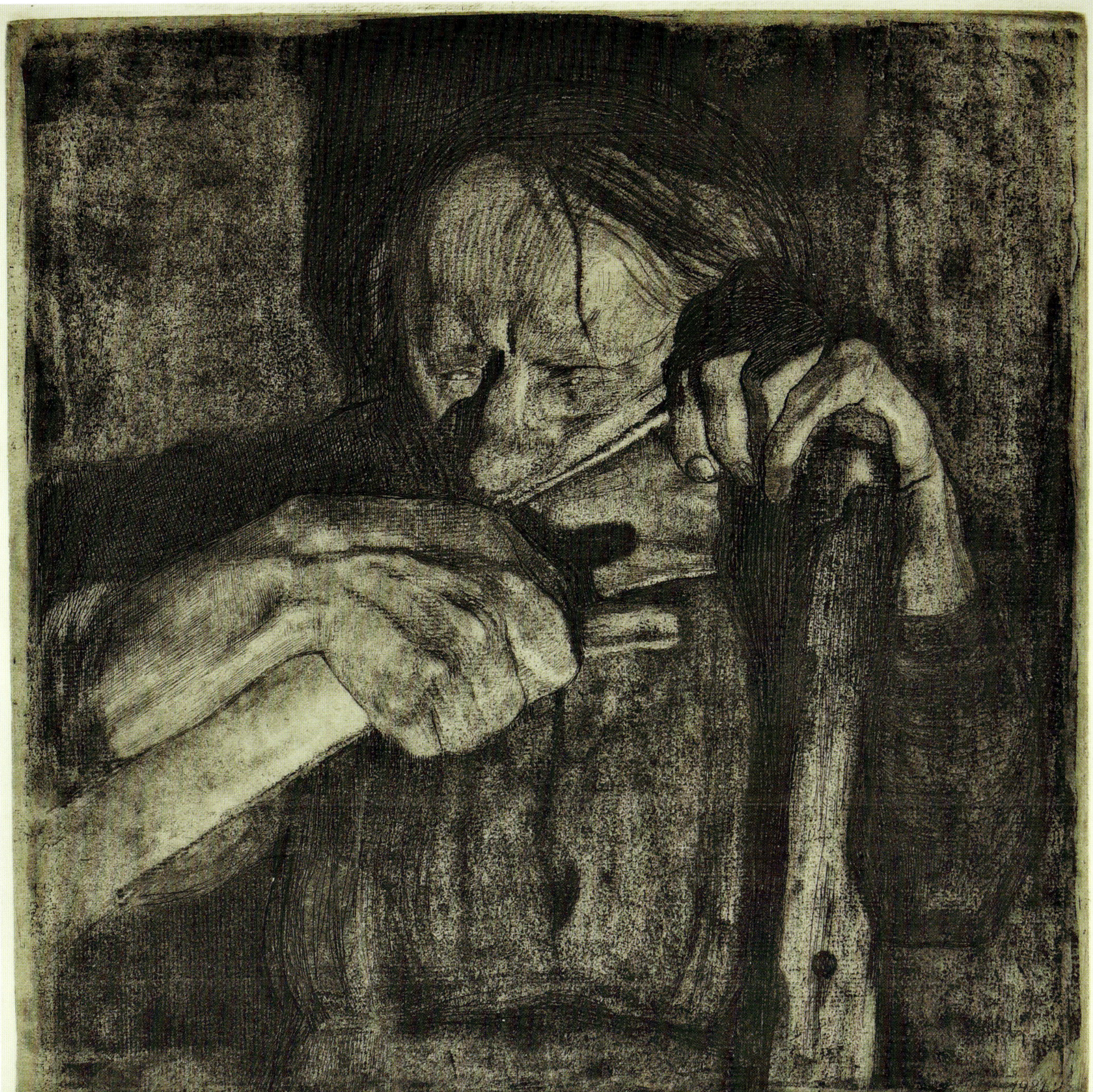

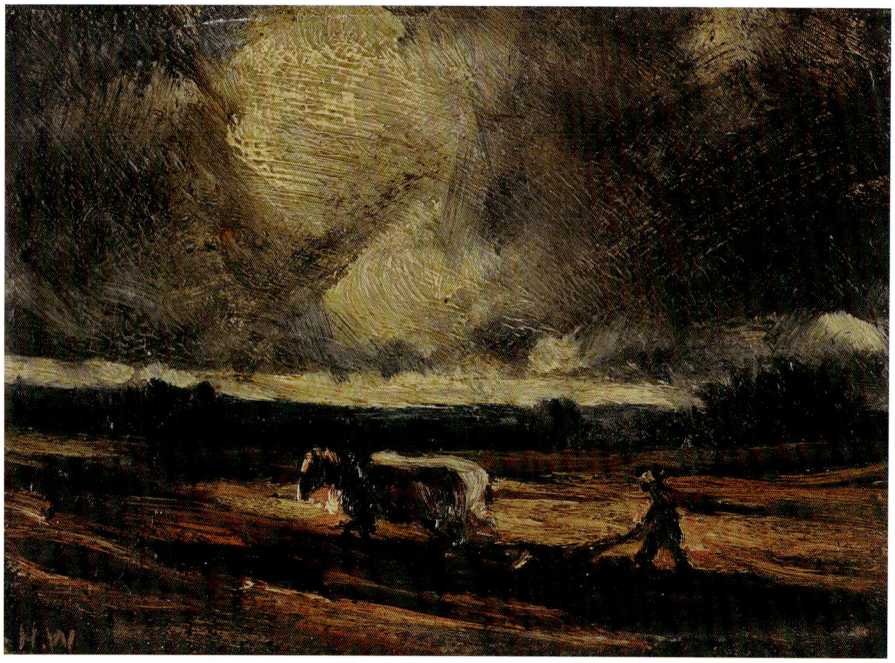

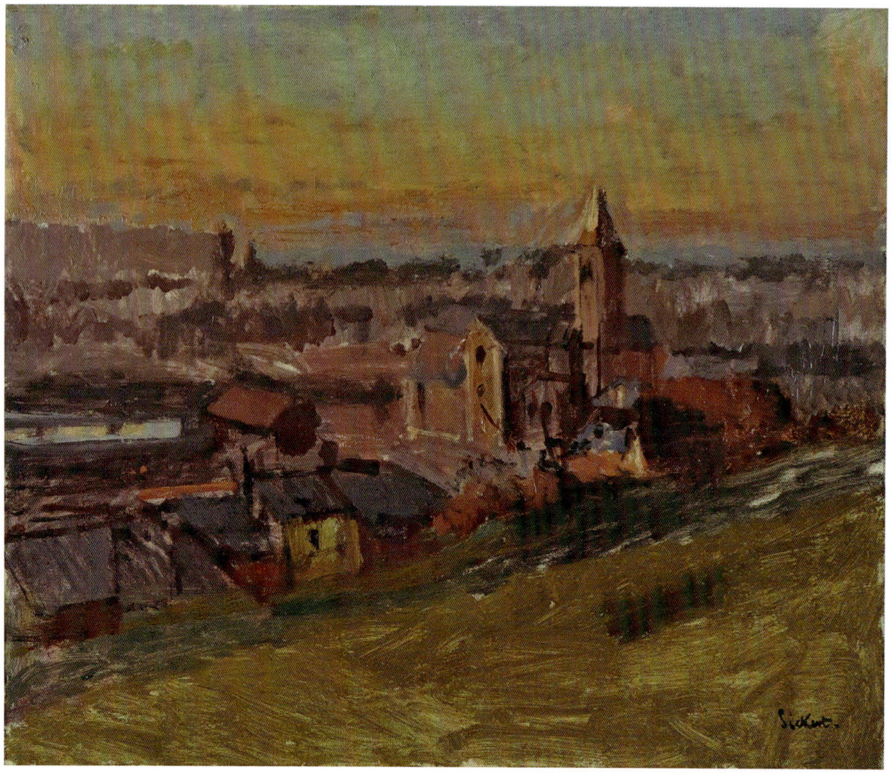

Homer Watson 1855-1936, Canadian, *The Ploughman*, nd, oil on card

Walter Richard Sickert 1860-1942, English, *L'Eglise du Poulet, Dieppe*, c.1920, oil on canvas

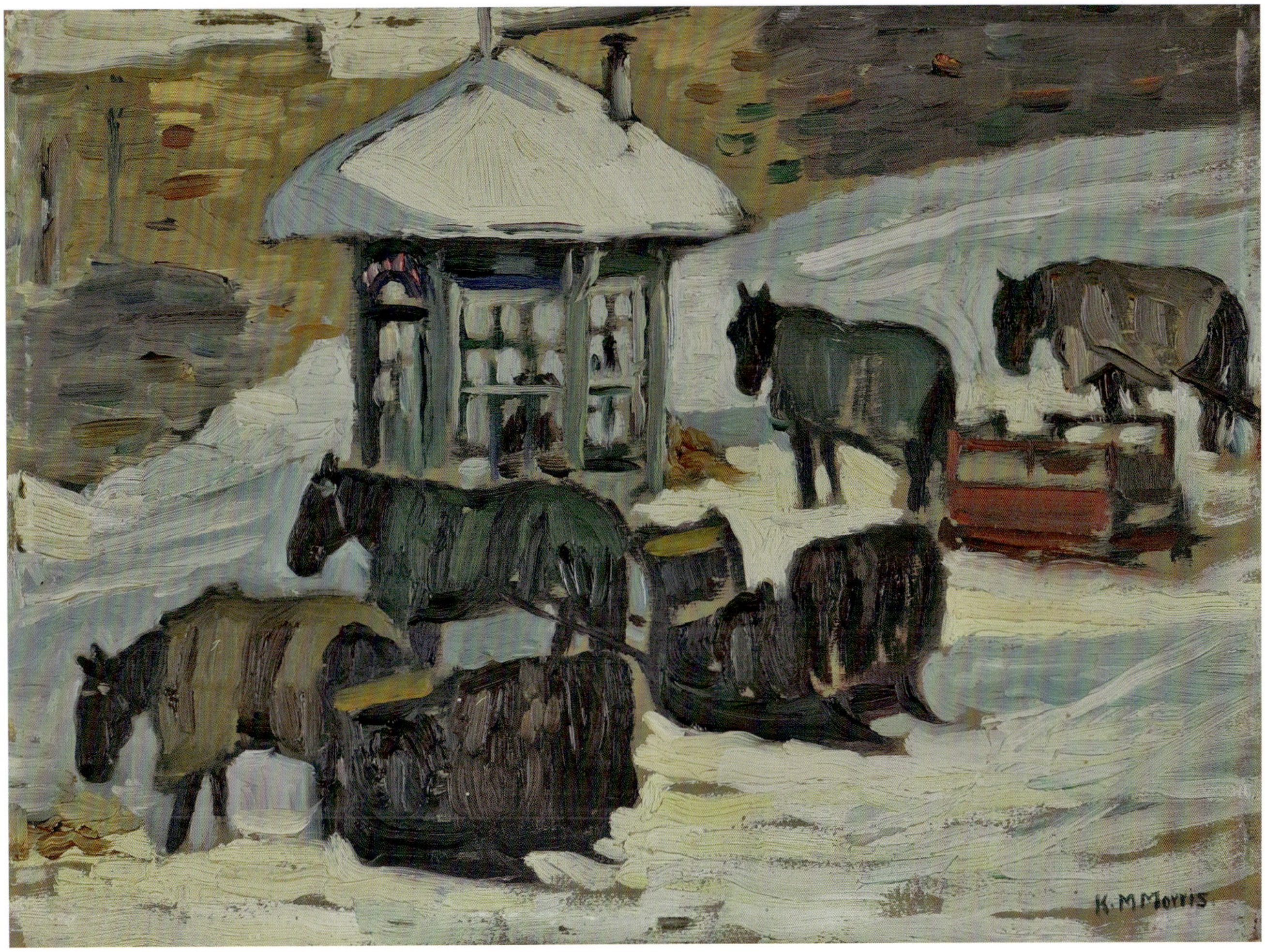

Kathleen M. Morris 1893-1986, Canadian, *Kiosk*, nd, oil on board

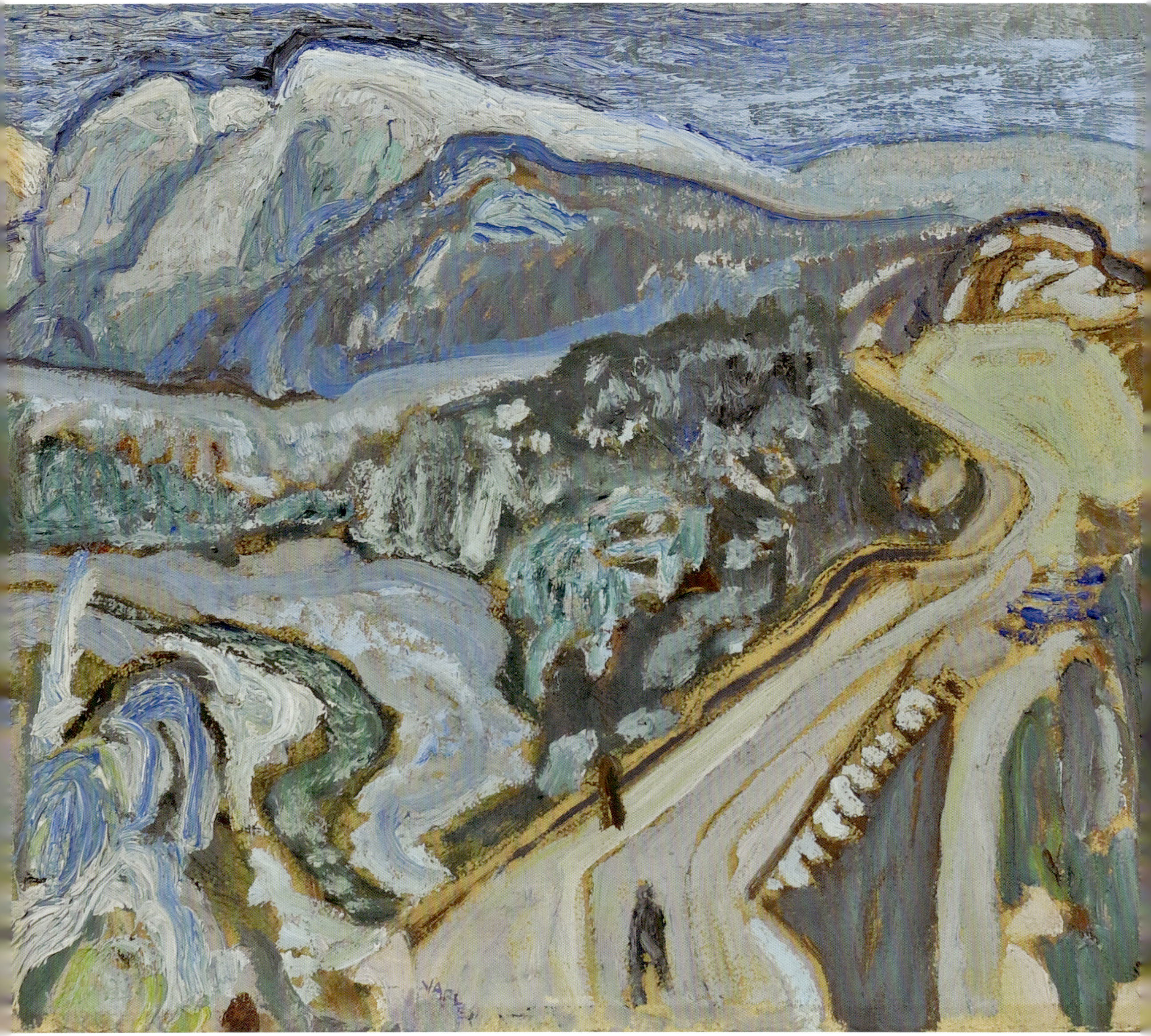

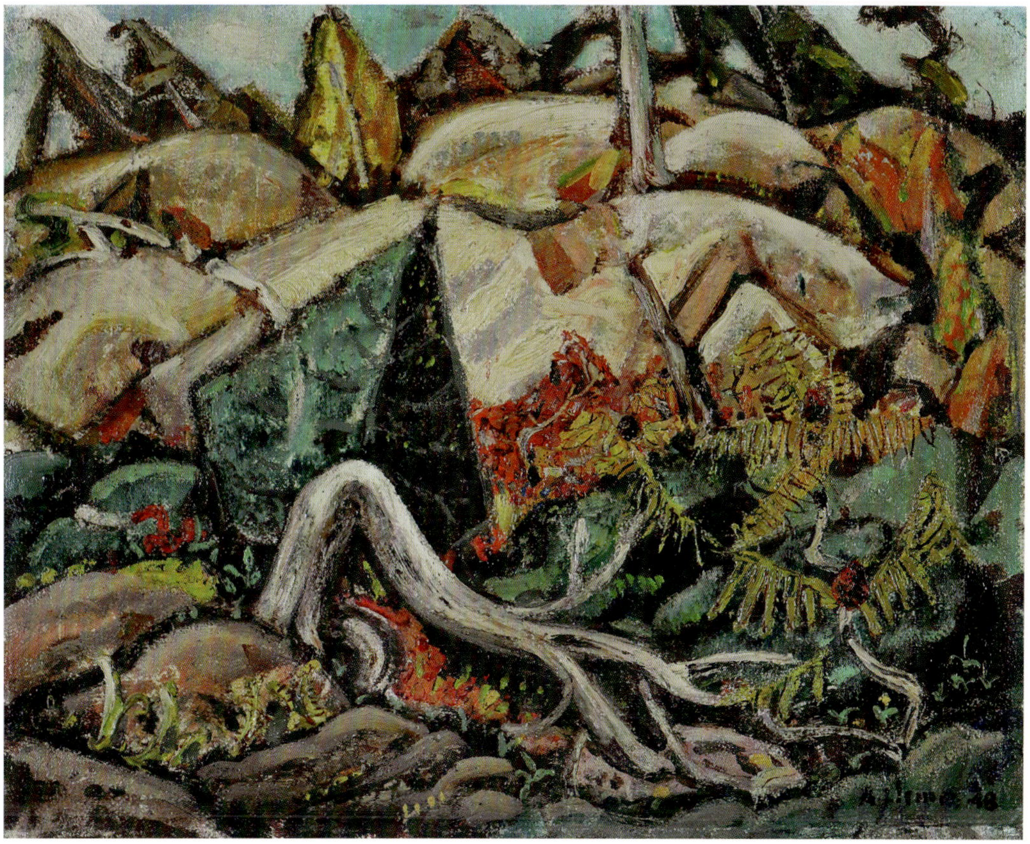

Frederick Varley 1881-1969, Canadian, *Winter, Lynn Valley, B.C.*, 1939, oil on card, © Varley Art Gallery, Town of Markham

Arthur Lismer 1885-1969, Canadian, *Rock & Sumac, Georgian Bay*, 1948, oil on canvas on board

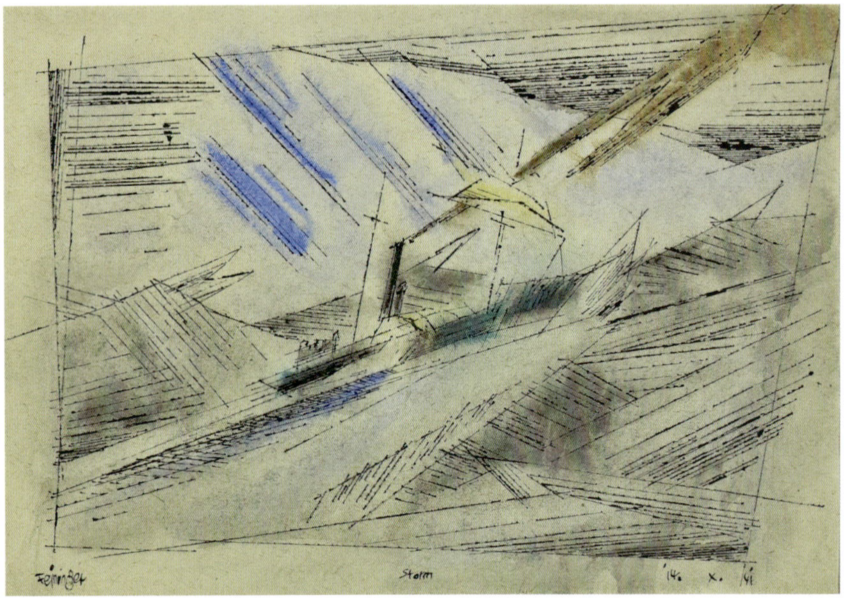

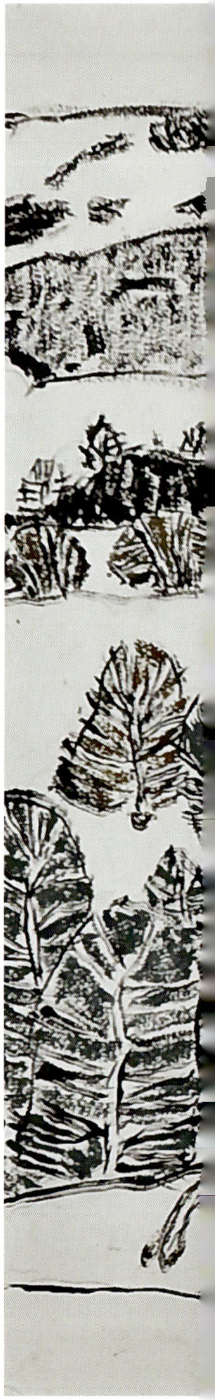

Lyonel Feininger 1871-1956, German; American, *Storm*, 1941, ink, watercolour on wove paper

David Brown Milne 1882-1953, Canadian, *Landscape (Boston Corners)*, 1920, graphite, watercolour on paper

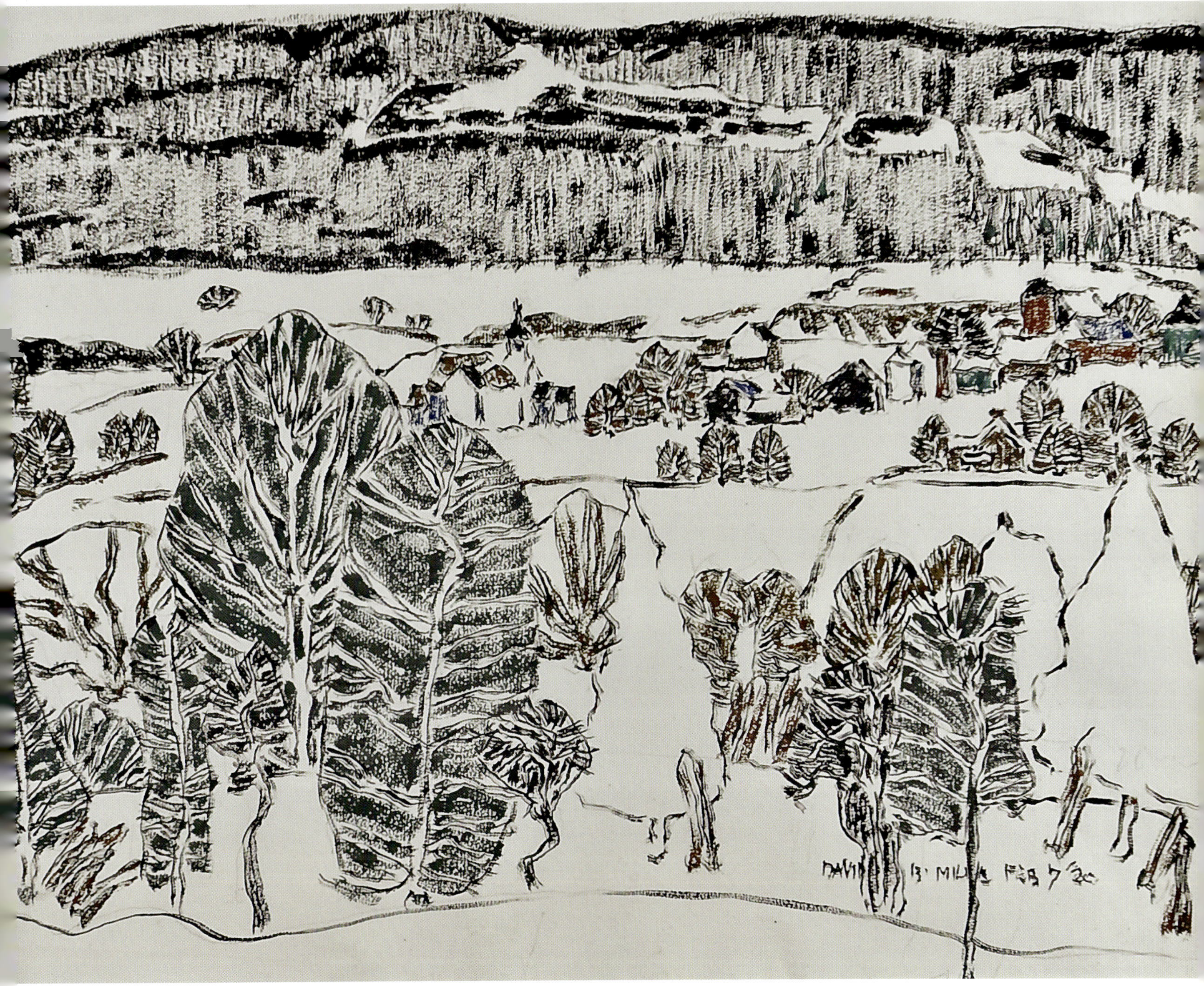
FEB 7 '30

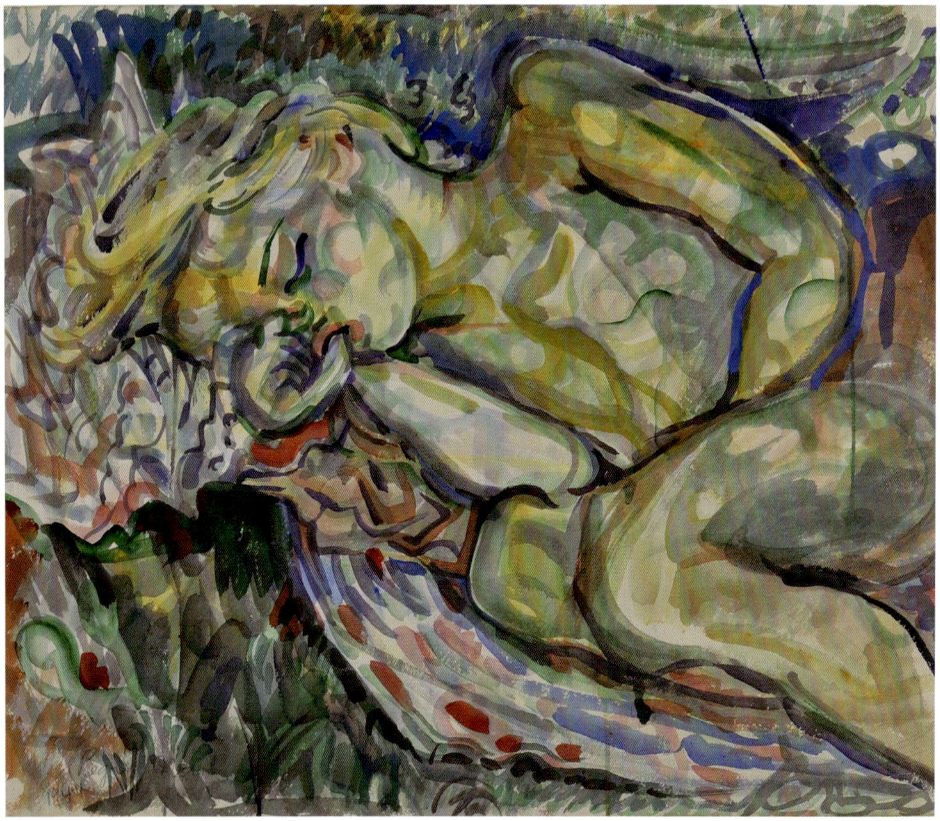

Pegi Nicol MacLeod 1904-1949, Canadian, *Jane Asleep*, 1944, watercolour on paper

Edythe Hembroff-Schleicher 1906-1994, Canadian, *Blue Girl in Boat*, 1968, oil on board

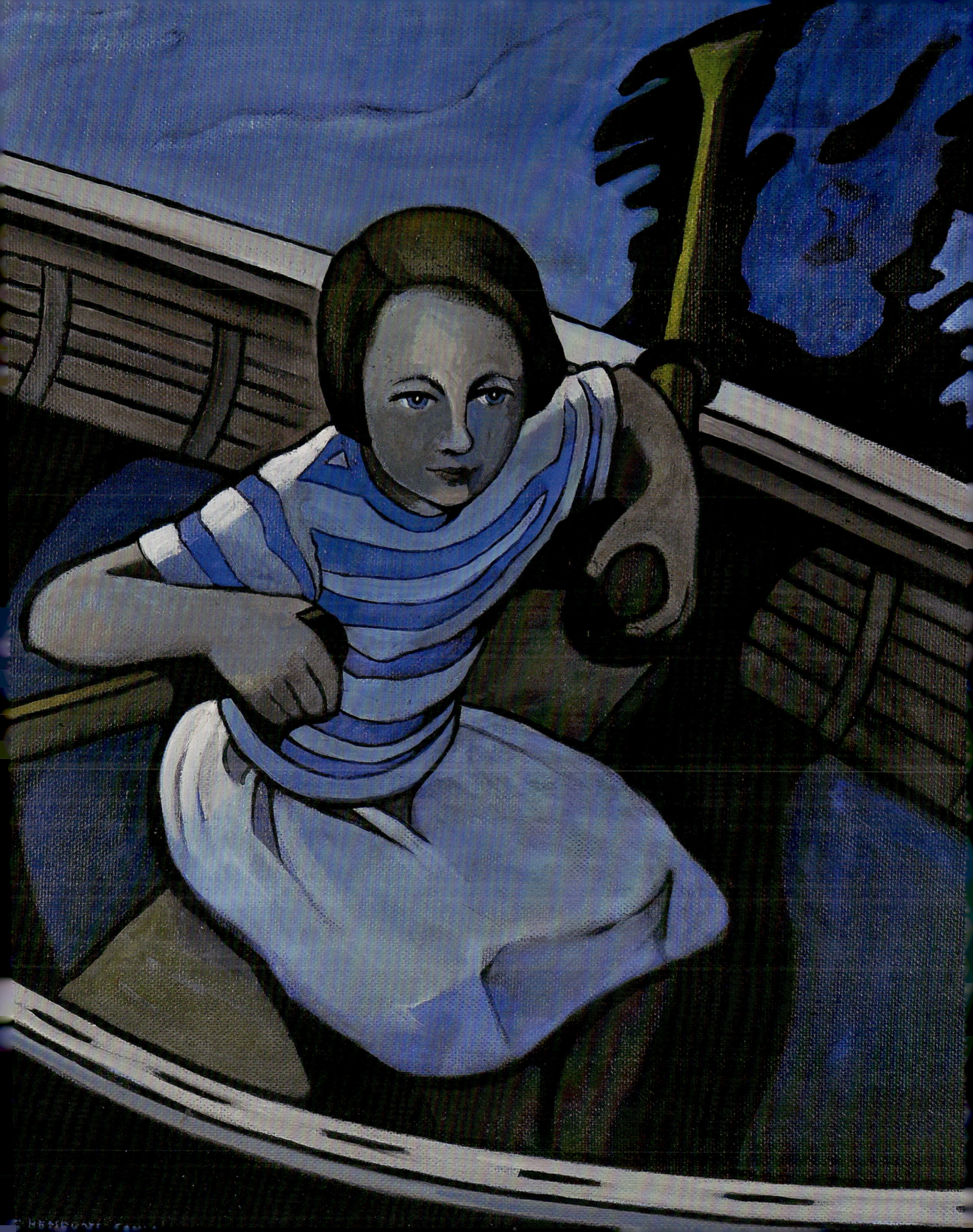

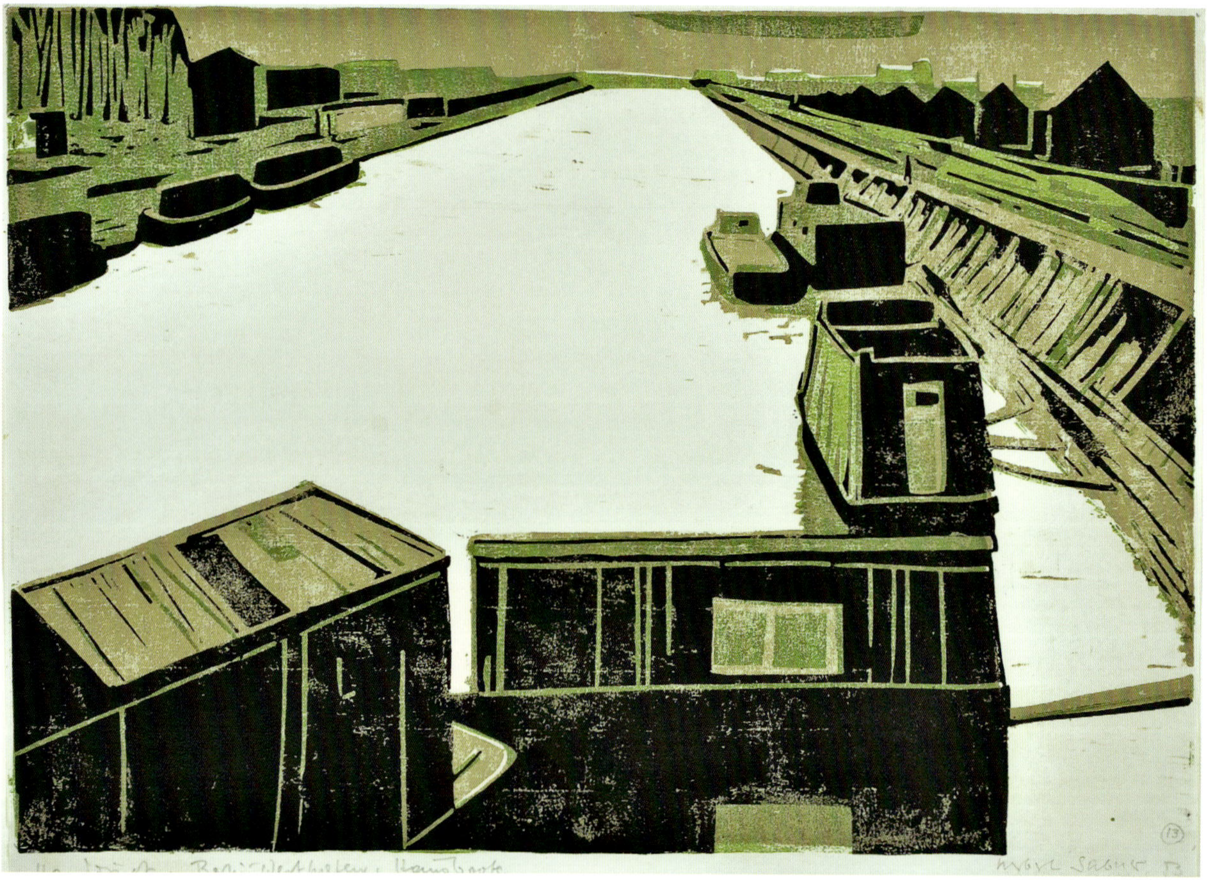

Herbert Siebner 1925-2003, Canadian, *Houseboats, Canal, West Berlin*, 1954, linocut on Gilbert Bond paper

Henry Moore 1898-1986, English, *Pandora & the Imprisoned Statues*, 1950, lithograph on wove paper, reproduced by permission of the Henry Moore Foundation

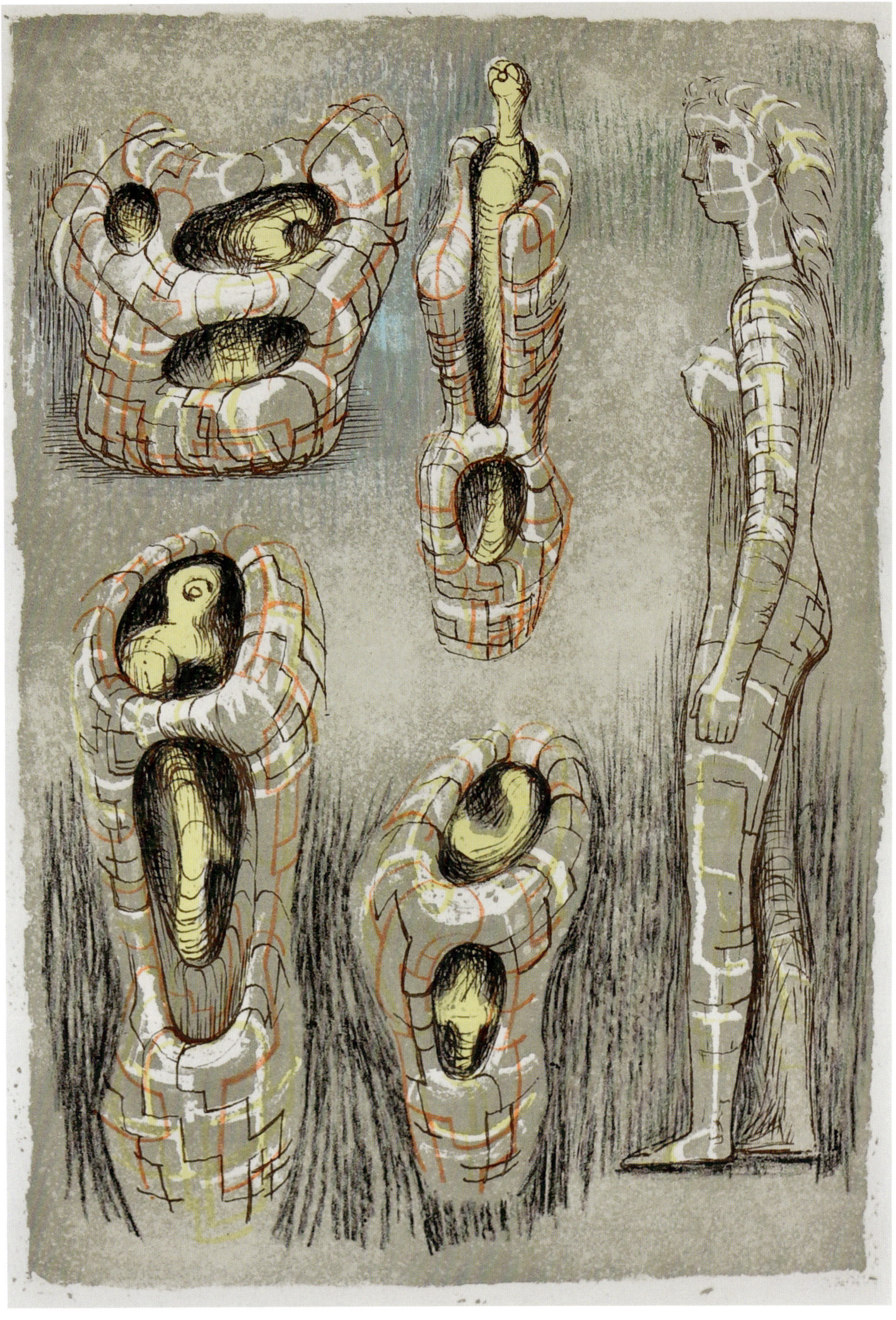

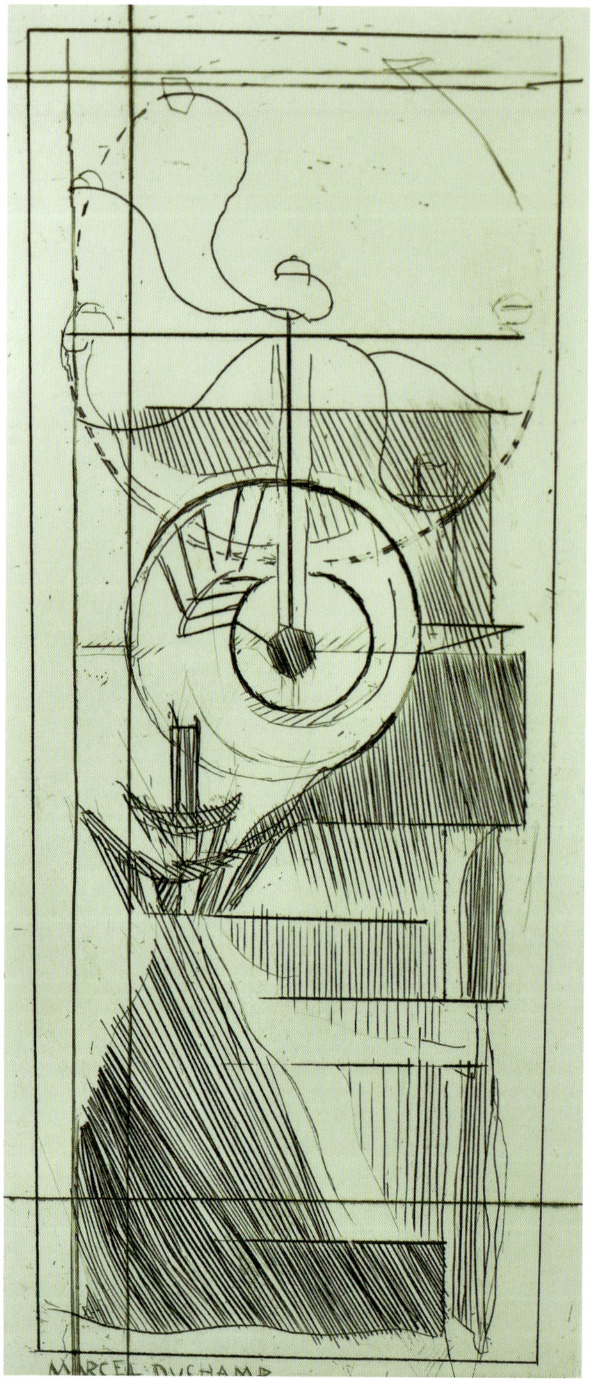

Marcel Duchamp 1887-1968, French, *Coffee Mill* (from *Du Cubisme*), nd, restrike etching on white wove paper

Wassily Kandinsky 1866-1944, Russian, *Stars*, 1938, lithograph on ivory coloured wove paper

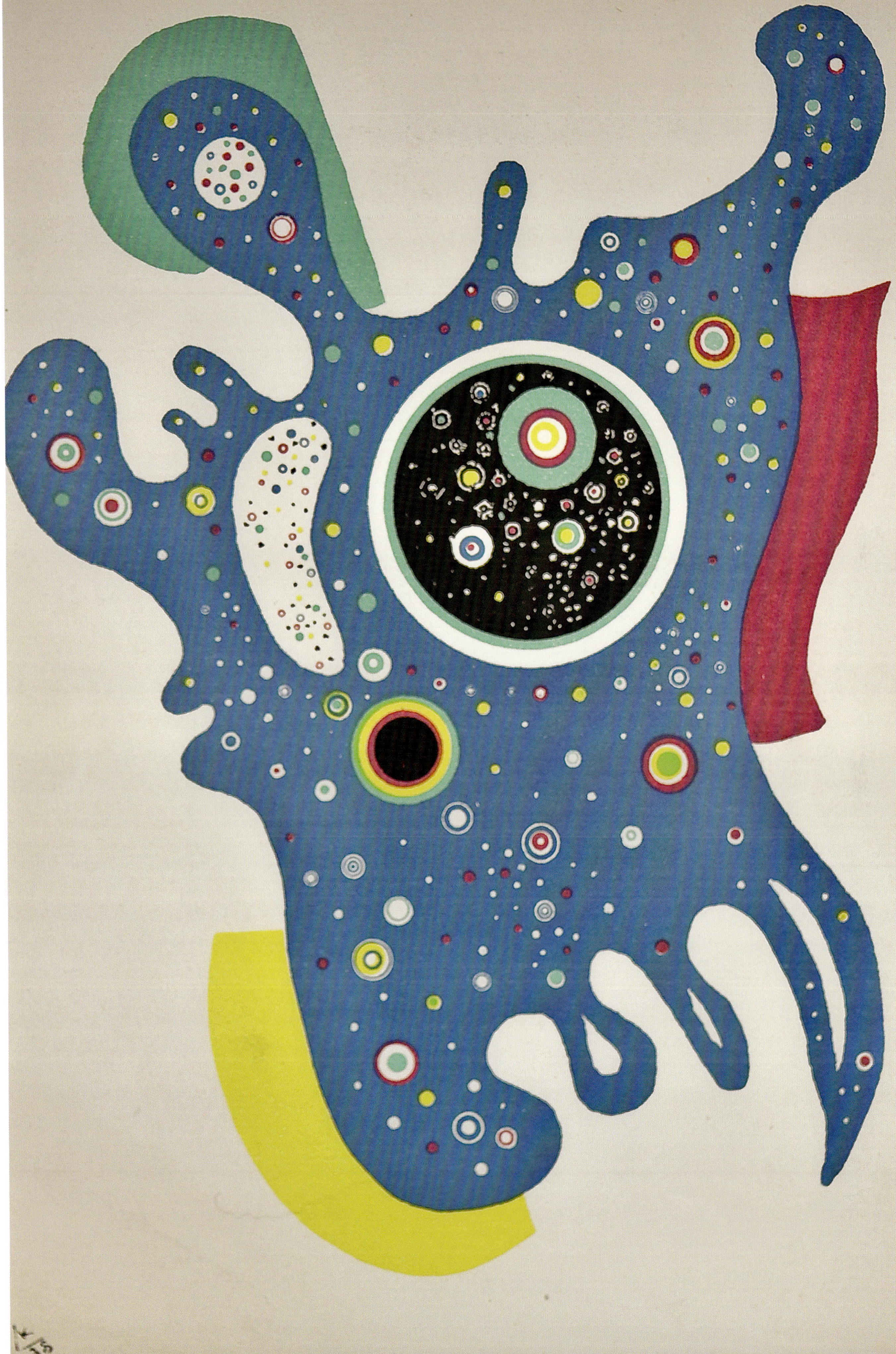

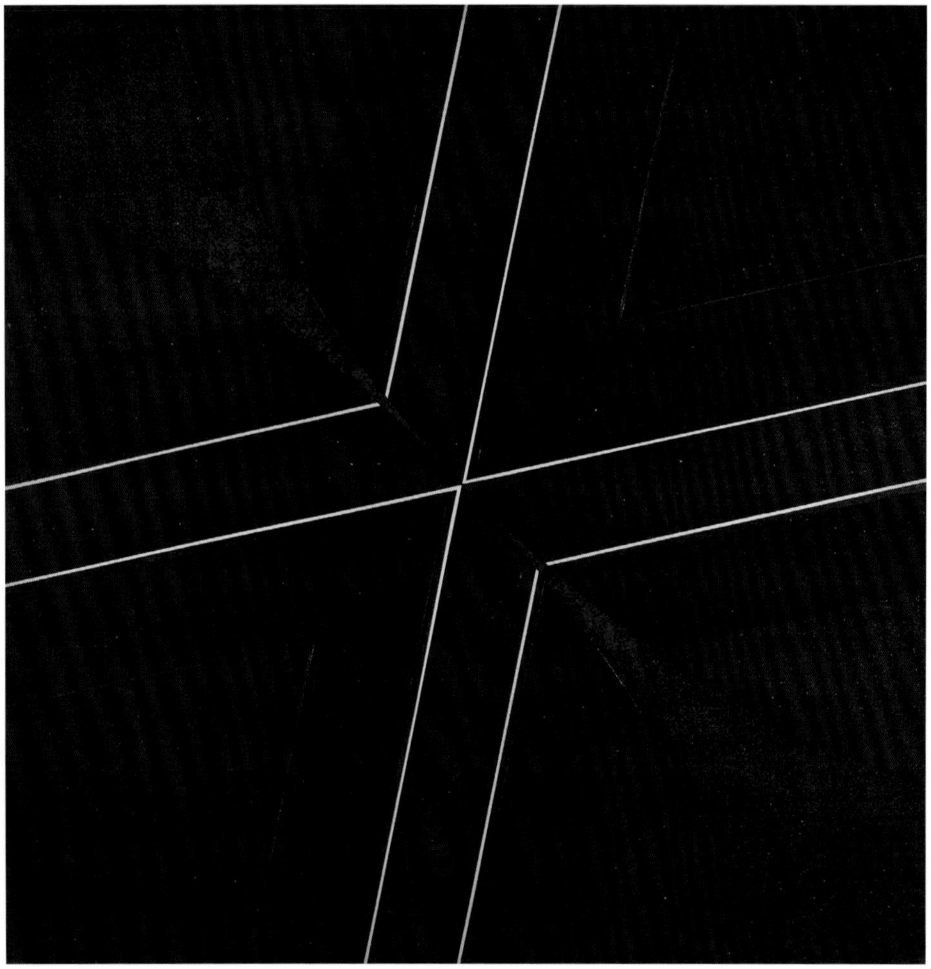

Roy Kiyooka 1926-1994, Canadian, *Menat*, 1963, acrylic on canvas

Harold Town 1924-1990, Canadian, *Cave*, 1957, ink on hardboard

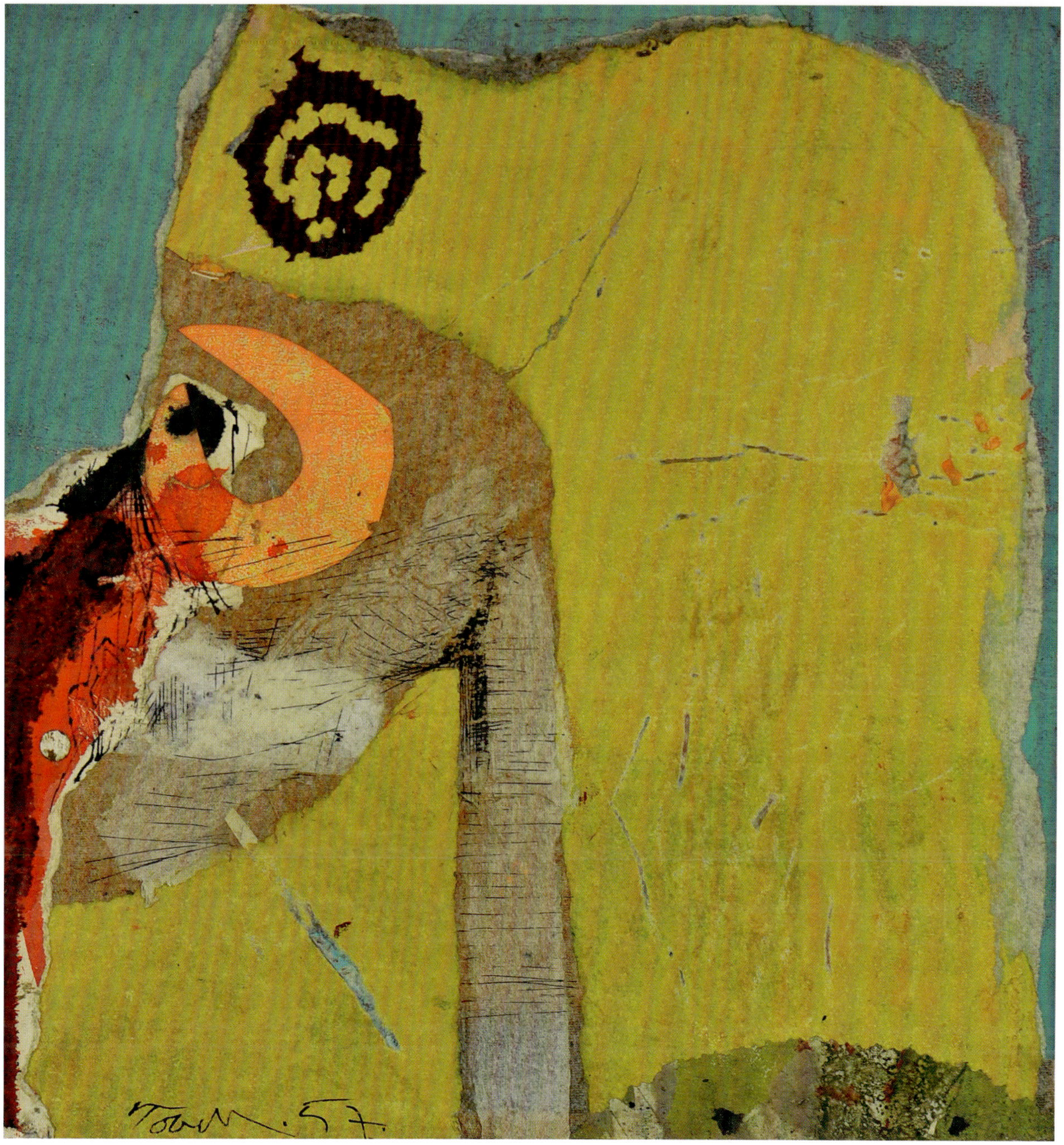

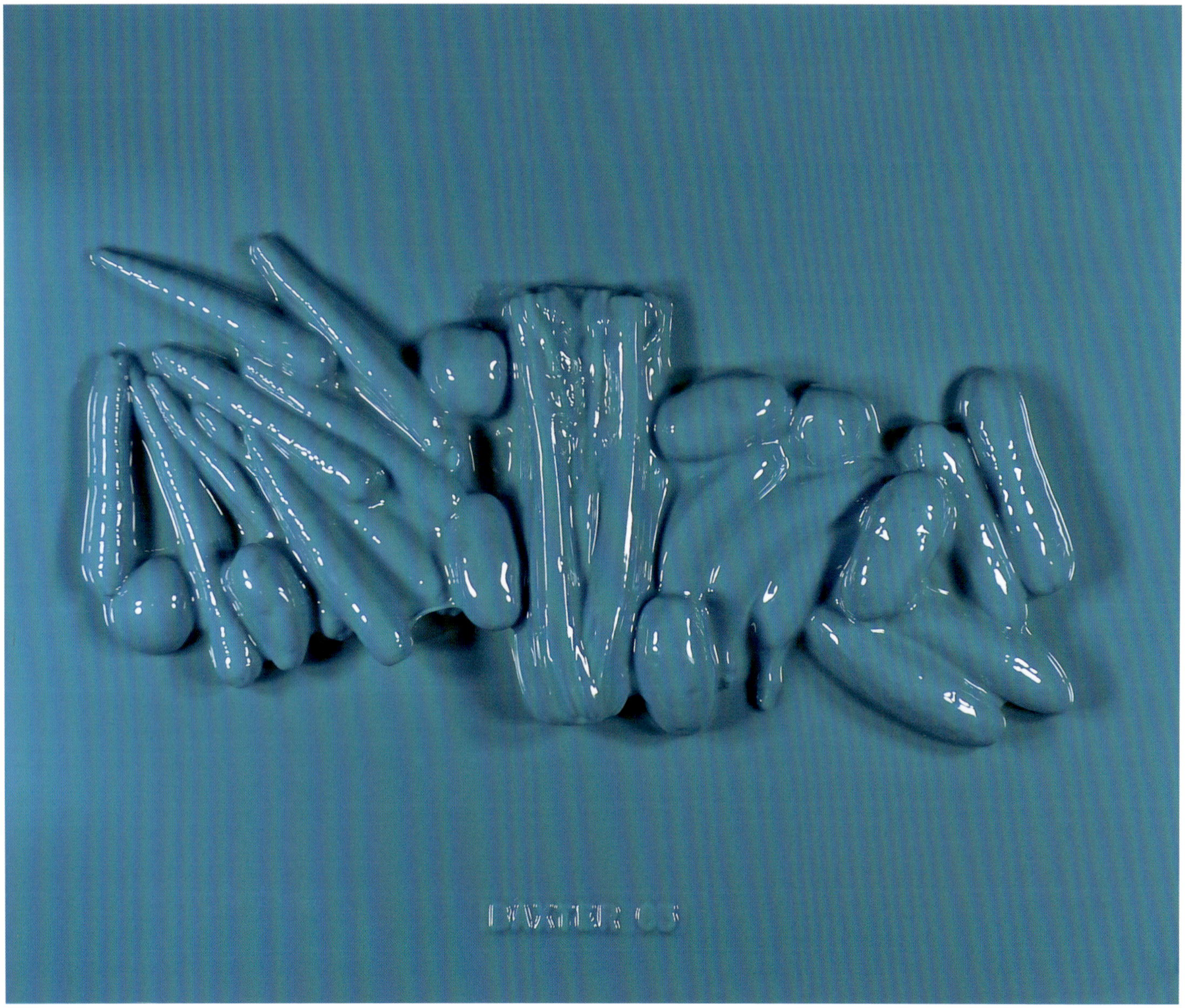

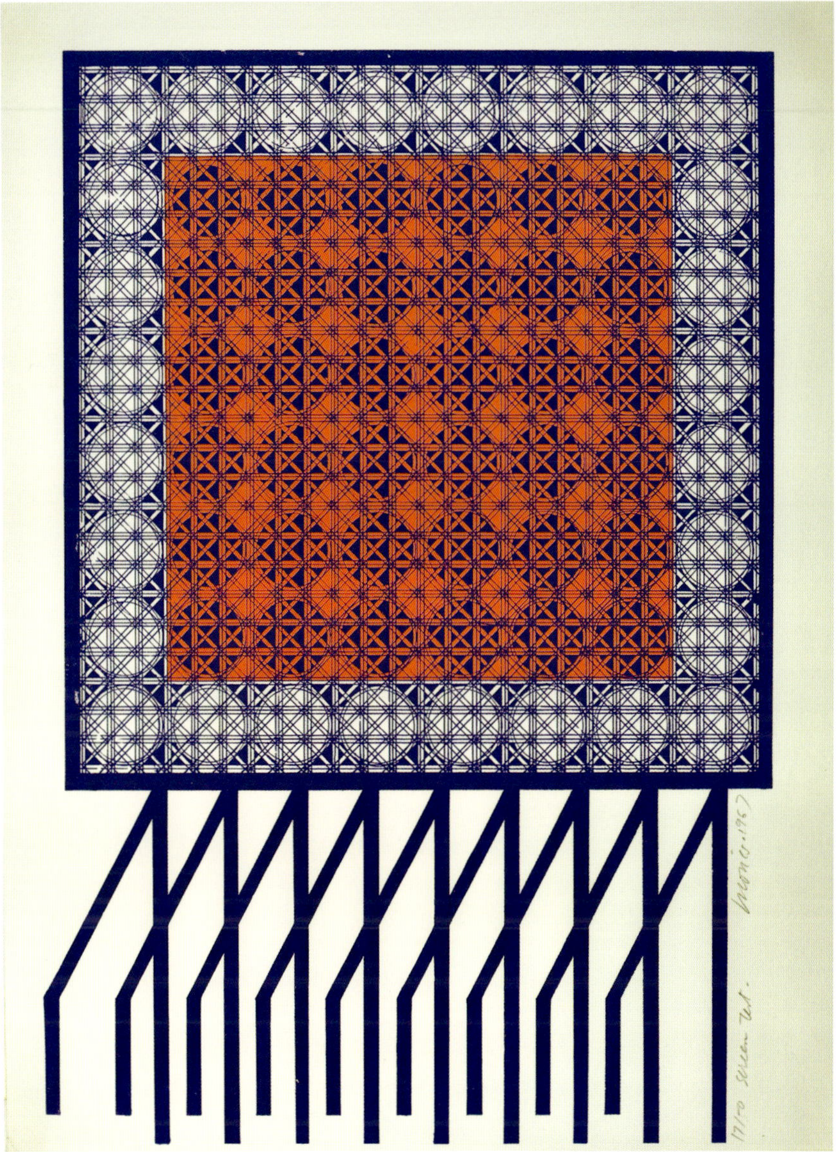

Iain Baxter b. 1936, Canadian, *Still Life*, nd, plastic moulded relief

Michael Morris b. 1942, Canadian, *Screen Test*, 1967, serigraph on paper

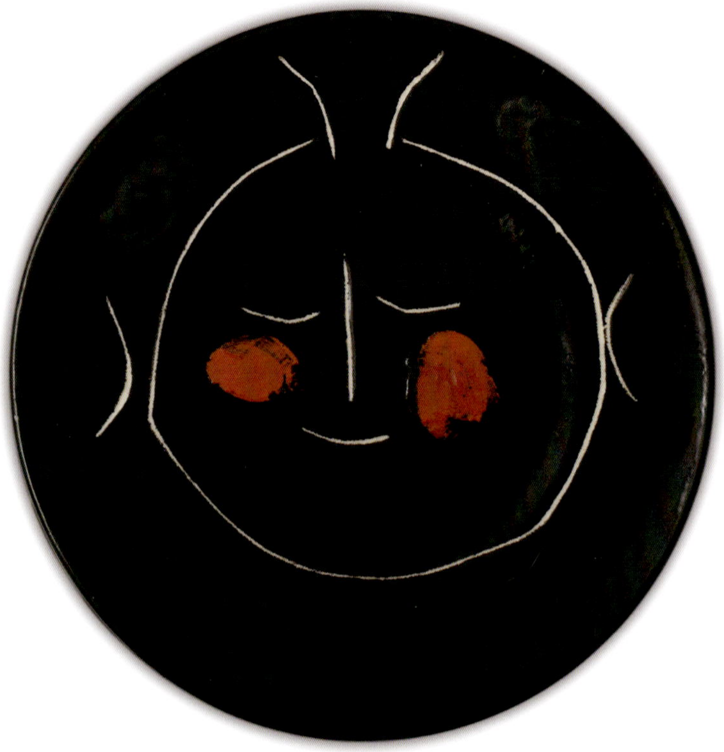

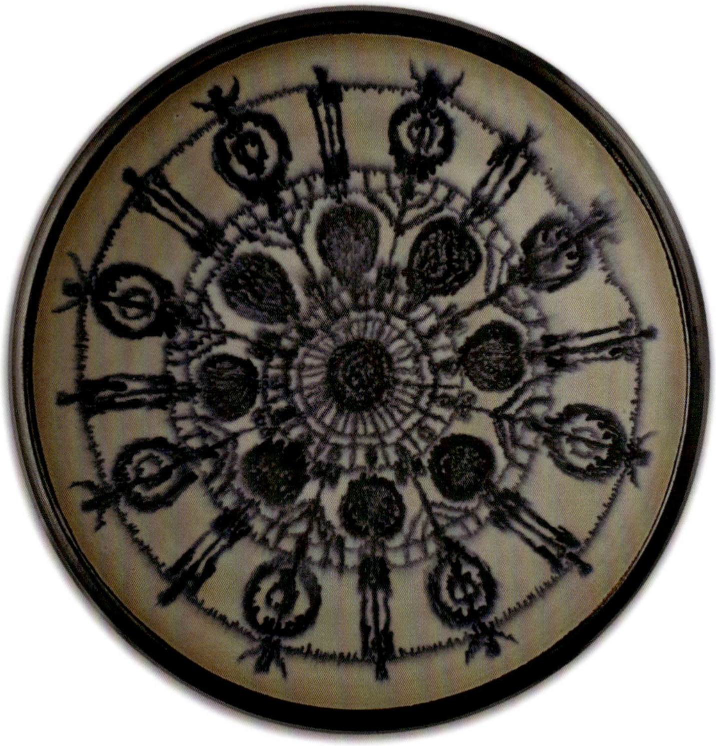

Madoura Pottery Studio Spanish, Plate Designed by **Pablo Picasso**, 20th C, earthenware; glaze; enamel decoration

Jan Grove b. 1930 and **Helga Grove** b. 1927, Canadian, Shallow Bowl with Radiating Design, 20th C, stoneware; glaze; enamel decoration

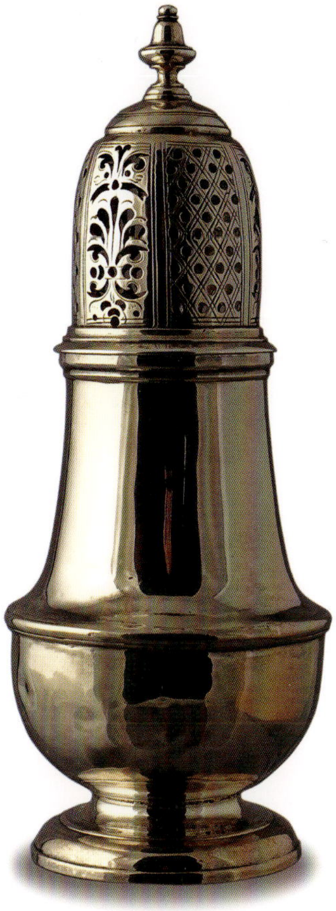

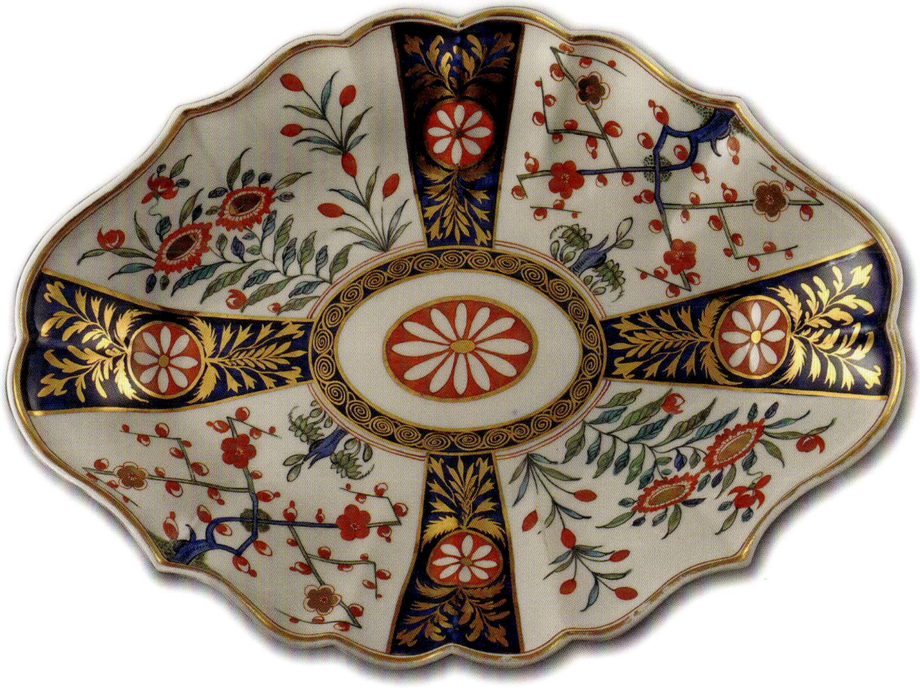

Sam. Welder English, Caster, 1720-21, Britannia (standard) silver

Worcester English, Dish with Imari/Kakiemon-Style Decoration, c.1775, soft paste/steatite porcelain; enamel decoration; gold

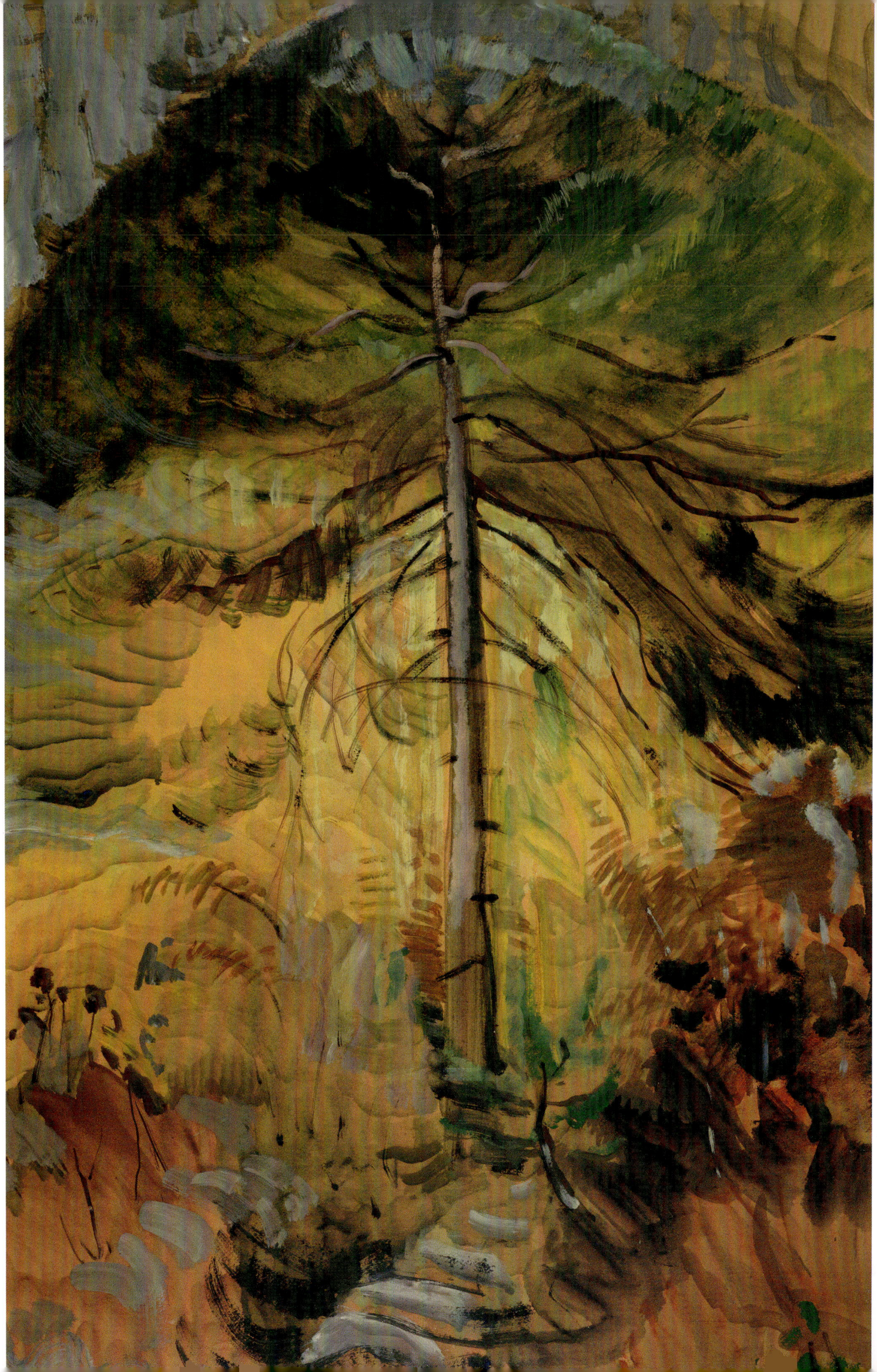

Colin Graham and West Coast Modernism

MICHAEL MORRIS

When the Art Gallery of Greater Victoria (AGGV) moved into its present location on Moss Street in 1951, it was run by a band of dedicated volunteers who were committed to the Gallery's survival and growth, despite a lack of funding and community support. The Gallery Board knew that success depended upon finding a charismatic and visionary person to serve as the Gallery's first Director and Curator, who would lead the AGGV forward into a new age. Colin Graham was the right person for this job, despite his self-proclaimed lack of administrative or curatorial skills. This young man brought with him the qualities that were needed to take on this risky and unknown venture. Colin's knowledge, commitment, and vision were the necessary complement to the volunteers' unwavering dedication and enthusiasm.

Colin's knowledge of art came from his Bachelor of Arts degree in history from Cambridge University, followed by a Master of Arts degree from University of California, Berkeley where he studied with the American-born artist Margaret Peterson who later moved to Victoria. He had also travelled extensively and had interacted with many modernist artists working and showing in the United States when he was lecturing at the California College of Art and Crafts, Oakland, and the Palace of the Legion of Honor, San Francisco. Colin's commitment manifested itself over the 20-year period he spent building the AGGV. Colin's vision for the Gallery was clearly demonstrated through his dedication to showing modern art—art of his generation—in Victoria and fostering acceptance of it, despite the incredible resistance of a city stuck in the Edwardian age.

Emily Carr 1871-1945, Canadian, *Happiness*, 1939, oil on paper

Colin's vision made all the difference. The AGGV would not be a mundane, status quo place to show comfortable and conservative art, which was largely what was offered by the Island Arts and Crafts

Society. Instead, it would be a fresh and exciting art centre that would do justice to a community awakening to the modern postwar era. Victoria in the 1950s was in a transitional period. A city that closely identified with British culture, it was slow to give up its traditions and retrospective mindset, and was thus not as quick as many North American cities to embrace the new ideas and principles that were developing after World War II. As such, Victoria's society was not about to change on its own. It needed people like Colin, as well as the artists he showcased at the Gallery, to incite change on a cultural level.

Colin Graham was fully aware that he would have to work especially hard to introduce modern cultural sensibilities to the community. However, what Colin soon realized was that he did indeed have a platform upon which to build. There was a history of modernism in Victoria, beginning with Emily Carr—who emerged as an artist at the beginning of the twentieth century—and was carried forward into the 1950s in a quiet way through Gallery volunteers and board members. These people had connections with Carr that spurred their vision forth. Colin played an active role in this task through the connections he developed with a network of artists of his own generation living in Victoria and Vancouver who, through varying degrees, shared the optimism and openness of modernism exemplified by Carr and the Group of Seven. These artists looked to establish Canadian art that was fresh and in keeping with their own time and place. Colin sought to make the Gallery an active part of this movement.

The tradition upon which Colin Graham built started with Emily Carr, who was born in 1871. Her first real exposure to modern art occurred from 1910 to 1911 in France, where she connected with the Fauves. Her experimentation with and promotion of new art forms fell flat in Victoria, however, where her works were summarily rejected upon exhibition. Her enthusiasm for experimenting with new art expressions would not be rekindled until 1927 when she met members of the Group of Seven while showing her art in an exhibition of West Coast artists at the National Gallery in Ottawa. The members of the Group of Seven, particularly Lawren Harris, encouraged Carr to return to her modernist painting investigations and search for a more honest expression that reflected her time, place, and personal yearnings. Carr returned to Victoria and entered the most productive period of her artistic career, further encouraged by the Seattle artist Mark Tobey who taught a master's class in her studio in 1928. In the 1930s Carr's art was becoming accepted outside of Victoria and slowly more visible within it. In 1932 she and a number of younger artists, including Jack Shadbolt, Max Maynard, Ina Uhthoff, and Edythe Hembroff-Schleicher, exhibited their work in what was called *The Modern Room* as part of an Island Arts and Crafts Society exhibition. Carr would continue to push the boundaries of her painting explorations, and up until her death would show regularly at the Vancouver Art Gallery.

At the time of Carr's death on March 2, 1945, Colin Graham was living in Berkeley, California. About three months later he was in Victoria visiting his parents when he met the Honourable Mark Kearley, the founder of the movement to create an art gallery in Victoria, which resulted in the creation of The Little Centre, which in turn eventually became the AGGV. Mark invited Colin to the late Emily's studio at 218 St. Andrew's Street. Colin recounted the event:

> In a room of that house there were, I estimated, roughly 600 Emilies, including large mounted drawings. Except for works she had sold or given away, here was Emily's entire life work. On the back of each work Emily had written its sale price. The highest price

I could find was $275.00. In an adjoining room was Lawren Harris (whom I knew from Vancouver days), a man who must have been Willy Newcombe, (a friend of Emily's and a trustee of her estate,) and a third man, Major Cuthbert Holmes, a leading Victoria realtor who was probably the city's only collector.

Prior to Emily's death, she and Lawren Harris had gone over the 600 works in the adjoining room and picked out 160 of what they felt were her best and most typical. These were to become the property of the province. The remaining 440 were to be sold, with the resulting income to provide scholarships for serious B.C. art students.[1]

Colin became keenly aware, upon seeing the paintings in her studio and meeting those who had known the deceased artist, that Carr was—and would continue to be—keenly significant to the cultural life of Victoria.

Just when Carr was discovering modern art in France, the next generation of B.C. artists was just being born. Their involvement with the AGGV in its early years would be instrumental in bringing modernism to the fore in Victoria. Artists such as Jack Shadbolt, Gordon Smith, E.J. Hughes, and B.C. Binning were all aware of Carr's influence on modernism in Canada. They became the significant figures in defining the culture of the 1950s. It is interesting that they brought to this period a utopian idealism, despite living in an era often referred to as the age of anxiety. These artists shared the common experience of being born into the First World War, maturing during the Depression, surviving the Second World War, only to then confront the spectre of the atomic bomb and the start of the Cold War. They were all alumni of the Vancouver School of Art (founded in 1925), which quickly established a reputation for developing new ideas promoted through teachers like Jock MacDonald, Charles Scott, and Group of Seven member Frederick Varley. This group of artists came of age during a period of ferment in the international art world, a time when all the major art movements—the "isms"—of the twentieth century emerged. These influences played a key role in helping them emerge from the dark period of the Depression and WWII with a desire to use art as a way to create social change.

In the fall of 1949, a few years before Colin's arrival in Victoria, the Community Arts Council in Vancouver held an important exhibition that brought modernism to life for British Columbians.[2] *Design for Living* was an eye-opener for many, demonstrating how design, art, and architecture were interconnected and vital to reflecting and even forming the optimism and ideals of the 1950s. Faced with a housing shortage, Vancouverites discovered through this exhibition innovative examples of modern dwellings. When Colin arrived in Victoria he connected with those Vancouver artists who were at the forefront of modernism provincially and nationally, artists Colin recognized as being B.C.'s innovators in the 50s. Relatively isolated on Vancouver Island, Colin had to work hard to establish and maintain these connections. However, as a result of his determination and vision, he showed the works of the best of that generation in Victoria, thereby encouraging Victorians to take note of and interest in the exciting possibilities contained within the modernist movement.

Not only did Colin tap into what was happening on B.C.'s mainland, he also used his connections in Seattle to exhibit artists such as Mark Tobey, Kenneth Callaghan, and Morris Graves, all of whom were at the forefront of the Pacific Northwest school. Colin recognized that Victoria had the potential to be a geographic hub for art enthusiasts, attracting audiences not just from

Vancouver, but Seattle as well, thereby exposing the community to art developments that were happening internationally. Furthermore, Colin embraced artists who had immigrated to Victoria, such as the American Margaret Peterson, the Czech Jan Zach, the Austrian Richard Ciccimarra, and the German Herbert Siebner. At the time, their arrival created some condescension on the part of Canadian artists who felt that the emigrant artists should assimilate Canadian ideals. For Colin, however, these newcomers brought a knowledge of international Modernism that was a vital addition to Victoria's developing arts community. Through these artists and those Canadians who were exploring aspects of international Modernism, Colin brought the world to Victoria.

The exhibition *Vision into Reality: Colin Graham and West Coast Modernism* explores the three decades after Emily Carr's death. It presents the setting Colin Graham established in Victoria and the artists he fostered and sought help from to invigorate the capital city. Colin introduced to Victoria European modern art movements and their influence on artists of that era. Binning brought a Bauhaus aesthetic in his art and architecture; Shadbolt introduced Surrealism; Bates, Siebner, Ciccimarra, and others brought their unique takes on Expressionism. The works in this exhibition represent 14 artists including Carr whose influences have enriched Victoria's understanding of modernism.

Vancouver School of Art Group

Originally from Victoria, Jack Shadbolt (1909–1998) would spend the majority of his career in Vancouver. He first met Emily Carr in the early 1930s through another young Victoria artist, Max Maynard. Both men saw her work in the 1930 Island Arts and Crafts Society exhibition and were impressed with how progressive her work was compared to her contemporaries in Victoria. Both men requested a studio visit and became friends with Carr. Certainly the early work of both artists demonstrates an affinity with Carr's painting, and Shadbolt credits his early interest in primitivism to seeing Carr's totem works.

In every way, Shadbolt was a modern man. Born in England in 1909, his family immigrated to Canada and settled in Victoria in 1912. In 1932, at the age of 23, he exhibited along with Emily Carr at the Island Arts and Crafts Society's *Modern Room*. Shortly thereafter he left Victoria to travel in the United States, where he met the Mexican painter and muralist Diego Rivera. When he returned to Canada, Shadbolt joined the faculty of the Vancouver Art School in 1937, teaching painting and drawing until 1966. During the war he served as a war artist in England and on the continent. His paintings from the war and postwar period were mostly executed in ink and watercolour and contain urban themes with a powerful social message. In 1948 he had a brief but important stay studying in New York at the Art Students League with the influential Abstractionist Hans Hofmann. Through his use of oil paint in the 1950s and 60s, Shadbolt developed his unique style of Abstraction. Later, his art became the celebration of the act of creation itself. As well as being regarded as a respected teacher, Shadbolt had numerous exhibitions and mural commissions, and represented Canada at the Venice and São Paulo Art Biennials. Colin Graham organized solo exhibitions of his work in 1954, 1958, 1961, 1965, and 1970 at the AGGV. Colin noted that when Shadbolt first showed in Victoria in 1950 very few of his paintings sold. However, when he held his next exhibition in Victoria in 1954, his work almost sold out. Victoria was beginning to warm up

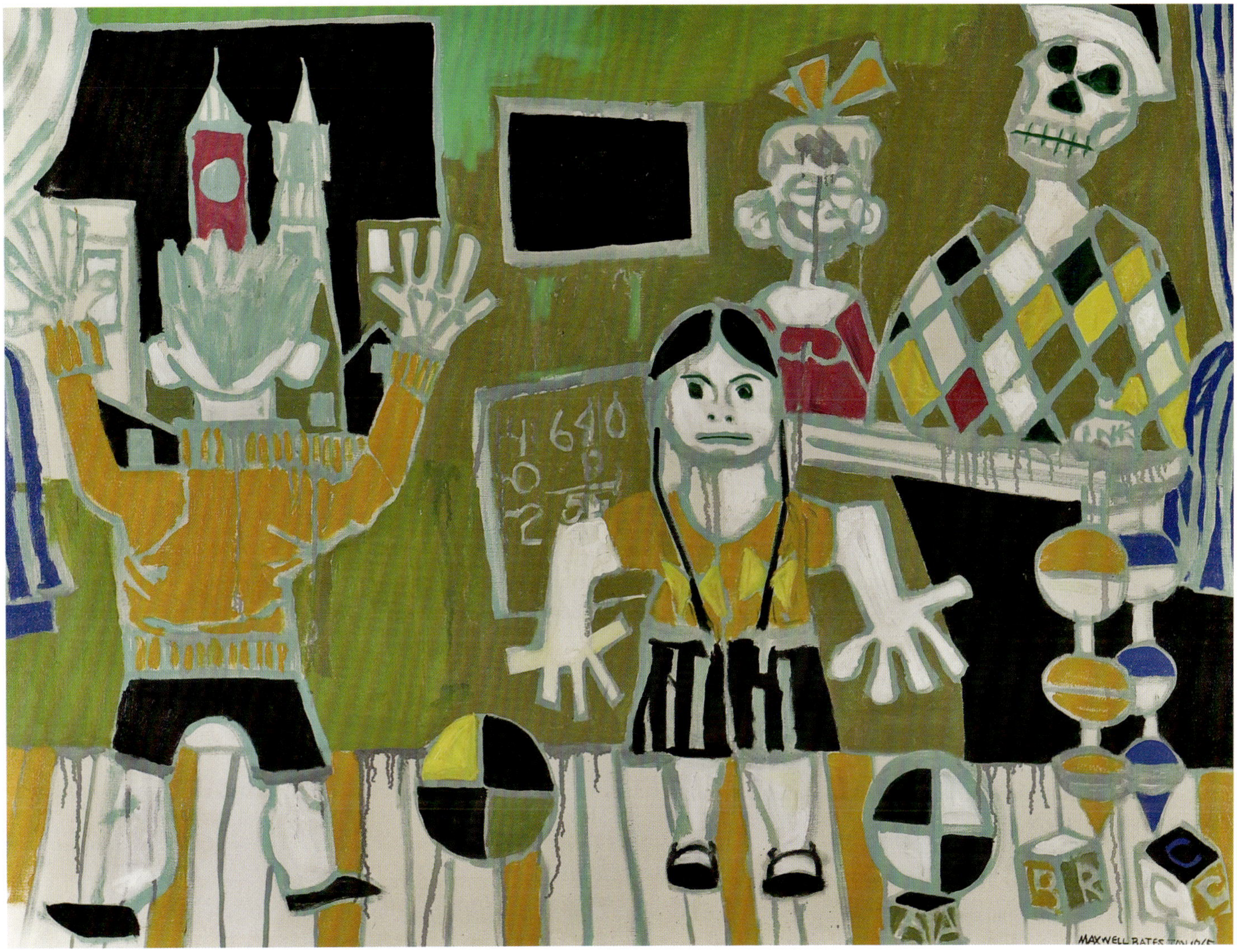

Maxwell Bates 1906-1980, Canadian, *Kindergarten*, 1965, oil on canvas

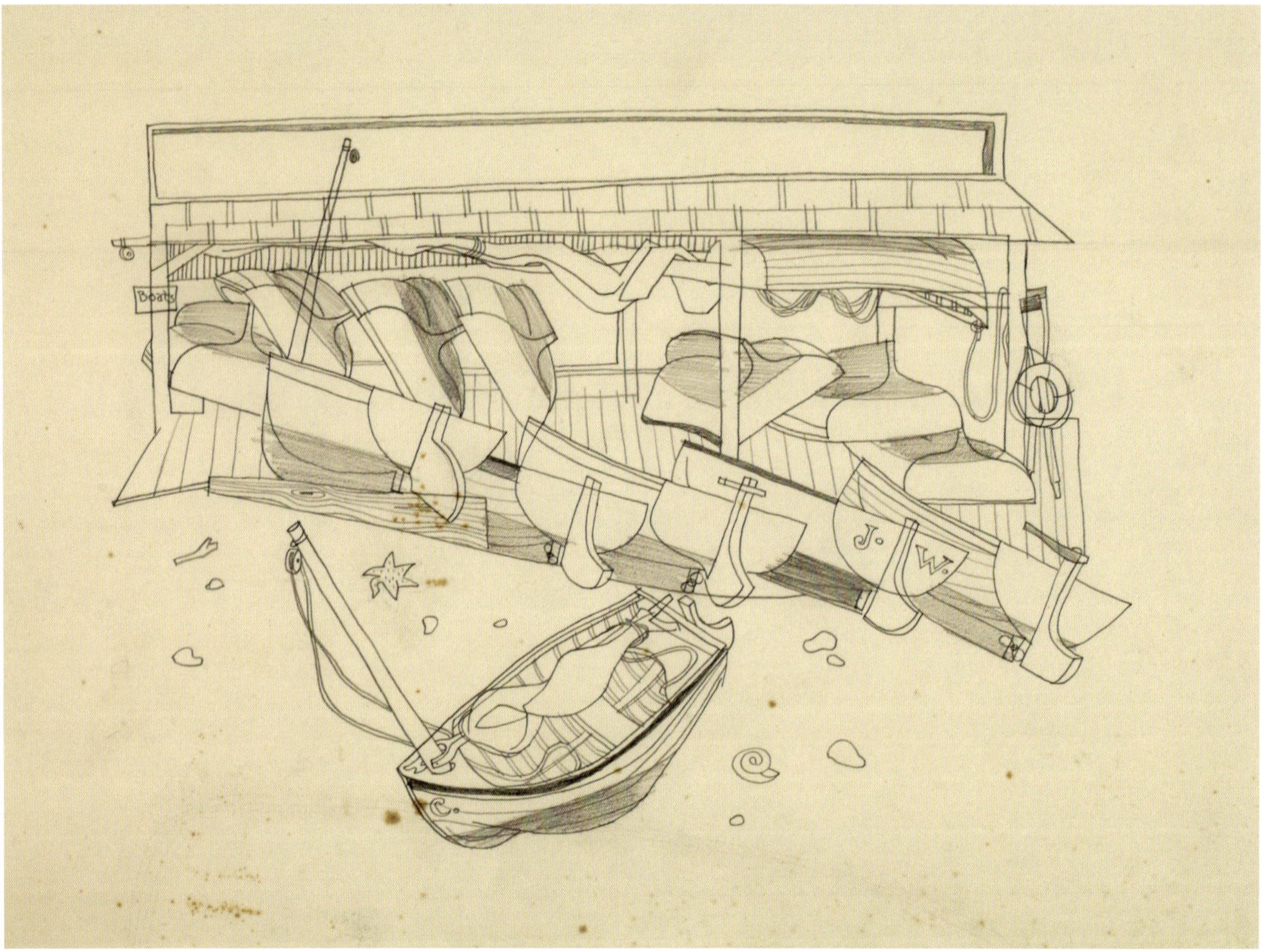

B.C. Binning 1909-1976, Canadian, *Boat Rental*, unknown, graphite on paper

to his modern style. Jack Shadbolt and his wife Doris made a major contribution to the cultural life of British Columbia and Canada.

Bertram Charles Binning (1909–1976) was born in Medicine Hat, Alberta, and was an artist, architect, educator, and committed modernist. In the 1940s he was known for his whimsical ink drawings that showed the delights of leisure: sail boats, coves, beaches, and care-free people enjoying the sparkling sea and sunshine illustrated a utopia within our reach. His work stood in stark contrast to Shadbolt's evocation of the bleakness of war and a world in turmoil. Binning graduated from the Vancouver Art School in 1932 and started teaching there in 1934. Binning's artistic vision benefited from the time he spent in London and New York in the late 1930s. In London he studied art with Henry Moore and Amédée Ozenfont who taught Purism, a theory that stressed the importance of clarity and discipline. Binning was also aware of the ideas circulating around Le Corbusier and the Bauhaus, which kindled his interest in architecture. He adopted those principles and applied them to his life, art, and teaching.

As the postwar scene developed, Binning's utopian view of what constituted modernism influenced every aspect of his life during that period: art, architecture, city planning, and education. He pioneered the concept of collaborative projects where artists worked together with other specialists to produce works that were regional, innovative, and private while at the same time practical, and highly applicable and adaptable to public needs. He was appointed to the University of British Columbia's Department of Architecture in 1949 and founded the Department of Fine Arts in 1955 where he served as department head until 1966. In addition to his paintings, he also designed large glass tesserae mosaic murals, the best known located in the Dal Grauer substation on Burrard Street in Vancouver. His contribution to the development of culture in British Columbia was enormous. In 1940 he designed and built his own modernist home, which became an inspiration to so many others to adopt a lifestyle that wholly reflected the modernist aesthetic. Jack Shadbolt, with his brother Doug, followed Binning's lead and built an impressive modernist house.

Gordon Smith was another of the Vancouver School of Art group to teach and promote modernism in Vancouver during this period. He was born in England in 1919, just as the First World War was ending. His family left England, and Smith grew up in Winnipeg, where he later worked at the commercial art firm Brigdens of Winnipeg as well as studied at the Winnipeg School of Art along with Group of Seven member L. L. FitzGerald. He moved to Vancouver in 1940, married Marion Fleming, and then proceeded to join the Canadian Army. Upon returning from service overseas in 1944, he continued his art education at the Vancouver School of Art and graduated in 1946. That year he joined the staff of the Vancouver School of Art and taught graphics and design for ten years. In 1956, he joined the Faculty of Education at the University of British Columbia where he taught art until his retirement in 1982.

Gordon Smith met Colin Graham in San Francisco in 1948 when Smith was taking a course with the well-known artist and teacher Elmer Bischoff. At the AGGV, Graham included Smith in a group exhibition with Molly and Bruno Bobak in 1954, and held a retrospective of Smith's career in 1966. Smith collaborated with architect Arthur Erickson on major commissions for Expo 67 in Montreal, Simon Fraser University in Vancouver, and the Canadian Pavilion for the Osaka World Fair in 1970. As well, Erickson designed Smith's home and studio in West Vancouver, which is considered one of the finest examples of Erickson's modernist architecture. Smith's paintings have been recognised with many national honours, including the Governor General award in 2009. Throughout his career, he has maintained an active presence in the Canadian art scene. To this day, Smith remains accessible to younger artists as both teacher and mentor.

Edward John Hughes (1913–2007) grew up in Nanaimo, British Columbia. At the age of 20, in 1933, he was accepted to the Vancouver Art School studying with Charles Scott, Jock MacDonald, and Frederick Varley. That same year he visited the *Century of Progress* exhibition in Chicago. Travelling through the American Midwest he saw the effects of the Great Depression and the terrible devastation that it brought to all. Hughes, like many young artists of his generation, was inspired by the paintings and murals of Diego Rivera. He was also moved by the works of Thomas Hart Benton, Grant Wood, and others from the Regionalist Movement who turned their backs on modernism. Instead, they created murals often commissioned by the U.S. government's Work Projects Administration program depicting allegorical sagas of everyday people working on the land.

Hughes returned to Vancouver in 1934 full of the influences and ideas he had seen in his travels. He joined a commercial art firm specialising in mural commissions with fellow Vancouver School of Art students Paul Goranson and Orville Fisher. In 1943 they enlisted as war artists where they saw action throughout the war, returning to Vancouver in 1946. Hughes was the recipient of an

Emily Carr scholarship in 1947 on the recommendation of Lawren Harris, and shortly thereafter he moved to Vancouver Island seeking a reclusive life. He seldom strayed far from familiar locations around Southern Vancouver Island including the Cowichan Valley and the Gulf Islands he so often painted. It was there that he found the source of his inspiration—the paintings of government docks, fishing boats, arbutus treed beaches, and coastal life in general—that represent his understanding of the place and its beauty. For the rest of his life Hughes remained committed to the principles of the Regionalist Movement, but his work was far from parochial. Ian Thom, Senior Curator at the Vancouver Art Gallery states, "Hughes has a deep affection for B.C. landscape and a vision that is unmistakably his own."[3] Despite not being a true modernist such as Shadbolt, Binning, and Smith, Hughes carried a sensibility that did reflect its time and place, and was a very important figure during this period on Vancouver Island.

The World Comes to Victoria: Making Victoria Home

Maxwell Bates (1906–1980) was born in Calgary. He visited Carr as a young artist in 1929. The year he met Carr was a critical period for her, as it was just two years after she returned to painting following her introduction to Lawren Harris and the Group of Seven. It was also just one year after Mark Tobey had taught his master class in her studio. Bates therefore would have witnessed the artist in her prime.

Shortly after meeting Carr, Bates took a cattle boat to England to pursue his career as an artist. It was the Depression and work was hard to secure, and yet he continued to paint and eventually was included in Lucy Wertheim's Twenties Group. The Twenties Group included the best of the generation growing up between the wars, artists like Paul Nash, Henry Moore, Christopher Wood, and Barbara Hepworth. Just as he was establishing a serious career in London the war began. He enlisted with the Territorial Army and within a year he was captured and spent the next five years as a prisoner of war, unable to paint. After the war he returned to Calgary in 1946, where he began a series of paintings on the harshness of prairie life that have established his reputation as an important Canadian artist. Bates went on to attend classes with the great German Expressionist Max Beckman in New York from 1949 to 1950. During the 1950s he practiced architecture, painting, and lithography.

Bates moved to Victoria in 1962, just after a devastating stroke that would hinder him the remainder of his life. Nonetheless he continued to paint, be an extremely active force in Victoria's arts community, and draw a following of artists around him. He formed the Limners group in 1971 with the German artist Herbert Siebner. The name refers to a medieval guild of artists. The group functioned as a support system for artists as well as a social network that enlivened the arts scene in Victoria in a way that has not been seen since.

The other founding member of the Limners, Herbert Siebner (1925–2003), worked in the Expressionist style. Siebner had studied in Berlin after the First World War under Max Kaus and Karl Hofer, both celebrated members of the first generation of German Expressionists. Siebner and his family emigrated to Canada, settling in Victoria in 1954. He set up his own studio where he taught a number of artists interested in modernism, including Nita Forrest, Molly Privett,

Flemming Jorgensen, and the author of this essay, Michael Morris. Siebner also became friends with Elza Mayhew, Robert De Castro, Richard Ciccimarra, and Colin and Sylvia Graham. Siebner brought a lot of energy with him, ensuring that Victoria would become a vital centre for artistic innovation. Siebner's attitude about work and life reflected his particular and fresh approach, not seen in Victoria before that time. He was instrumental in bringing Victoria's repressive and restrained society back to life. His work was sophisticated and contained the important elements of irony, paradox, and—most importantly—a sense of the absurd. Part of the reason Victoria received him openly was the great friendship he developed with Colin Graham. Colin welcomed professional artists to the city at a time when immigrants, especially artists, were not always accepted. Graham exhibited Siebner's work numerous times during his tenure at the Gallery. Siebner went on to exhibit widely across Canada, receiving numerous awards and commissions. Since his death in 2003 Siebner's work has gained appreciation and his contributions to the art of this period continue to attract critical attention.

Richard Ciccimarra (1924–1973) arrived in Victoria in 1955 one year after Siebner. He was born into a cultured bourgeois Viennese family. After the war he moved to England in 1948 and married there. In 1949 he and his wife moved to the West Indies. The couple and a friend bought a yacht in Barbados to run charters for tourists hopping between the islands. There he began making sketches, usually loose, watercolour landscapes, charming in their simplicity and discreet use of vibrant colour. At this time the lives of the Bahamian people fascinated him, although many of his strongest impressions did not emerge in his completed works until six or seven years later, after he settled in Victoria in 1955.

The work he created during his first few years in Victoria reflected West Indies' subject matter, such as *Laughing Woman* and *Woman with Oranges*, both painted in 1958. Like Bates and Siebner, Ciccimarra's work explores Expressionism, especially the influences of the Viennese Expressionist painters. Like the work of Egon Schiele before him, Ciccimarra's work has a haunting sense of ennui. At the start of the 1960s he suffered bouts of serious depression and his work, such as *Descent* (1968), became more tentative and more existential. By 1973 his health was failing and, not long after the Limners officially formed, Ciccimarra died. Colin Graham exhibited Ciccimarra's work in exhibitions in 1958, 1962, 1964, and curated his memorial exhibition in 1974.

Another European artist who lived only a short time in the city was Jan Zach (1914–1986). He came to Victoria from Czechoslovakia, via Brazil and the United States, where he was commissioned to create a sculpture for the Czech Pavilion at the 1938 New York World's Fair. When World War II broke out he stayed on in North America. Zach arrived in Victoria in 1951, the same year as Colin Graham. Zach and Graham gravitated to one another as two kindred spirits interested in generating a vital modern art scene in Victoria. According to Anthony Emery (columnist and historian who served on the Board and as Acting Director of the Art Gallery during Colin's illness in 1956),

> After [Emily Carr's] death the cause of art in Victoria was left to the care of a few devoted souls who saw to it that interest in painting and sculpture was not allowed to die. These few...were the people who gave us our art gallery. Their task was lightened by the arrival of an artist-scholar and an artist-teacher in the persons of Colin Graham and Jan Zach.[4]

Before the end of Colin Graham's first year as Director of the AGGV, he offered Zach a one-person exhibition. In the exhibition brochure, Colin wrote, "As the paintings in this exhibition so forcefully attest, Victoria, and indeed Canada as a whole, have gained in the arrival of Mr. Jan Zach, an artist of major rank." Colin offered Zach teaching stints at the AGGV, and Zach soon opened his own studio downtown where he taught classes. In 1958 he was offered a position at the University of Oregon in Eugene where he made a huge impact mentoring several generations of young American sculptors. His most significant contribution to the Victoria art scene was his mentoring of Robert De Castro and Elza Mayhew who would become two of B.C.'s most significant modernist sculptors.

Robert De Castro (1923–1986) was born in Winnipeg and served with the Canadian Army during the Second World War. He moved to Victoria where he studied sculpture with Zach from 1953 to 1957. Both men were part of Expo 67 as their work was shown in the *Sculpture '67* exhibition that was held outside Toronto City Hall that same year. Both De Castro and Elza Mayhew absorbed a strong sense of European Modernism from Zach, making it entirely their own. De Castro's works, primarily carved out of rough timber and rubbed to a dark, elegant black with creosote and boot polish, are purely abstract and are mostly untitled. Their uneven surfaces full of grooves and seemingly arbitrarily spaced drilled holes have a vague timeless feeling associated with psychological states rather than the figure or landscape. Colin Graham held an exhibition of his work in 1954 in the show *Pupils of Jan Zach*, again in 1964 along with paintings by Myfanwy Pavelic, and with work by the Limners in 1972.

In Emily Carr's Steps: Modernist Women Artists in Victoria

Elza Mayhew (1916–2004) is perhaps one of Canada's best known sculptors from the modernist period. She was chosen to represent Canada at the 1964 Venice Biennial with Harold Town, at Expo 67 in Montreal and at Expo 86 in Vancouver, and also was awarded numerous commissions in various parts of the country, such as the grounds of the Royal BC Museum and the Confederation Centre of the Arts in Charlottetown, Prince Edward Island. She had one-person exhibitions during Colin's tenure at the AGGV, in 1964 and 1971. Her independence, her dedication to modern form, and her determination to create despite many challenges, marks Mayhew as one of a number of strong women artists in Victoria who picked up and ran with Carr's vision for the kind of art that was possible in Victoria. Mayhew, who was a war widow with two children, studied with Zach from 1955 to 1958 and became entirely committed to her sculpture. In 1963 she graduated with a Master of Fine Arts degree from the University of Oregon. Like Carr, Mayhew was driven and determined to create the kind of art that spoke of the modern world, while at the same time making reference to other ideas and traditions. Although her sculptures are often totemic in form and have a certain modern primitivism to them, her influences lean more towards European traditions of mythology rather than West Coast Aboriginal traditions.

Margaret Peterson (1902–1997) was also a strong force in the modern scene in Victoria. She was truly a West Coast artist, born in Seattle and a teacher for 22 years at the University of California at Berkeley. When Colin attended this university, Peterson was one of his teachers. During the McCarthy era she resigned from the university in protest when she was asked to denounce Communist sympathizers. Because her writer husband was a Canadian, the couple retreated to Canada. Originally they lived on the Cowichan River in a cabin where, like Carr, Peterson

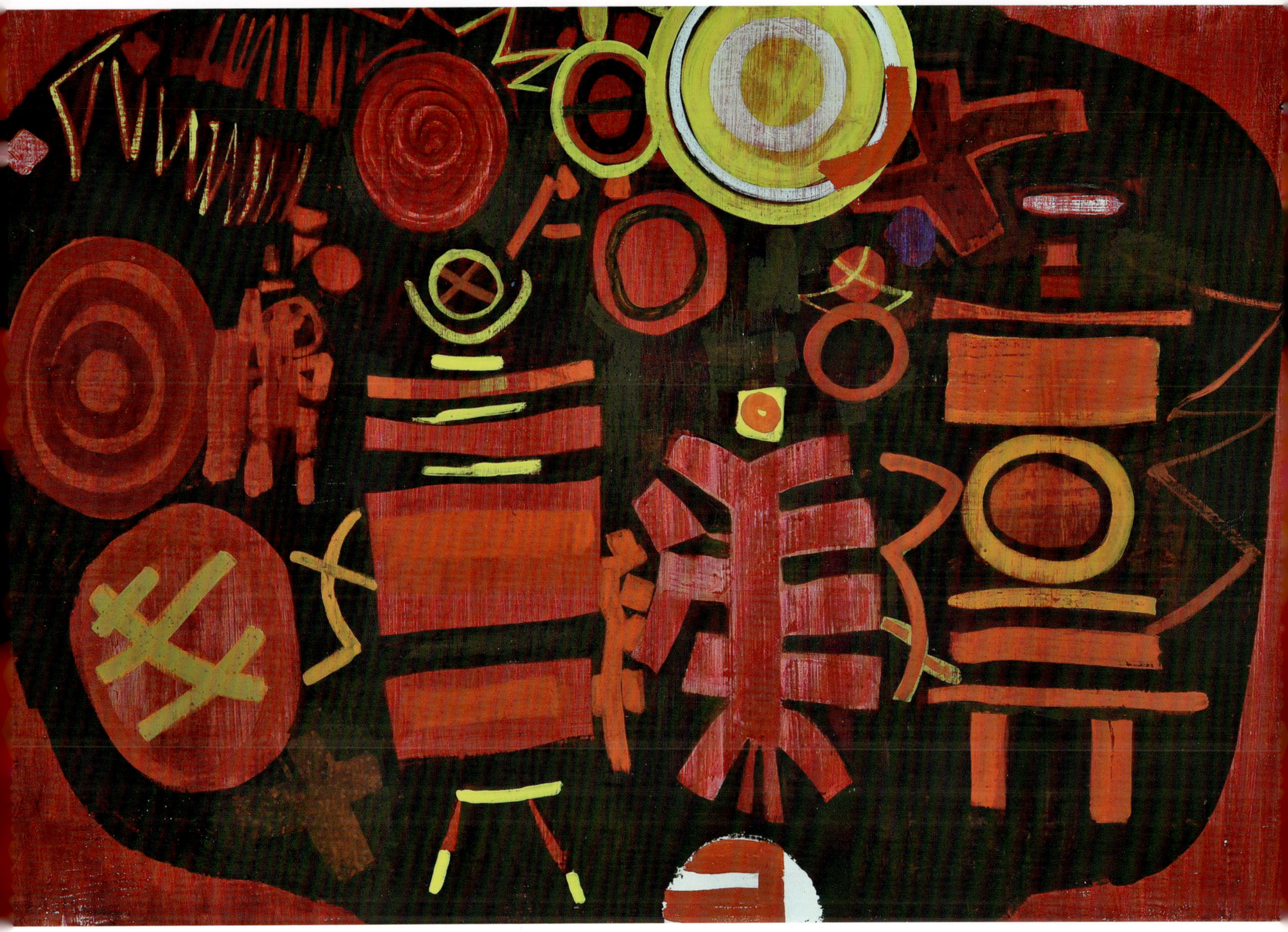

Margaret Peterson 1902-1997, Canadian, *The Zodiac Keepers*, nd, egg tempera on gesso on board

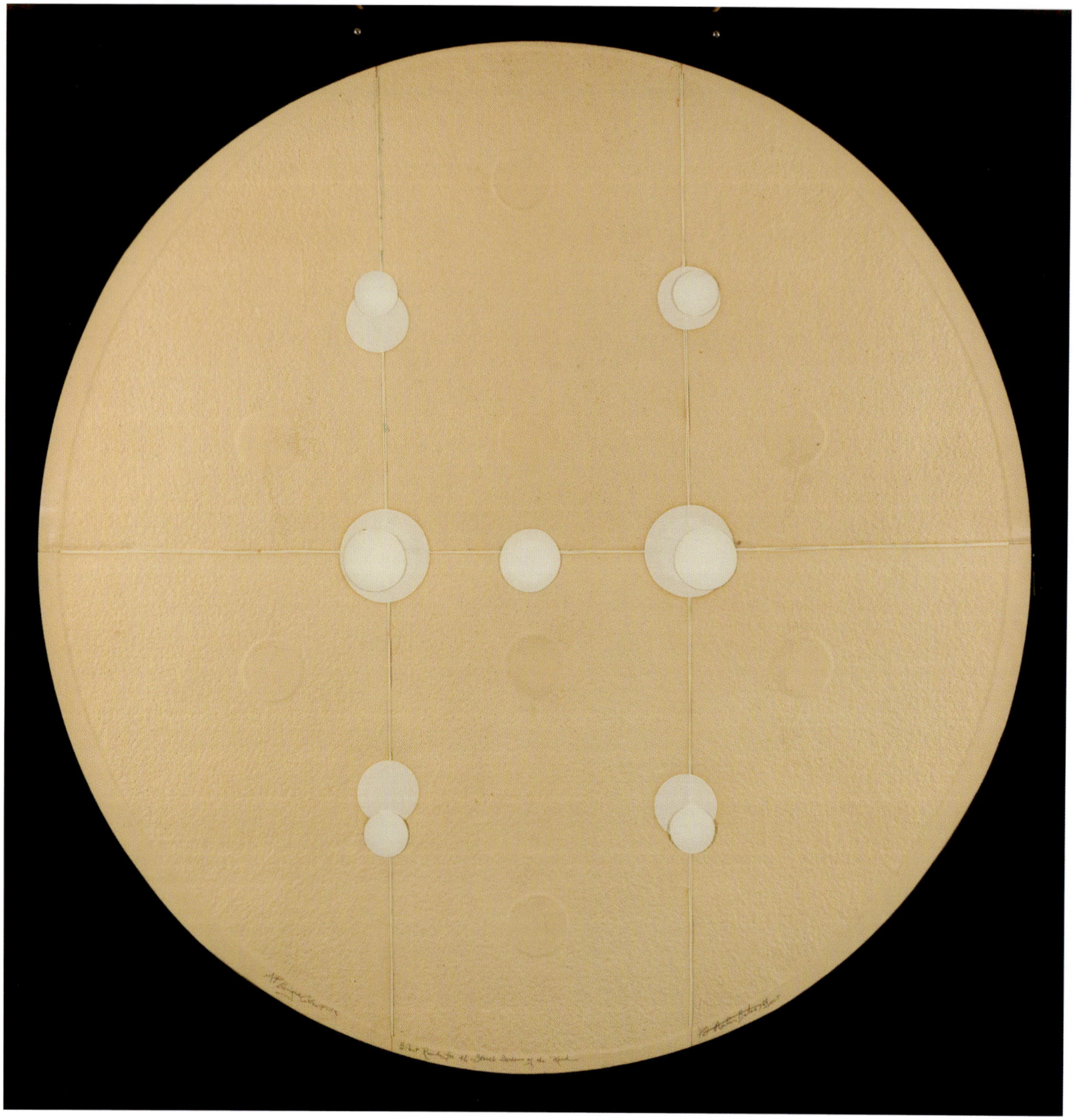

Pat Martin Bates b. 1927, Canadian, *Silent Round for the Gravel Gardens of the Mind*, 1968, perforated pressing with paint, plexi, and collage developed relationships with and an admiration for her First Nations neighbours. Colin Graham recognized how significant it was to have a modern artist of this calibre living in Victoria and gave her one-person exhibitions in 1953, 1959, and 1962. Her work reveals an interest in Byzantine art and the primitivism of Aboriginal art, as well as an interest in the formal aspects of Cubism and Abstract Expressionism.

Pat Martin Bates was born in 1927 in Saint John, New Brunswick, and is of proud Acadian heritage. She graduated from the Royale Académie des Beaux Arts, Brussels, and continued her postgraduate studies at the Institut National Supérieur des Beaux-Arts in Antwerp, the Sorbonne in Paris, and the Pratt Graphic Centre in New York. By the late 1950s her mystical contemplative work made a break from the traditional boundaries of printmaking and earned her national and international recognition. The respected French critic and art historian Pierre Restany said "Madame Martin Bates has firmly placed Canadian printmaking on the international scene, her artwork takes a path few dare follow."[5] In 1962 Bates moved to Victoria, and two years later Colin Graham invited her to exhibit her elegant black and white heavily embossed prints at the Gallery. He gave her a full retrospective in 1971. She recalls the experience of working with Colin, "The way he hung my work was superb. I myself was surprised; what an eye, what caring."[6] Her knowledge and understanding of her medium allowed for experimentation, moving to the realm of multi-media. She pioneered the use of light boxes to illuminate delicate arabesques of pin points of light creating her unique cosmology. Anne Hurtig, who curated Martin Bates's 2005 solo show *Destinations, Navigation, Illuminations* notes, "The lightbox works starting in the 60s were marvelously innovative precursors that anticipated by several years the now familiar backlit advertising form."[7]

Pat Martin Bates received an Honorary Doctorate from the University of Victoria in 1994, and was elected a fellow of the Royal Academies of Canada in 2008. Amongst her many awards includes the Gold Medal Award from the Norwegian International Printmaking Biennial in 1986 and the Global Graphics Award from Holland's First International Graphic exhibition in 1993. She was the first recipient of the Victoria YWCA Woman of Distinction – Arts & Culture Award. Other awards include critics' choice Ljubljana Biennial, Canada Arts Council fellowship to Persia, and Edinburgh Arts Festival Bursary. Bates was named Ambassador of the Arts in 2005 and received a Commendation of her dedication to advancing the status of Woman from Zonta International.

Modern Architecture and Design in Victoria

John Di Castri (1924–2005) was born in Victoria and was one of the original architects of the West Coast Style, which included B.C. Binning, Arthur Erickson, and Doug Shadbolt in Vancouver and Peter Cotton, John Wade, and Alan Hodgons in Victoria. In the late 1940s Di Castri attended the University of Oklahoma studying under Brice Goff, a follower of Frank Lloyd Wright. John Di Castri admired the architecture of Frank Lloyd Wright and believed that architecture should not be a monument to the architect.

Di Castri returned to Victoria in 1952 and started his own practice. He designed shops, churches, private homes, and public buildings. Besides architecture, he was an accomplished painter in the modernist tradition. He chaired the Community Planning Association of Canada from 1958–68 and the Canadian Housing Design Council from 1976–80. He designed many houses of distinction, including the award-winning Trend House for Gwendoline Cash in 1954 and Colin and Sylvia Graham's home in 1953 (featured on the cover of the magazine *Western Living*). His public works include the Canadian National Institute for the Blind building in Victoria (1951), and the Student Union Building (1963) and the Interfaith Chapel (1985), both at the University of Victoria. The city granted heritage status to Di Castri's 1957 home in 2002.

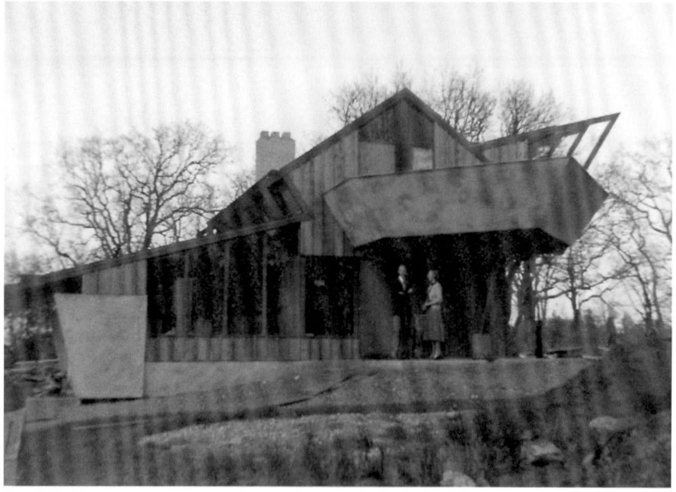

Colin and Sylvia Graham in front of their new house designed by John Di Castri, c. 1953. Photographer unknown.

Peter Cotton (1918–78) was also born in Victoria at a time when the city's aesthetic sensibilities were still strongly attached to the Edwardian era. The Arts and Crafts Movement was greatly admired, as were the architecture and ideals of Samuel McClure, Francis Rattenbury, Charles Rennie Macintosh, and William Morris. Cotton shared this appreciation. He trained as an architect, but his contribution is remembered chiefly from his innovative angle iron, steel rod, and moulded plywood furniture from the late 1940s and 1950s. Cotton, and his Victoria contemporaries in the design firm Morrison-Bush, were part of the West Coast designers who shared the ideals of the artists showcased in the *Design for Living* exhibition of 1949, ideals echoed by members of the Vancouver Art School and the Architecture department of the University of British Columbia. The technological advances in the development of new materials, such as plastic and plywood, pioneered by European designers (such as those at the Bauhaus) before the war became popular for a postwar budget-conscious public in British Columbia during the years when Colin Graham was Director of the AGGV. As well, industry in the province was supportive of promoting new uses for manufacturing, which encouraged the production of such furniture. In 1949 Peter Cotton opened his Perpetua Furniture firm, with a showroom in Vancouver and outlets in Eastern Canada. He was later recognized by the National Industrial Design Council of Canada. Magazines like *Western Living* featured illustrations of local design that favoured modern ideals and helped foster their acceptance. Peter Cotton's furniture captured the spirit of the times. His understanding of the principles behind good design gives us an appreciation of what it is to be modern.

It is twenty years since the political situations that characterised the modern age have shifted, with the collapse of Communism and the dissolution of the Cold War threat. And now that the first decade of the new millennium is coming to an end we can step back and have perspective on modernity, which in effect has become today's antiquity. It is pertinent for us to look at Canada and its art from this immediate past to gain further perspective on where we are now. The modern scene in Victoria, although slow to gain momentum, was vibrant during the years of Colin Graham's tenure and reflected the larger scene of the rapidly shifting postwar era. Graham appreciated the significance of reflecting his own time through the visual culture that he brought to and established at the Art Gallery of Greater Victoria. Indeed, in the exhibitions he presented and the collection he developed, and even in the modernist house he built for his family, Graham lived the modern life and endeavoured to establish it as a vibrant presence in Victoria.

ENDNOTES

1. Letter from Colin Graham to curators Michael Morris and Mary Jo Hughes explaining his relationship to the Emily Carr Estate, November 18, 2007.

2. See Community Arts Council of Vancouver website for more information: http://www.cacv.ca/

3. Ian Thom as cited on the McMichael Canadian Art Collection Web site in *E.J. Hughes: The B.C. Landscape*: http://www.mcmichael.com/exhibitions/ejhughes/index.cfm

4. Anthony Emery, "The Community and Artist – Victoria's Loss," Daily Colonist, undated and unpaginated clipping as cited in *Intersections: The Life and Art of Jan Zach*, Seattle: University of Washington Press, 2002.

5. Interview with Pat Martin Bates with Michael Morris, spring, 2009.

6. Ibid.

7. Annette Hurtig, *Pat Martin Bates: Destinations, Navigations, Illuminations*, Art Gallery of Greater Victoria, 2005, np.

Colin Graham and West Coast Modernism

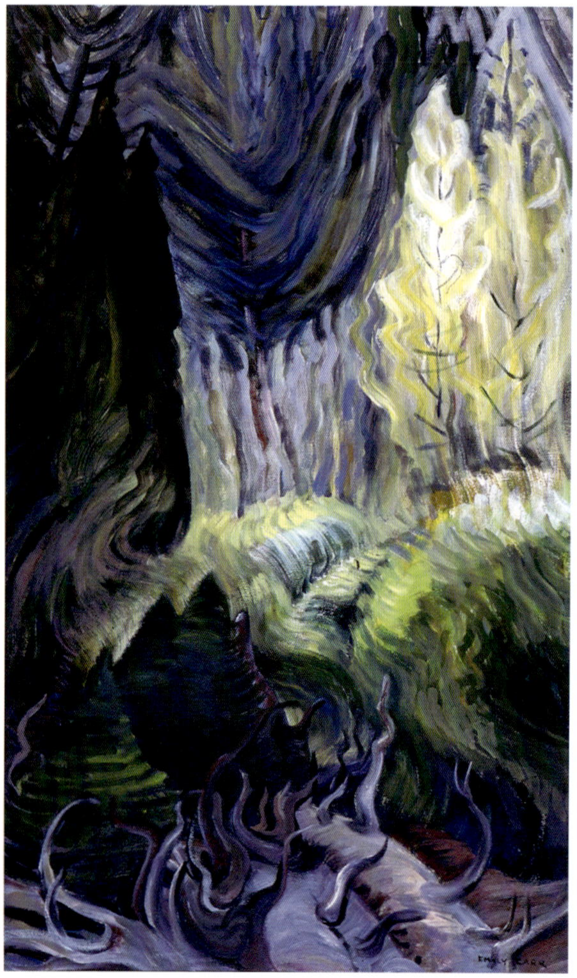

Emily Carr 1871-1945, Canadian, *Light Swooping Through*, 1938-39, oil on canvas

Emily Carr 1871-1945, Canadian, *Odds and Ends*, 1939, oil on canvas

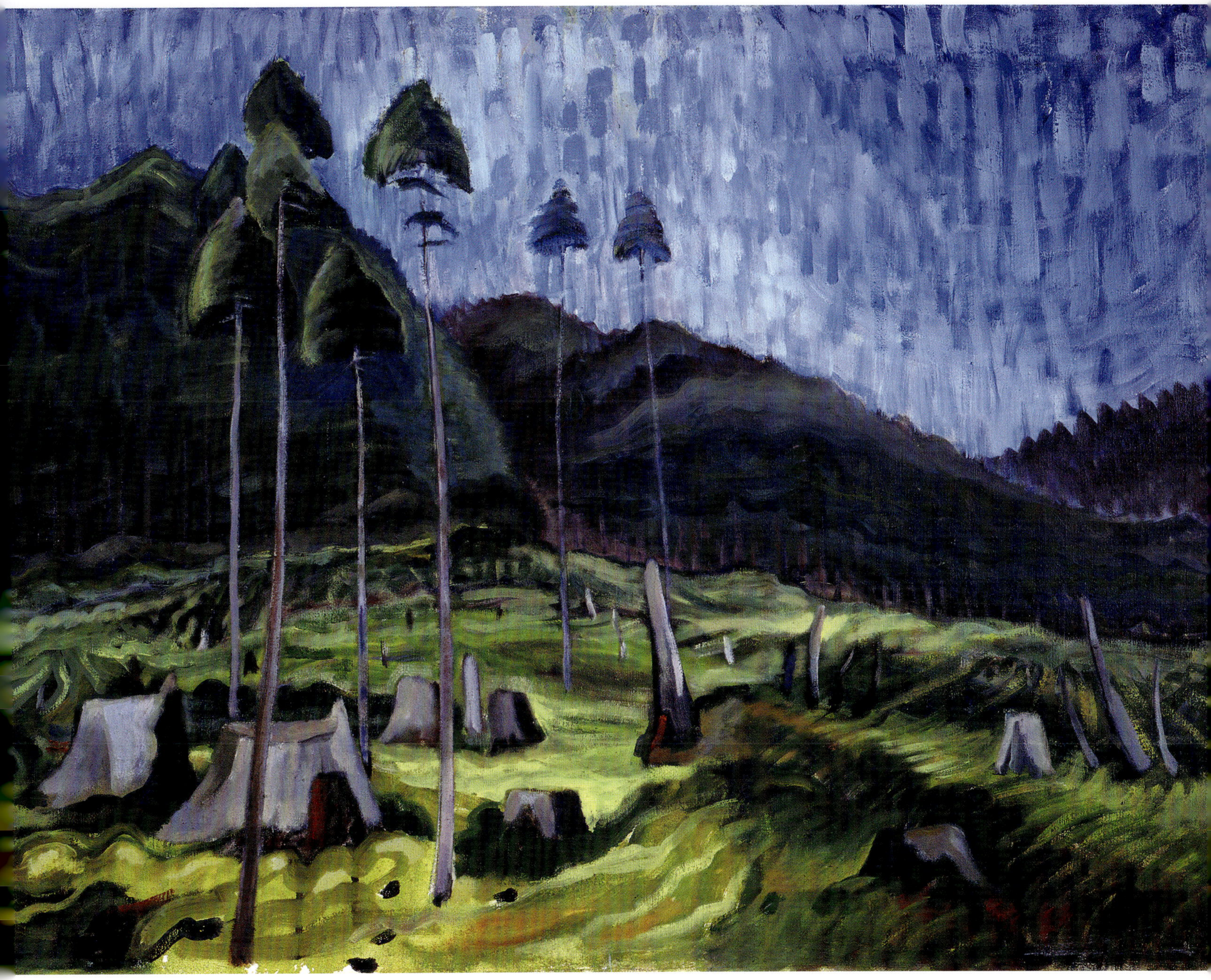

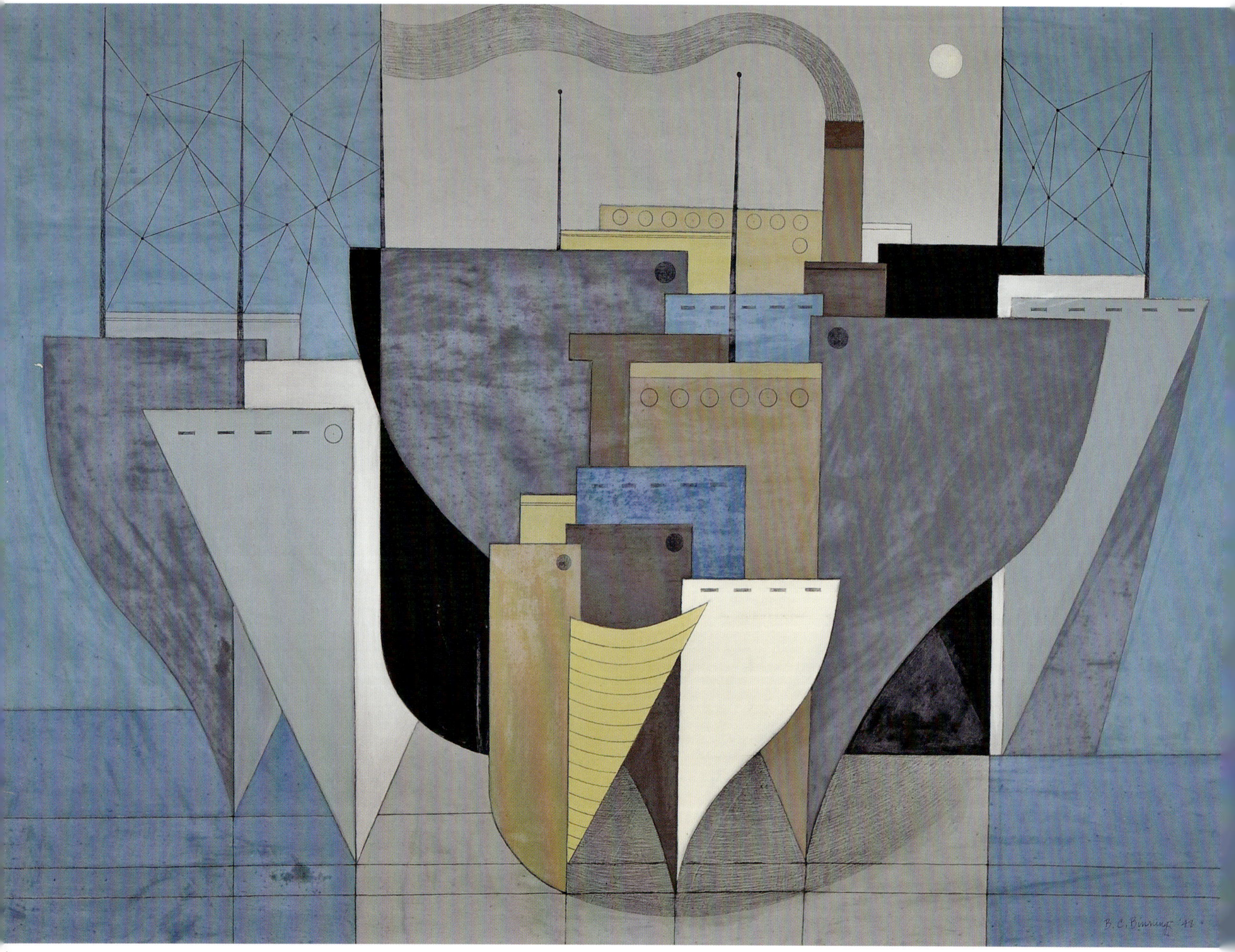

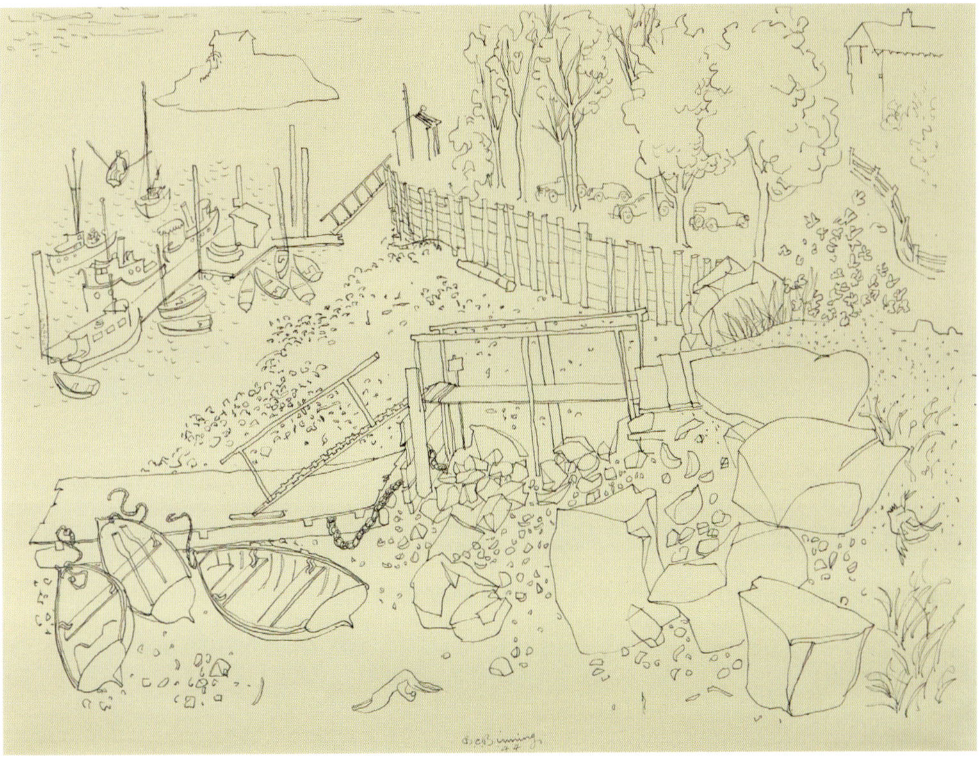

B.C. Binning 1909-1976, Canadian, *Convoy Under Way*, 1948, oil on board

B.C. Binning 1909-1976, Canadian, *View of Fisherman's Cove* 1944, ink on paper

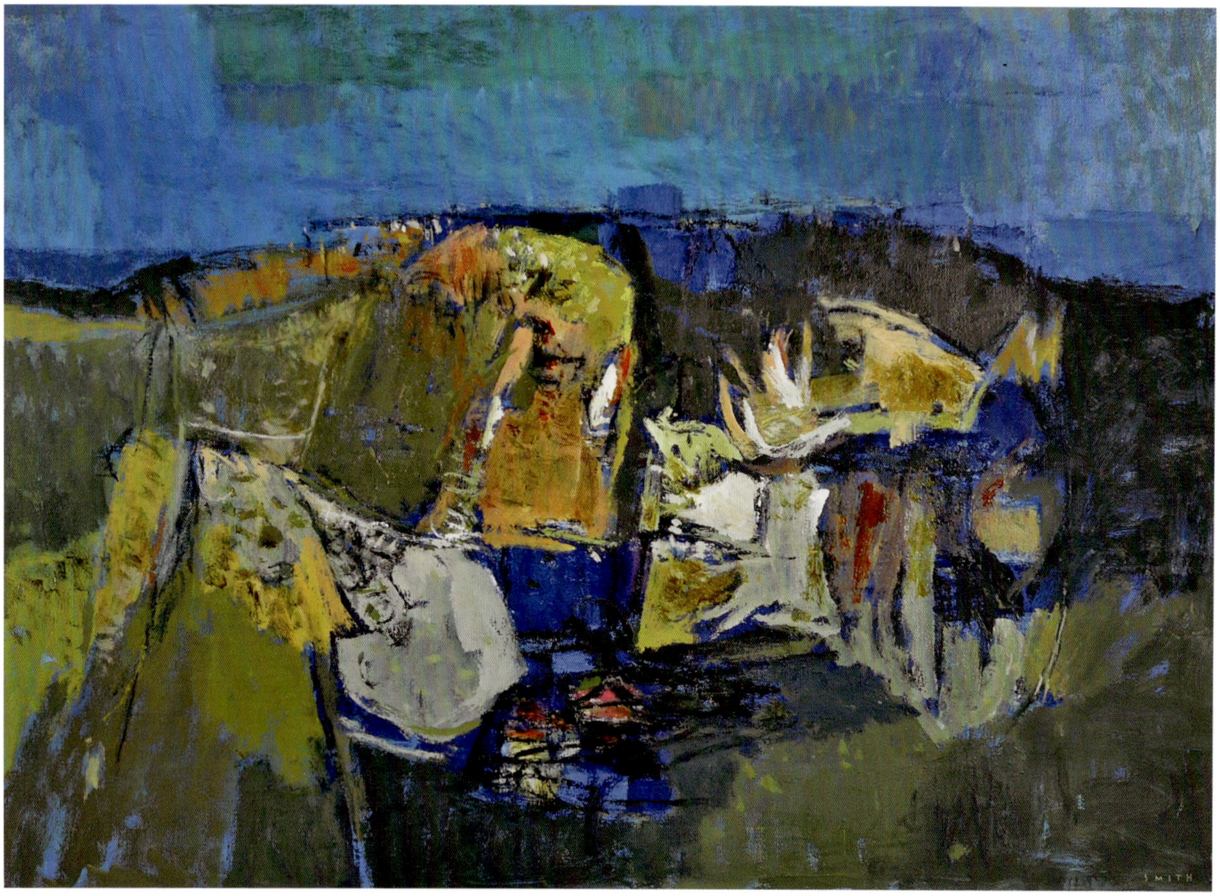

Gordon Smith b. 1919, Canadian, *Coast Range*, nd, oil on canvas

Gordon Smith b. 1919, Canadian, *Wet Night*, 1953, oil on canvas

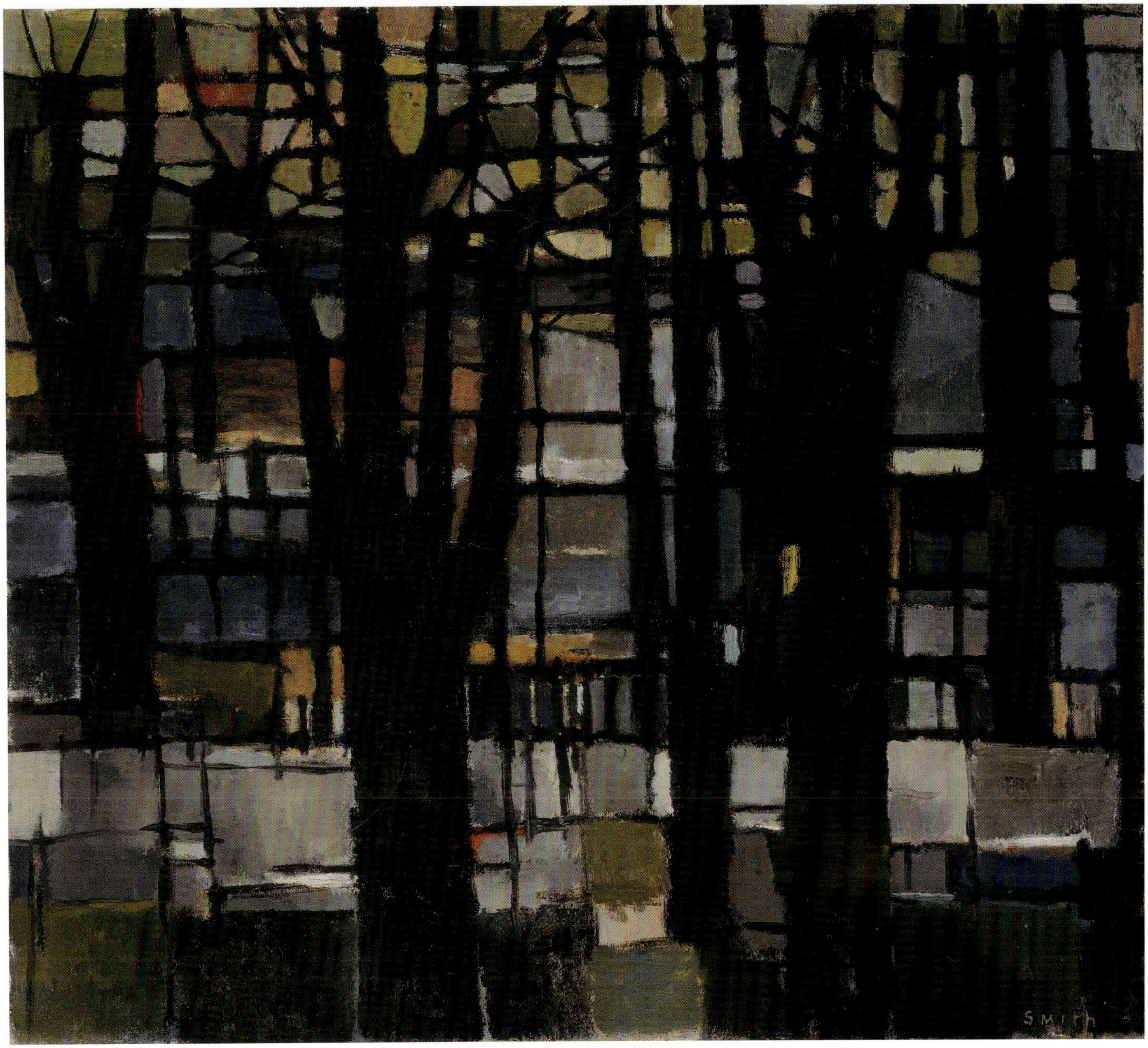
SMITH

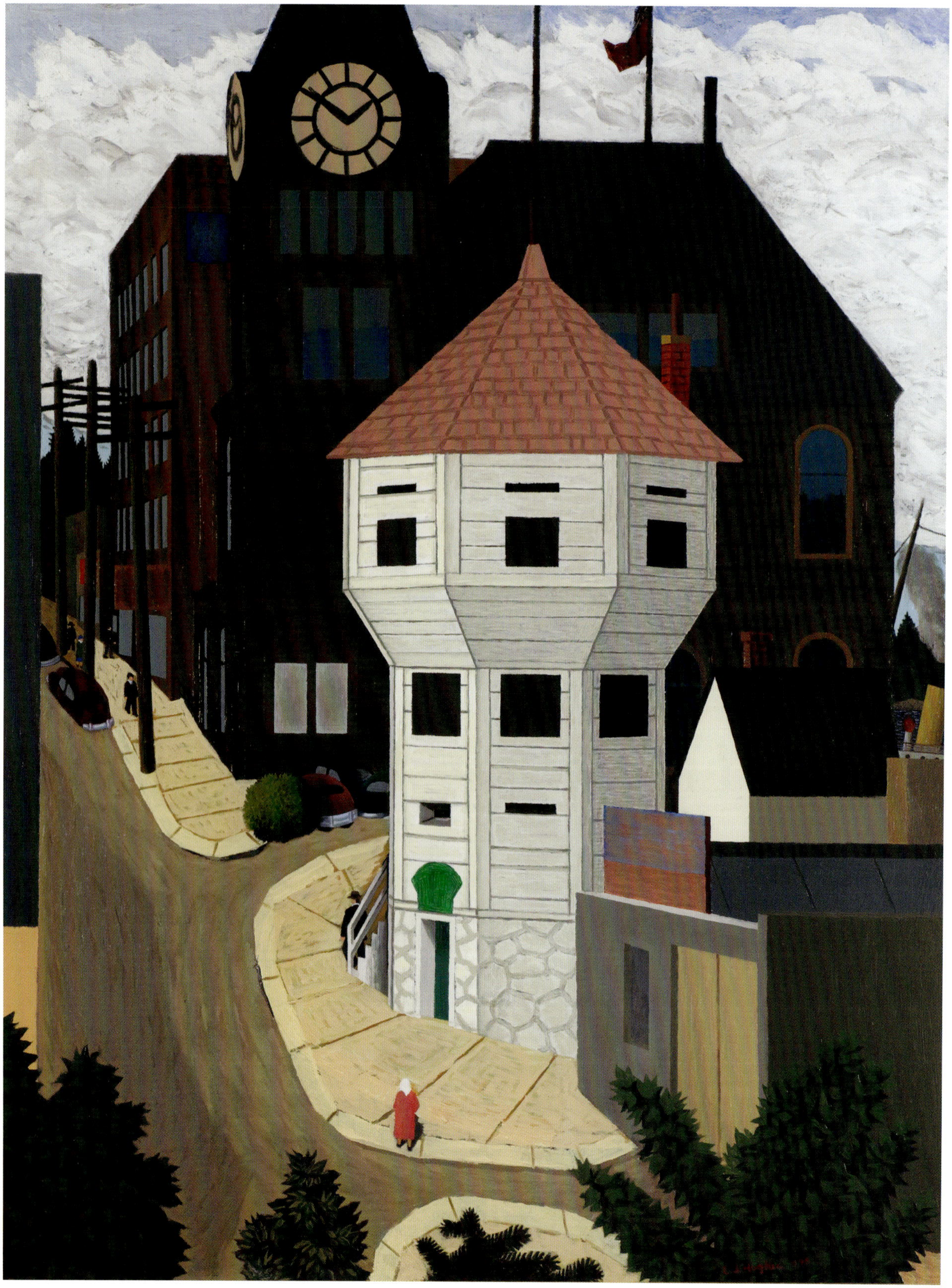

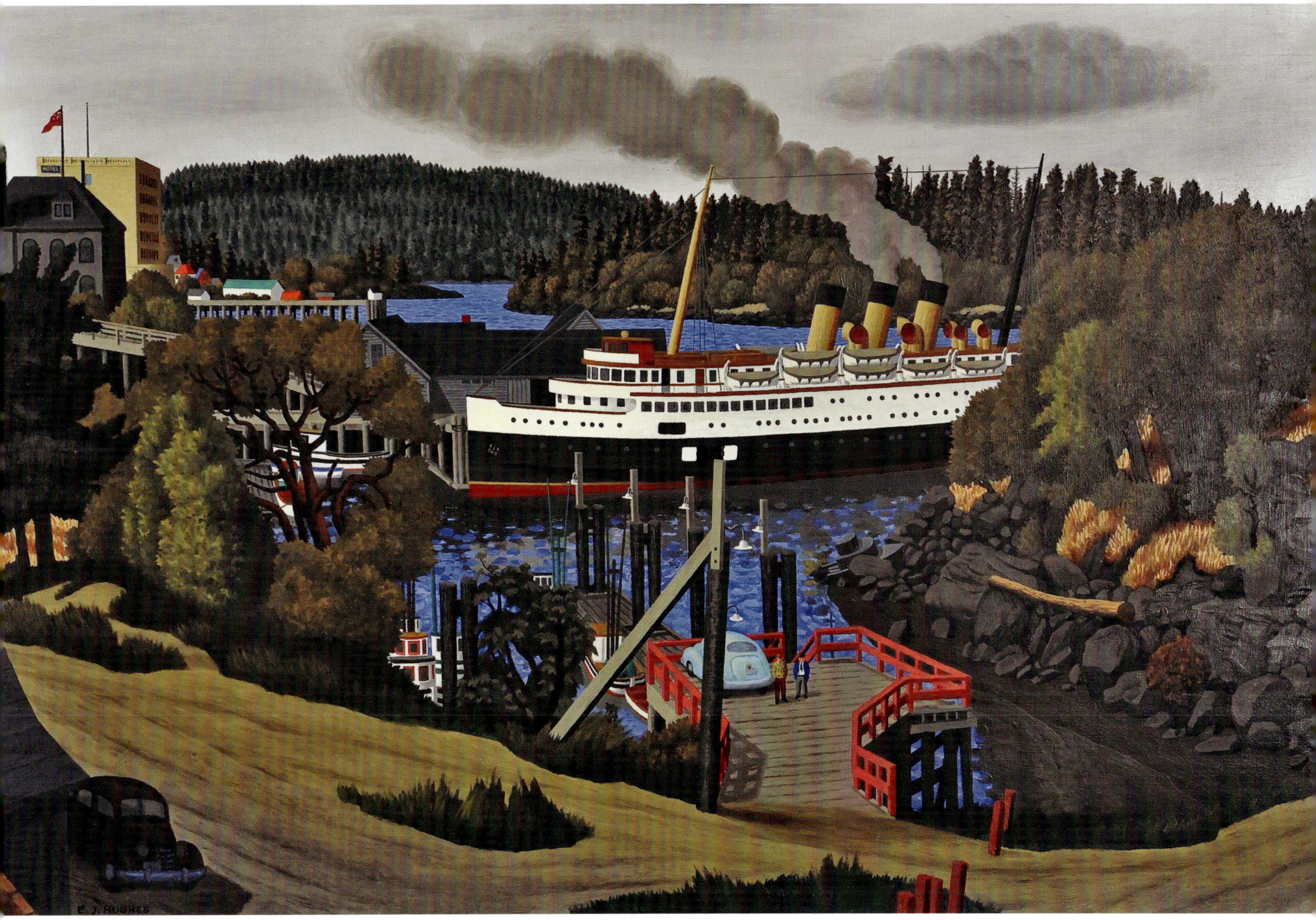

Edward John Hughes 1913-2007, Canadian, *Bastion, Nanaimo*, 1954, oil on canvas

Edward John Hughes 1913-2007, Canadian, *Steamer at the Old Wharf, Nanaimo*, 1958, oil on canvas

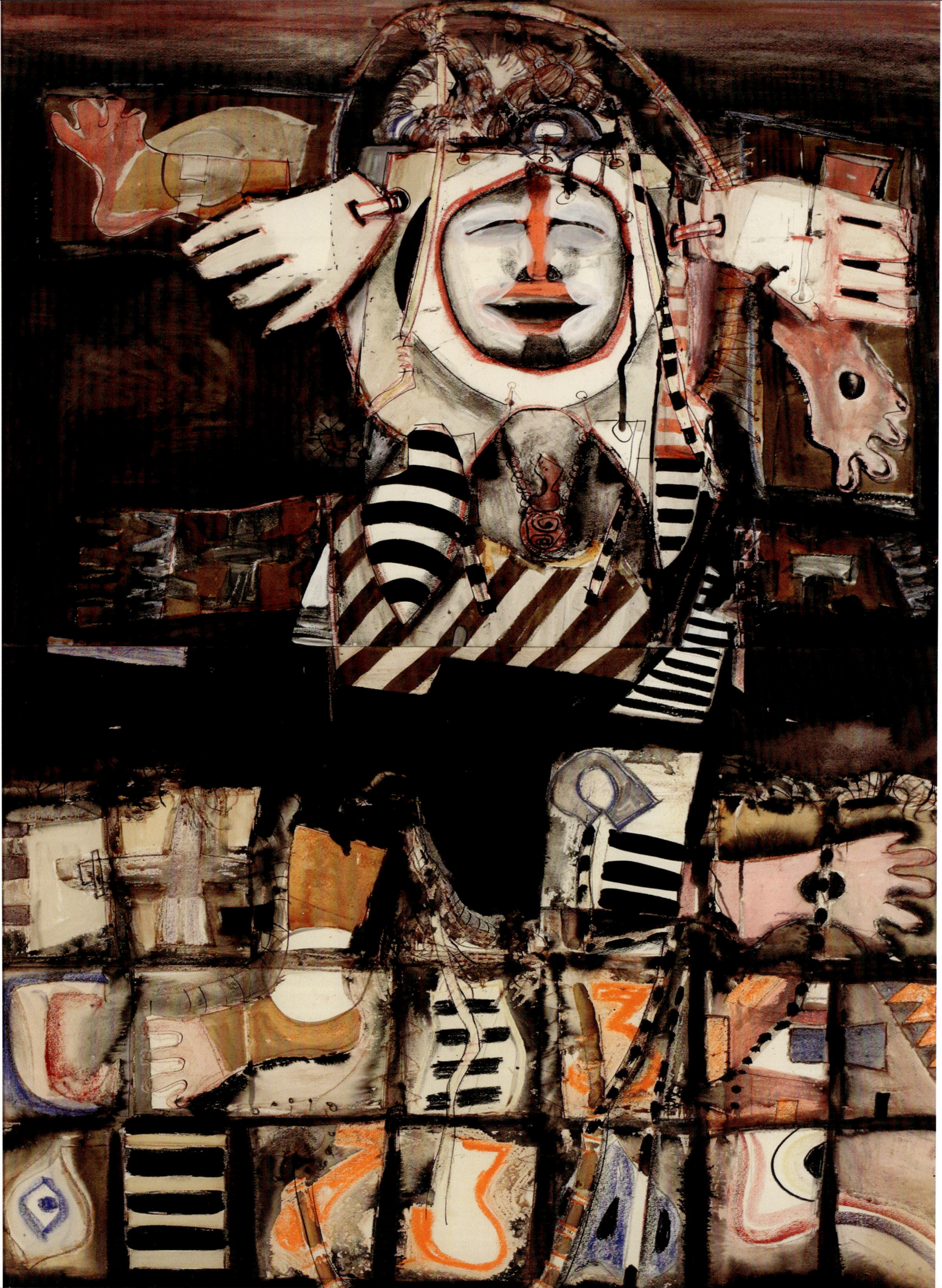

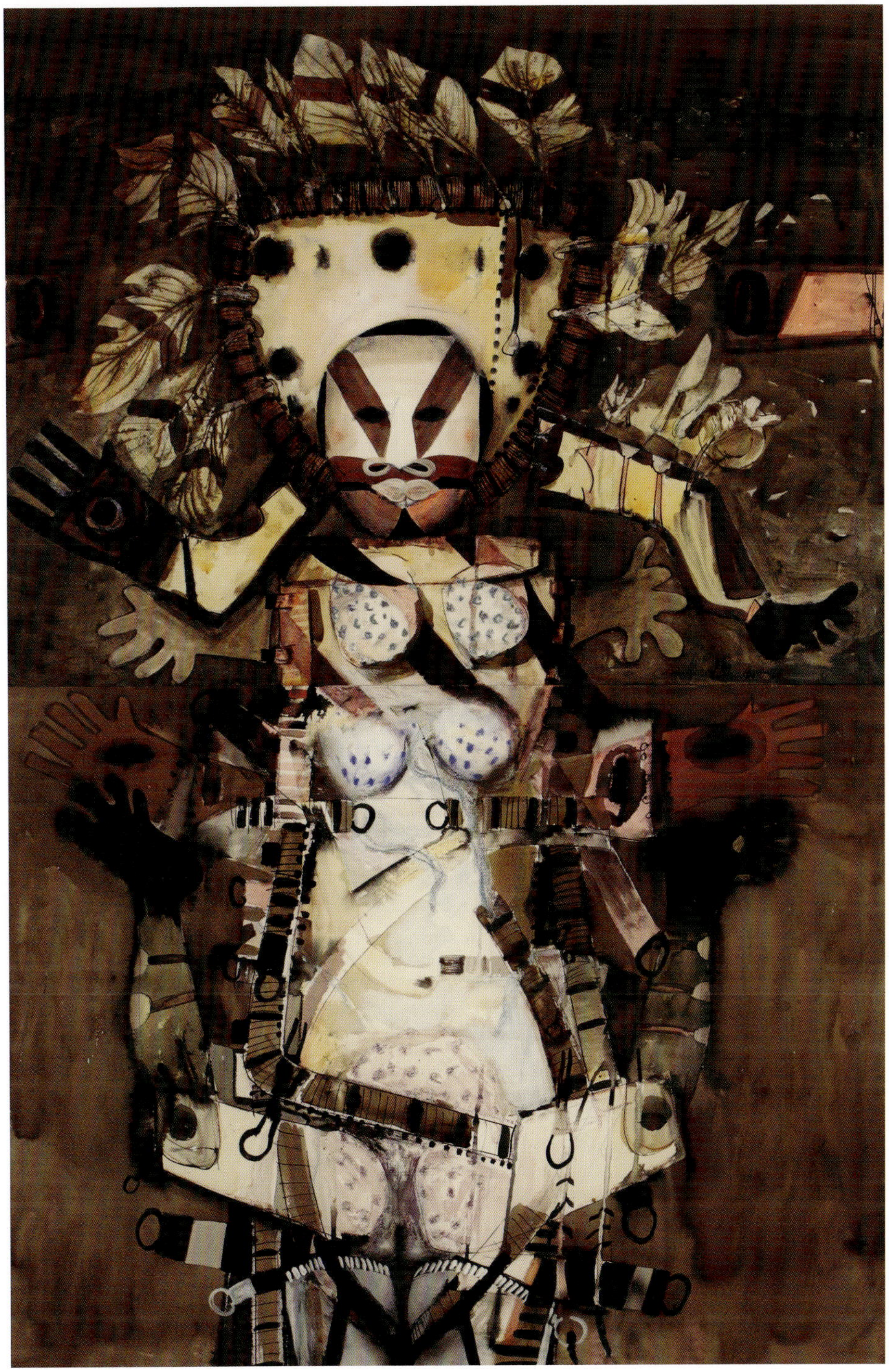

Jack Shadbolt 1909-1998, Canadian, *Masks & Fetishes*, 1966-70, watercolour and ink on paper

Jack Shadbolt 1909-1998, Canadian, *Adjustable Venus*, 1969-70, watercolour, ink, colour chalk, acrylic and gouache on board

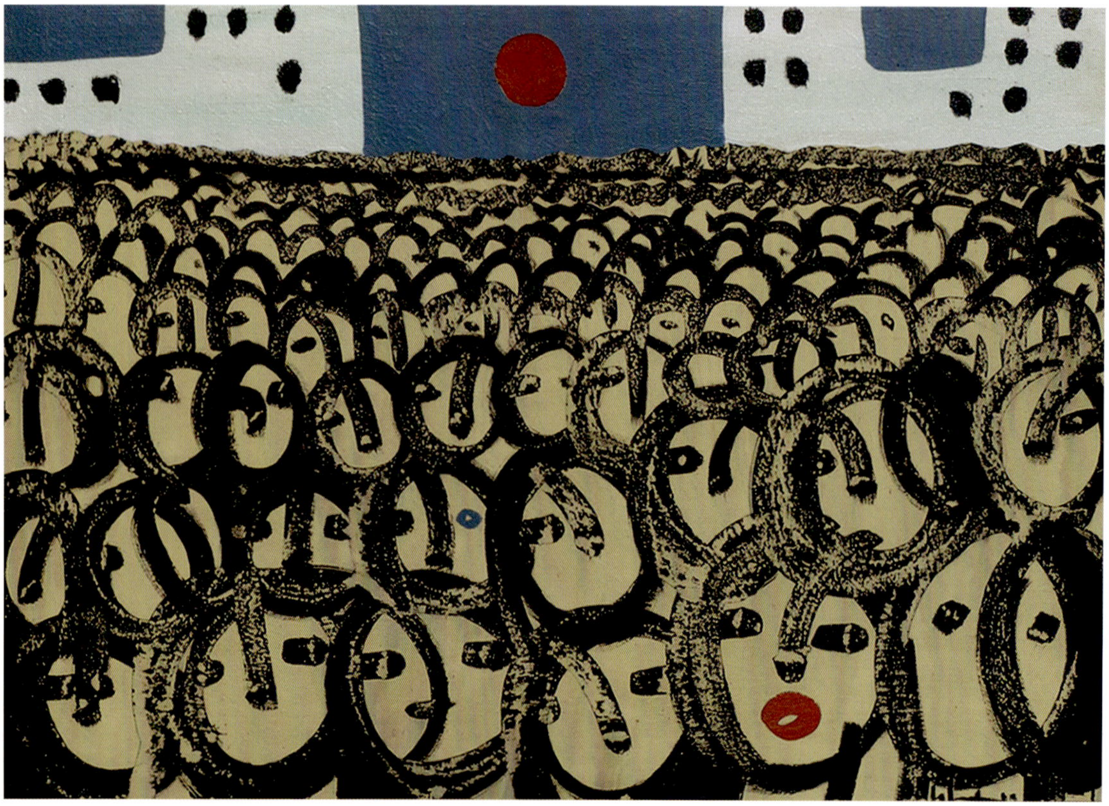

Herbert Siebner 1925-2003, Canadian, *Crowd Looking for a Friend,* 1973, acrylic on canvas

Herbert Siebner 1925-2003, Canadian, *Afternoon, Lake Como,* 1953, oil on canvas

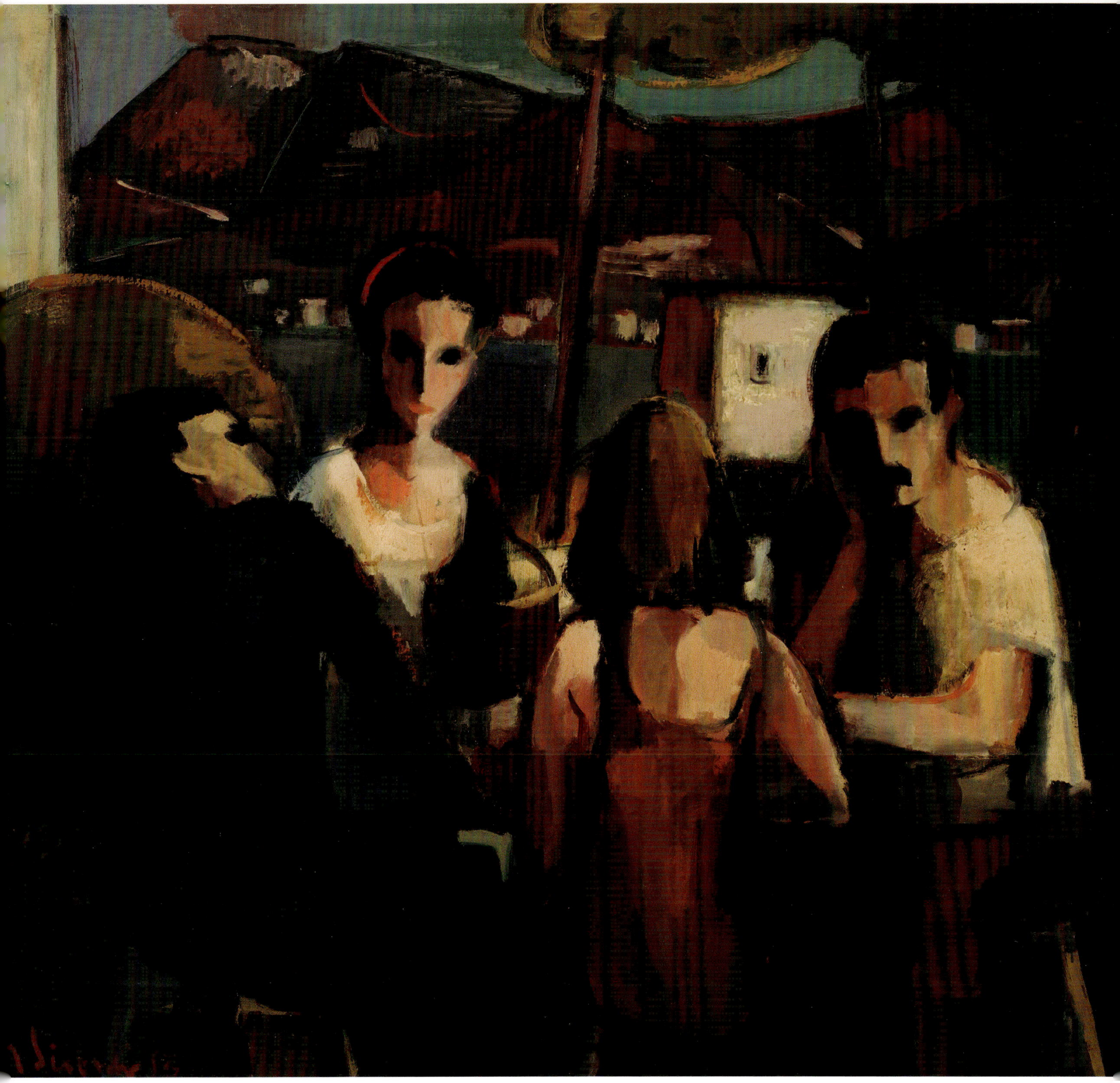

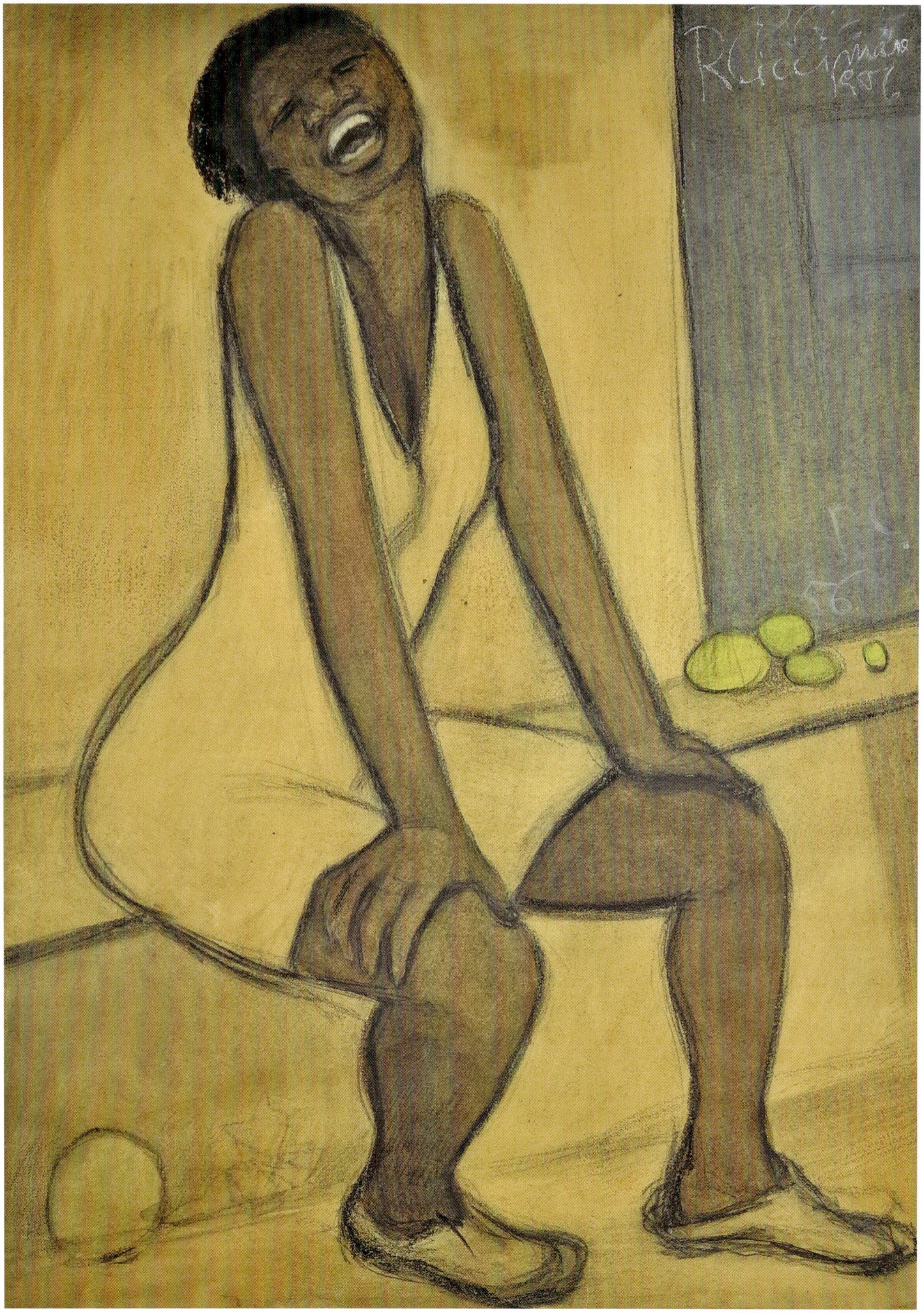

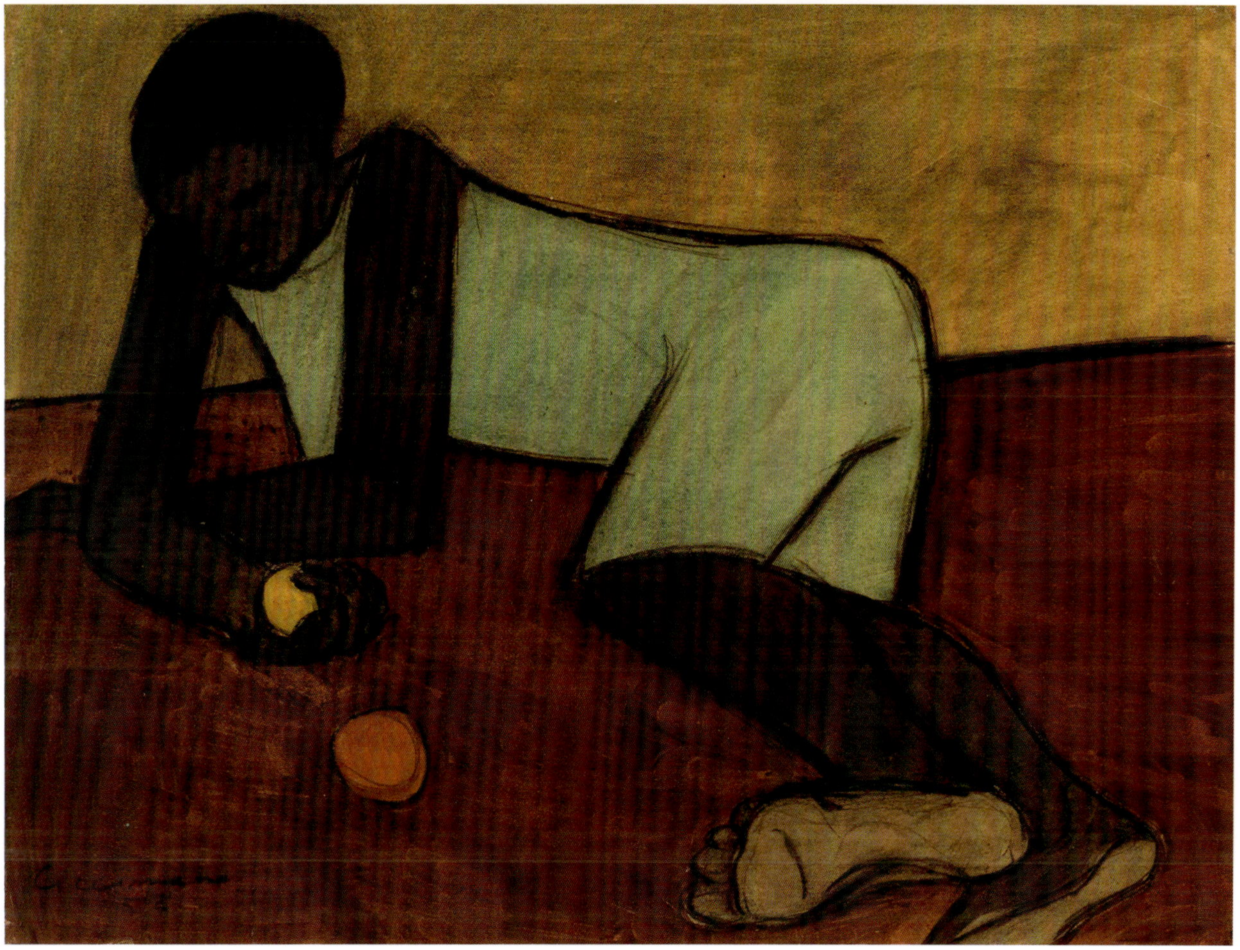

Richard Ciccimarra 1924-1973, Canadian, *Laughing Woman*, 1956, chalk, charcoal, wash, tempera, varnish on ochre coloured wove paper

Richard Ciccimarra 1924-1973, Canadian, *Woman with Oranges*, 1956-1957, gouache and varnish on board

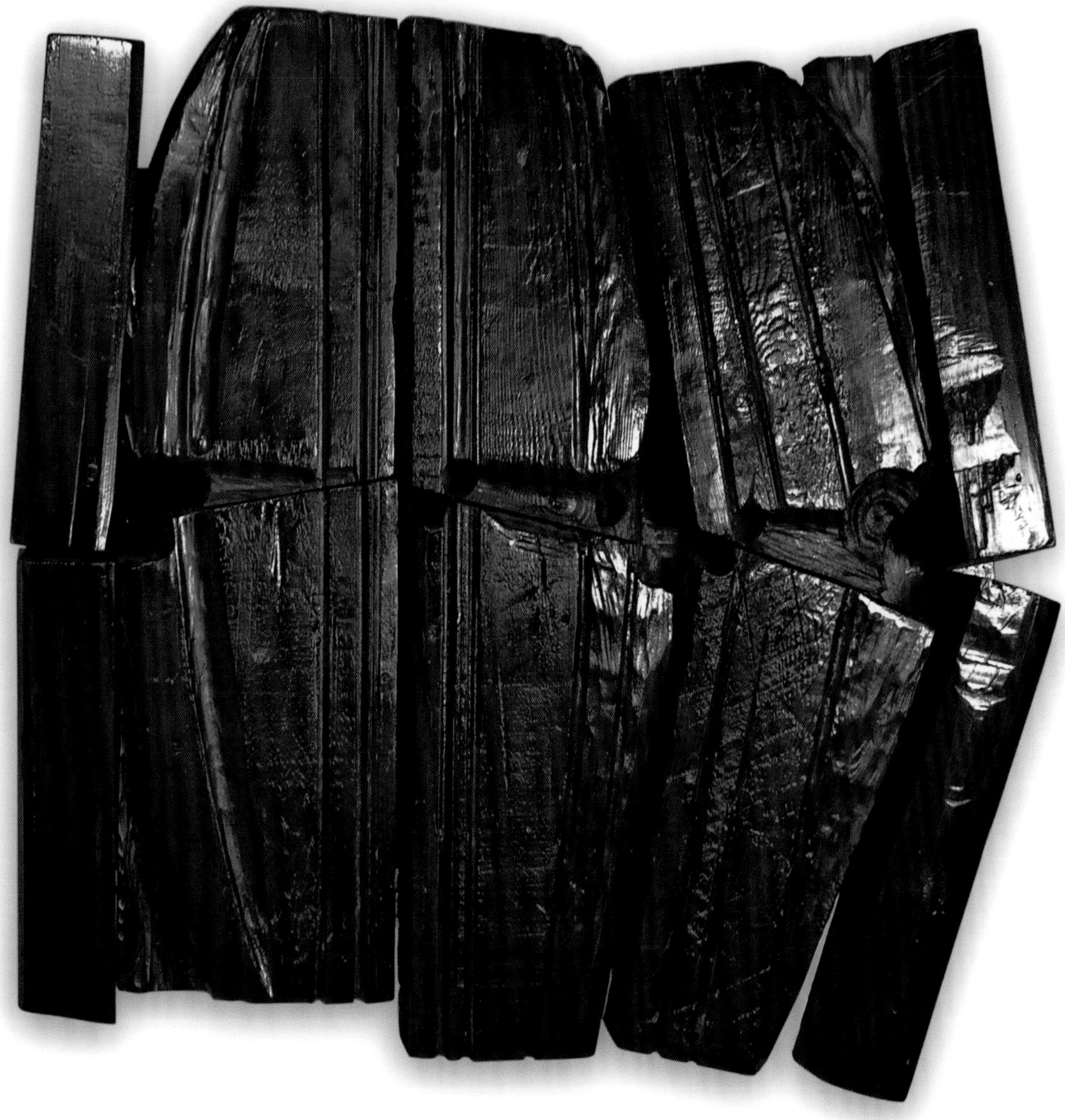

Robert De Castro 1923-1986, Canadian, *Untitled (Ten Wood Sections with Holes)*, wood; paint

Robert De Castro 1923-1986, Canadian, *Bingo*, nd, wood

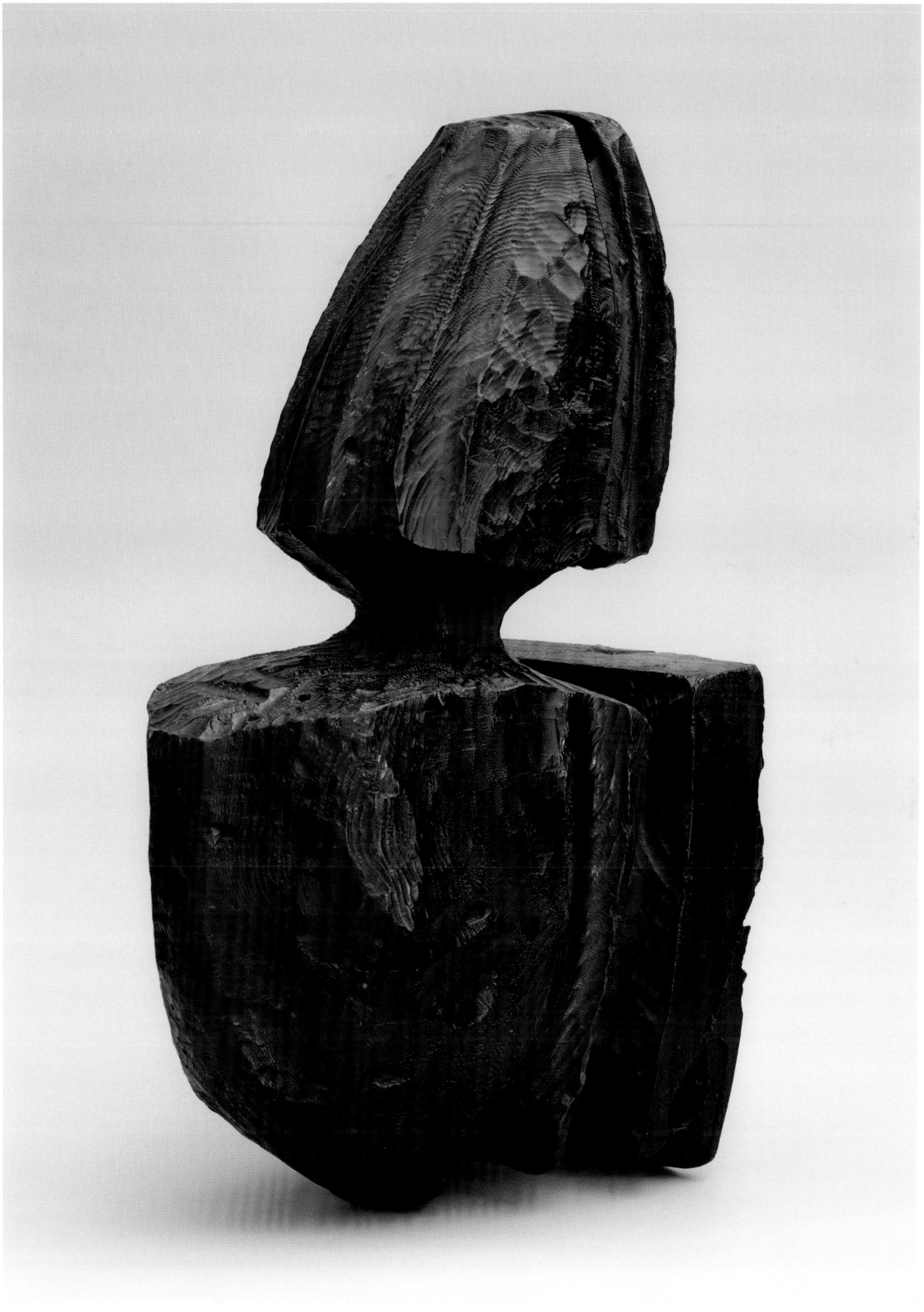

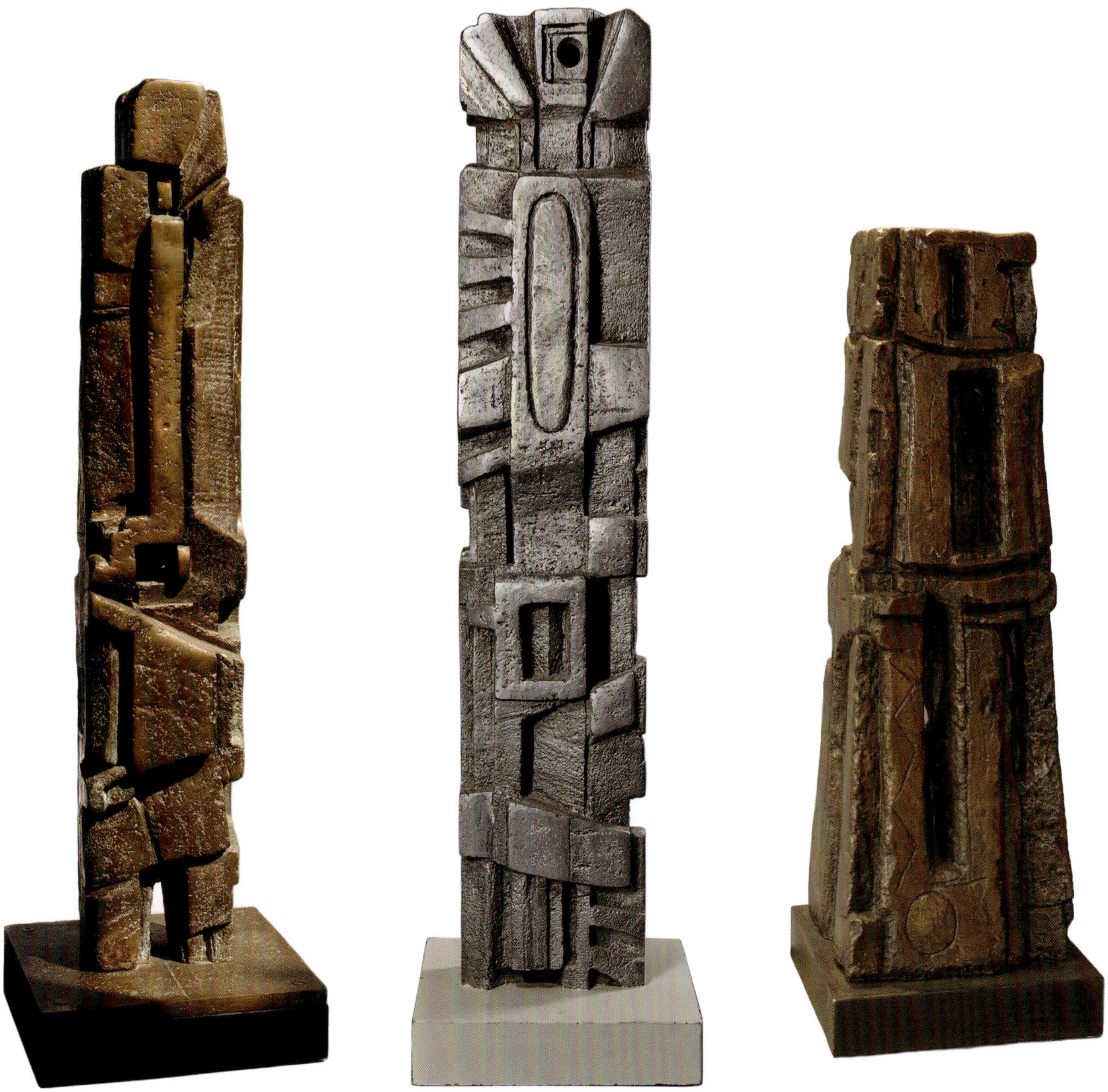

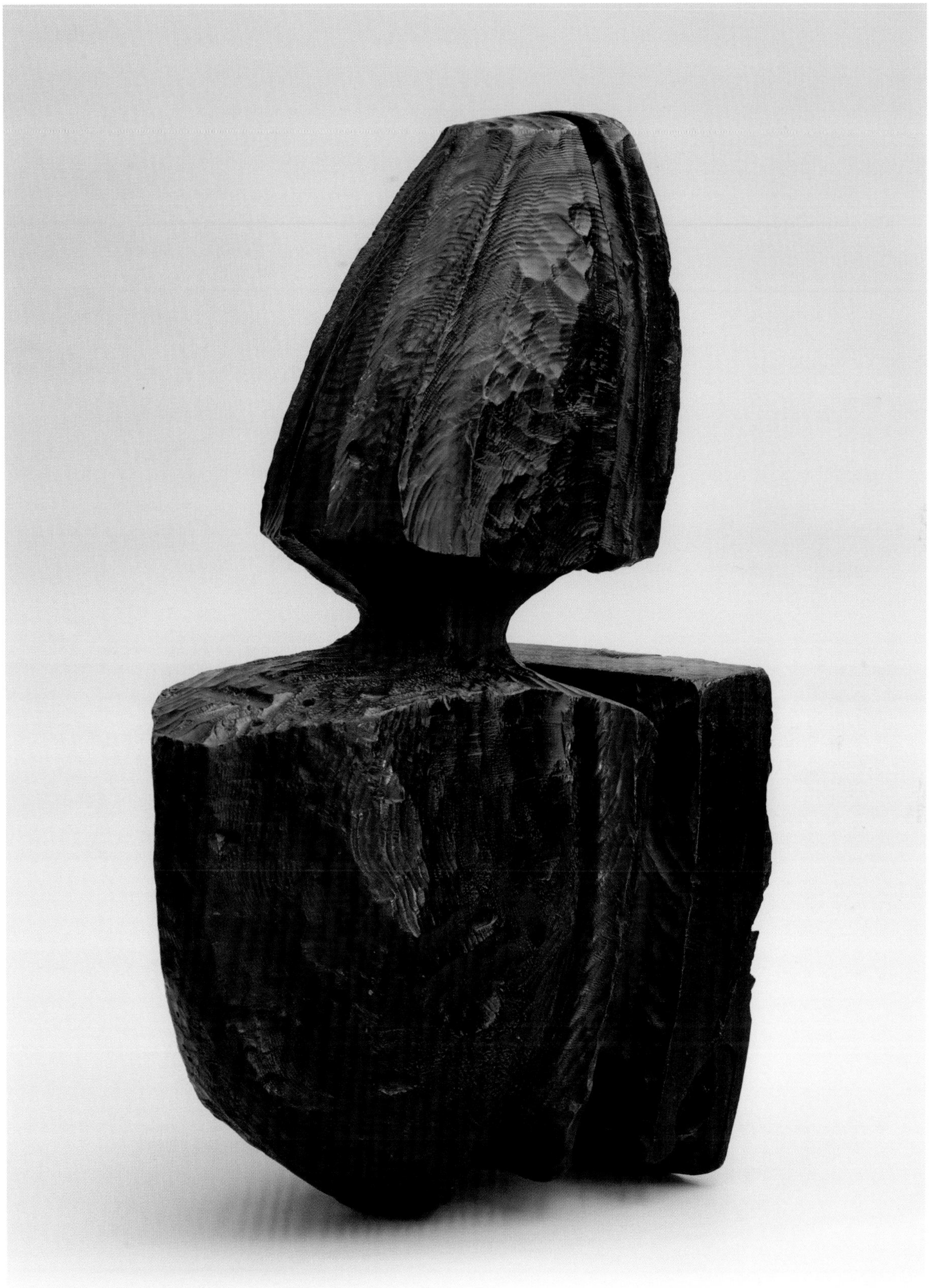

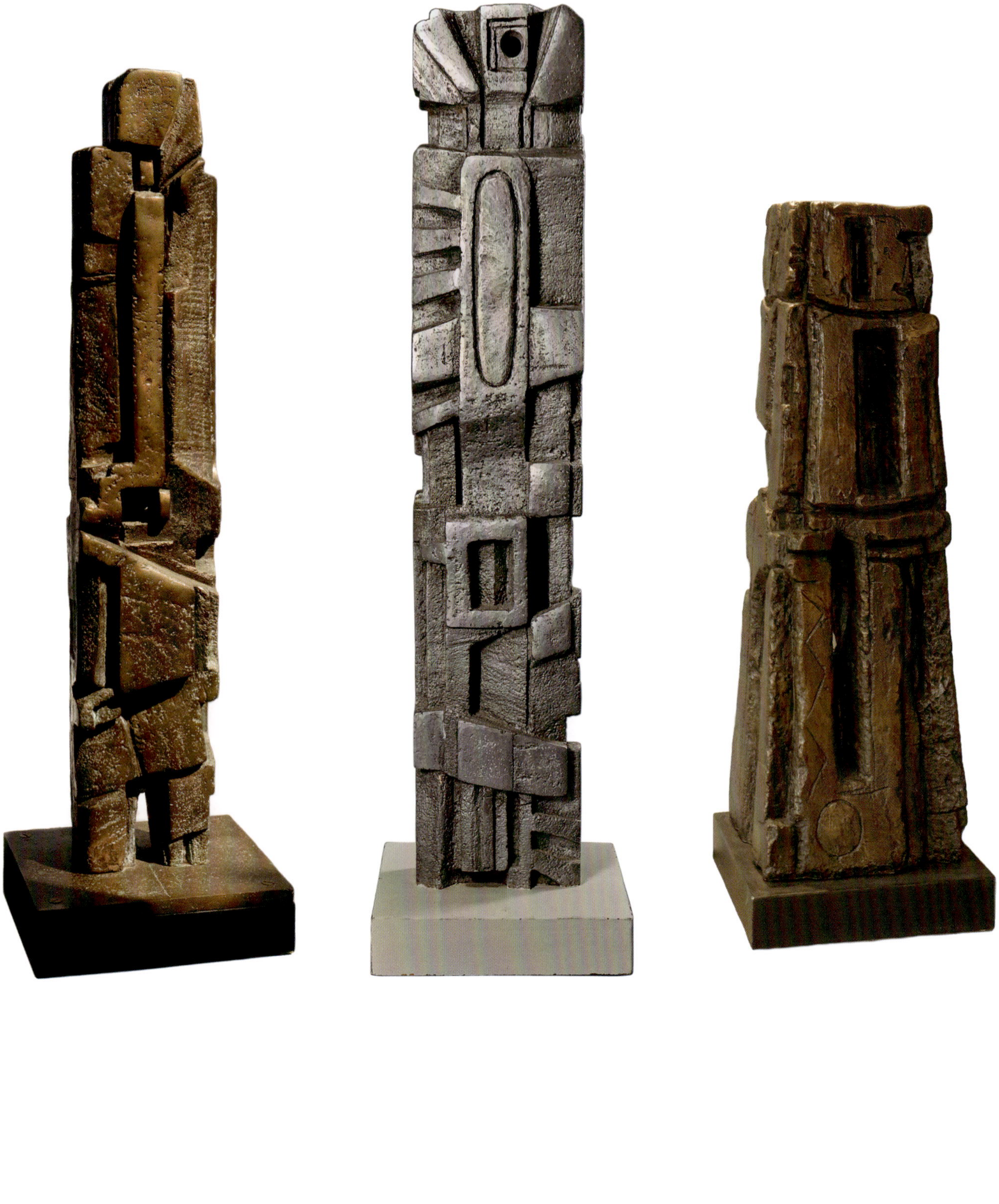

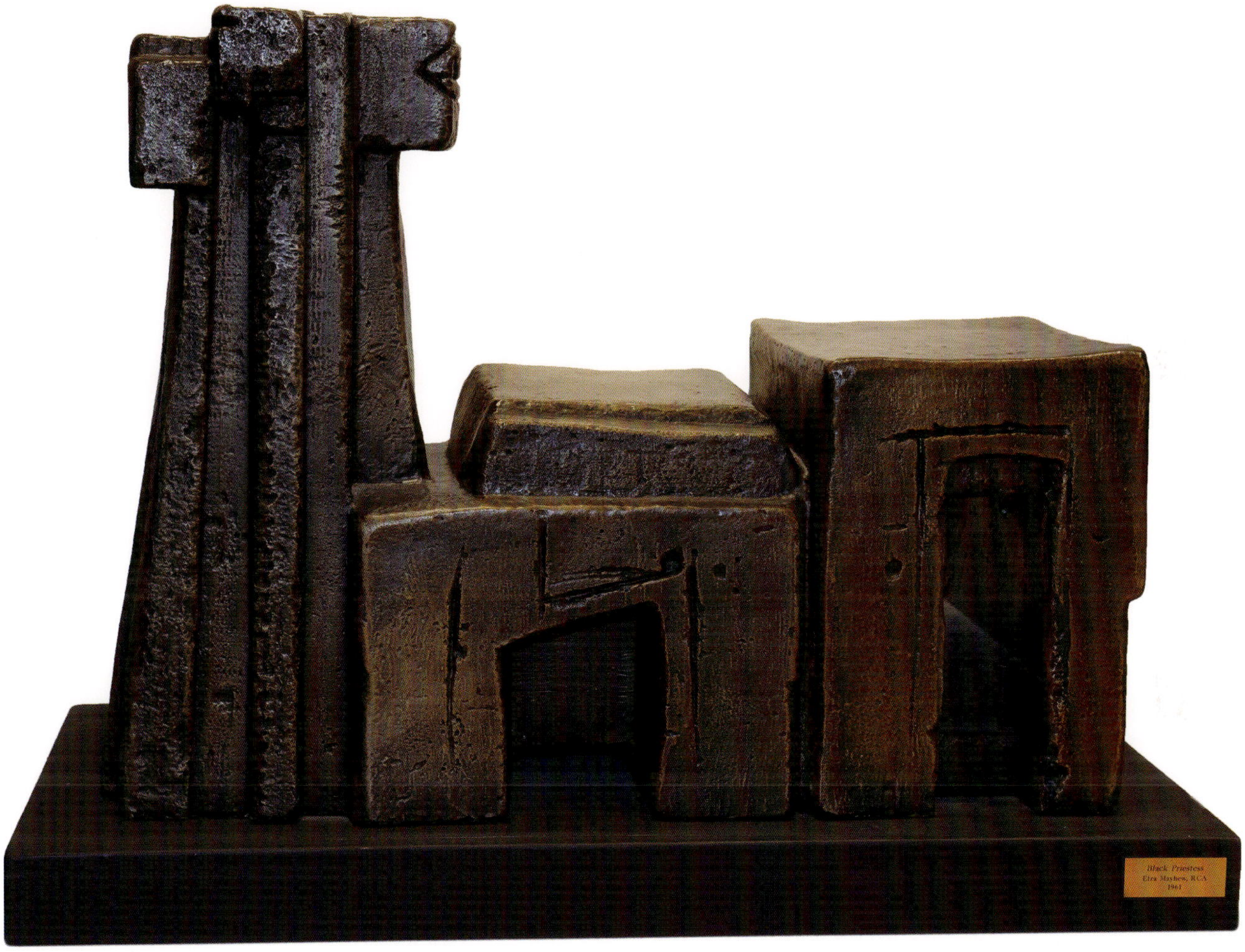

Elza Mayhew 1916-2004, Canadian, from left to right, *Procession*, 1960, bronze, *Princess*, 1963, aluminum; wood, paint, *The Supplicant*, 1963, bronze

Elza Mayhew 1916-2004, Canadian, *Priestess*, 1961, bronze

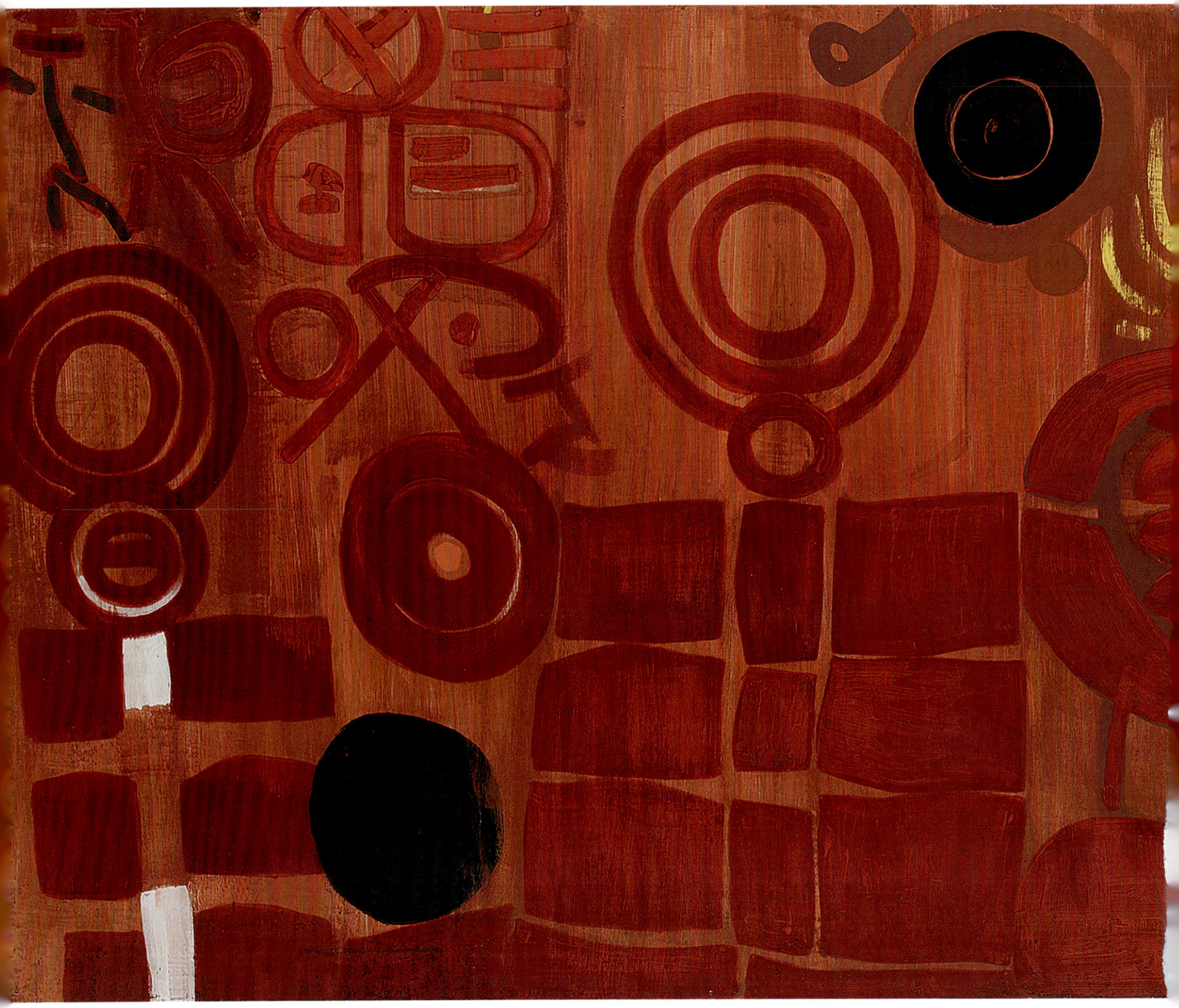

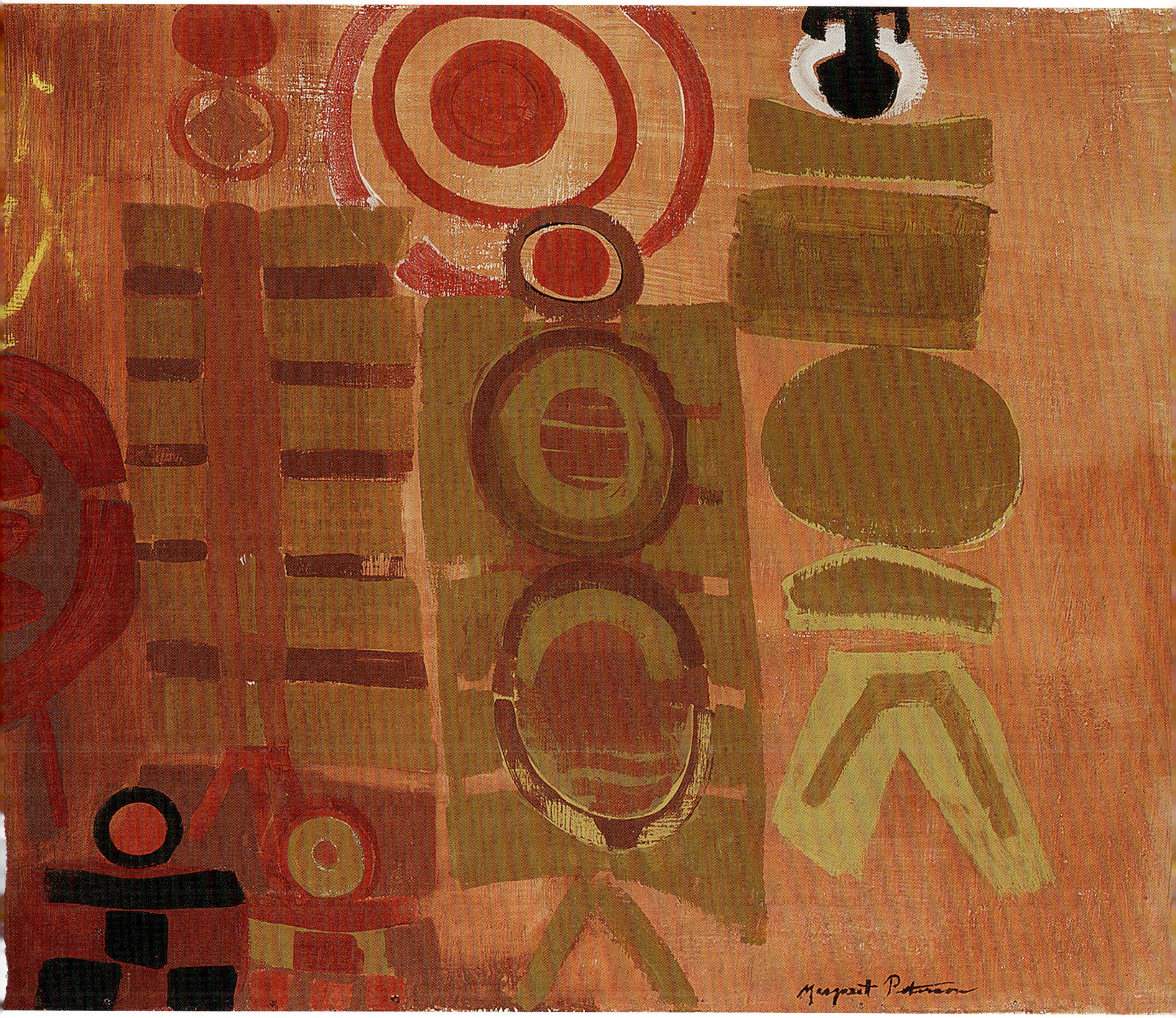

Margaret Peterson 1902-1997, Canadian, *Gods Rising from the Abyss*, 1961, egg tempera on board

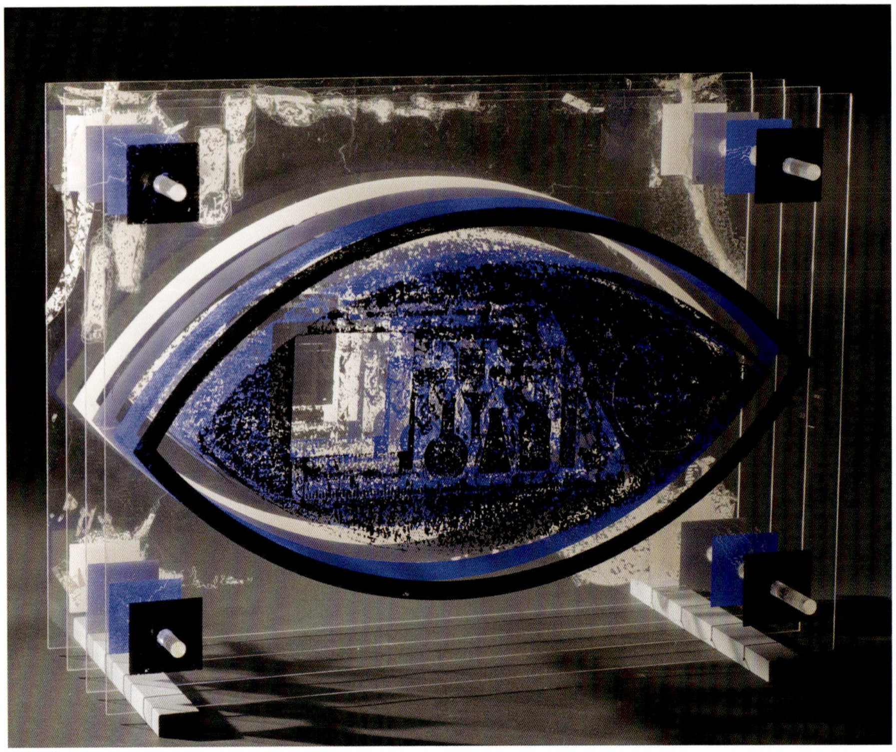

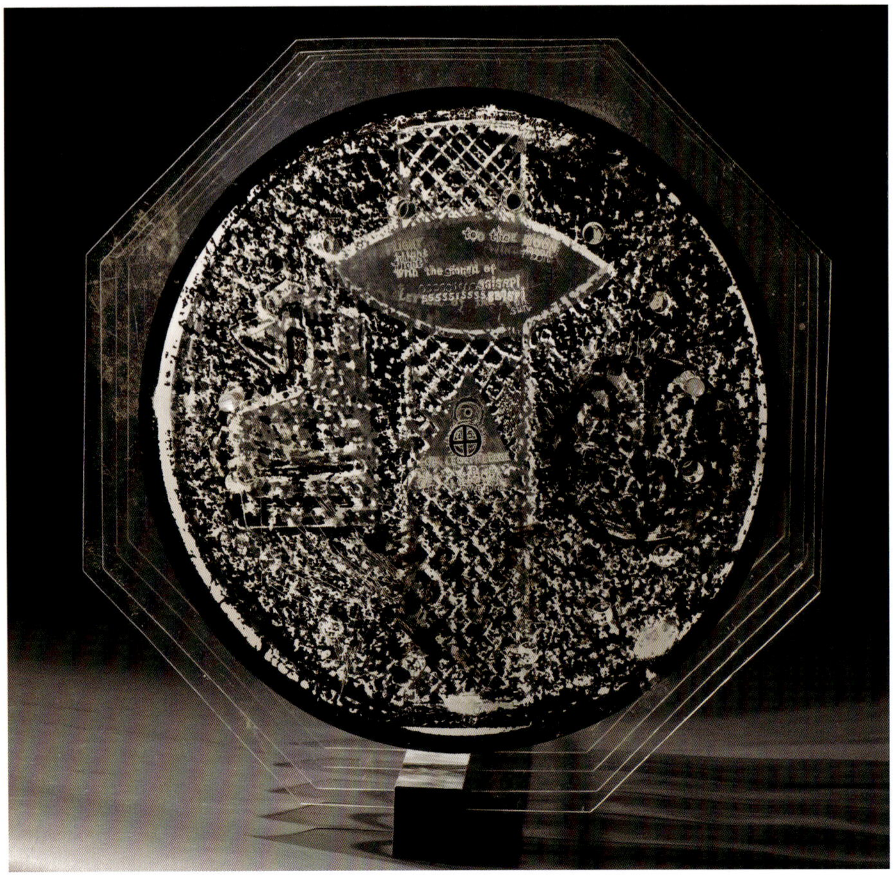

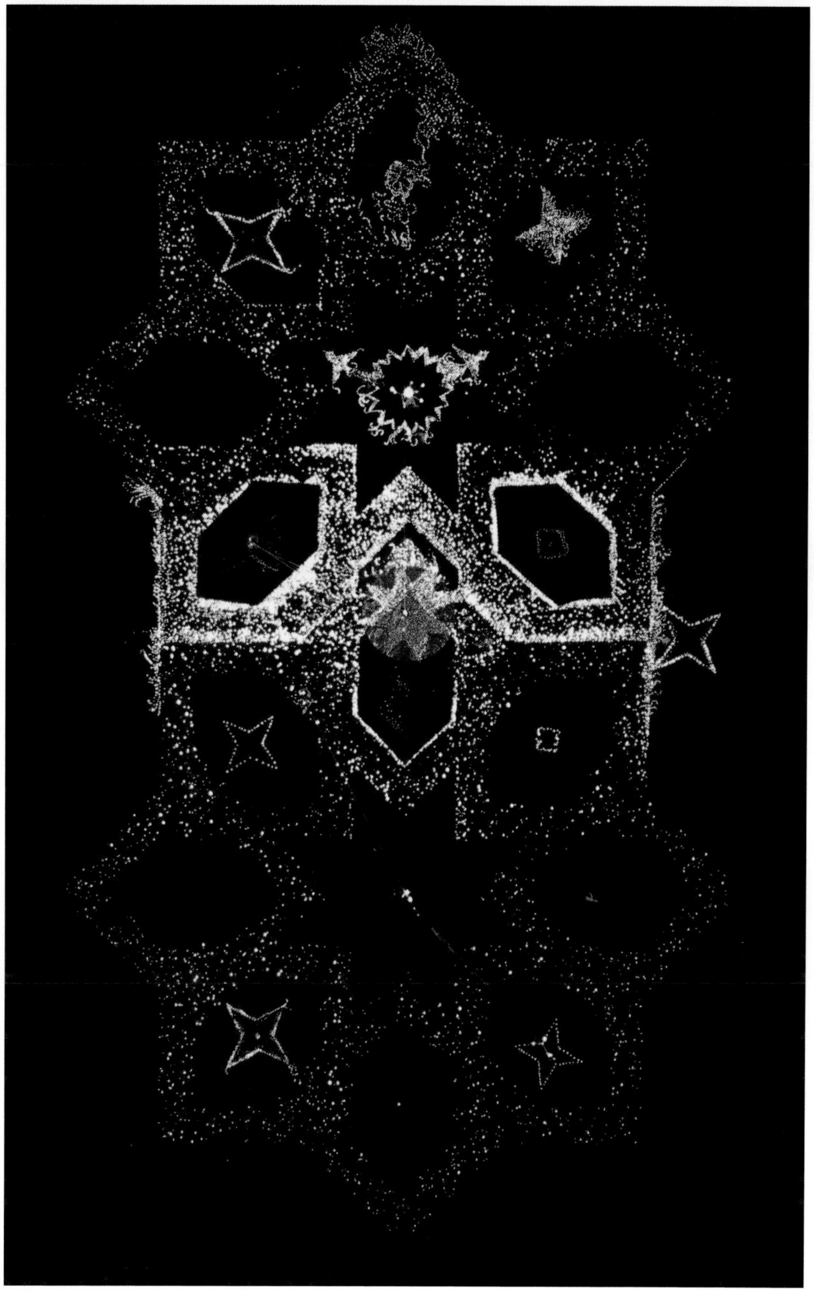

Pat Martin Bates b. 1927, Canadian, top, *Letter Through the Window from the Sun to the* Moon, 1967, lacquer paint silkscreen on plexiglas
bottom, *Flight Window of the Alchemy Letter from the Sun to the Moon*, 1968, lacquer paint silkscreen on plexiglas

Pat Martin Bates b. 1927, Canadian, *Silent Mandala for Gravel Star Garden* 1968
silver foil, grommets, ink, silver threads, silver leaf, perforated relief and bas-relief pressing with chine collé in screenprinted lightbox

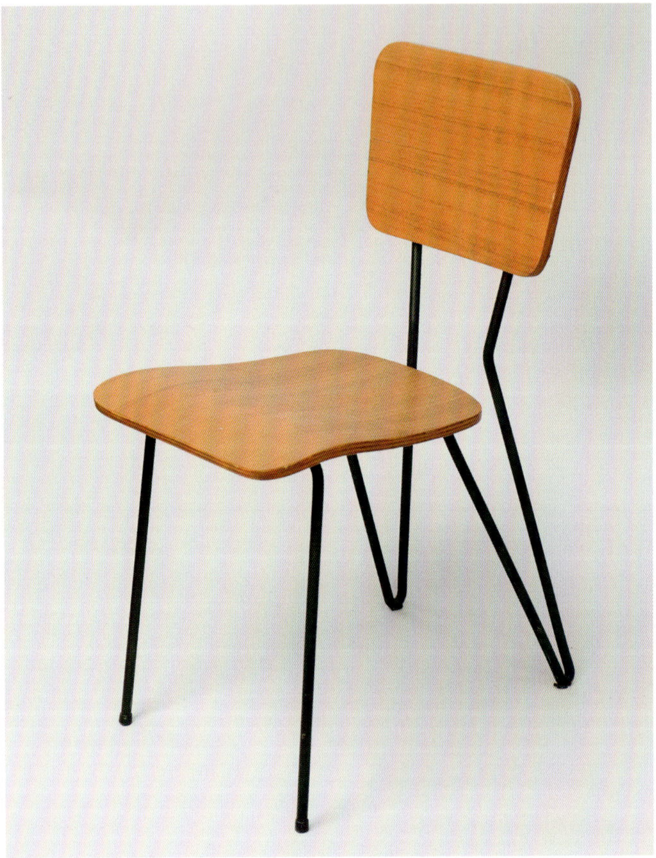

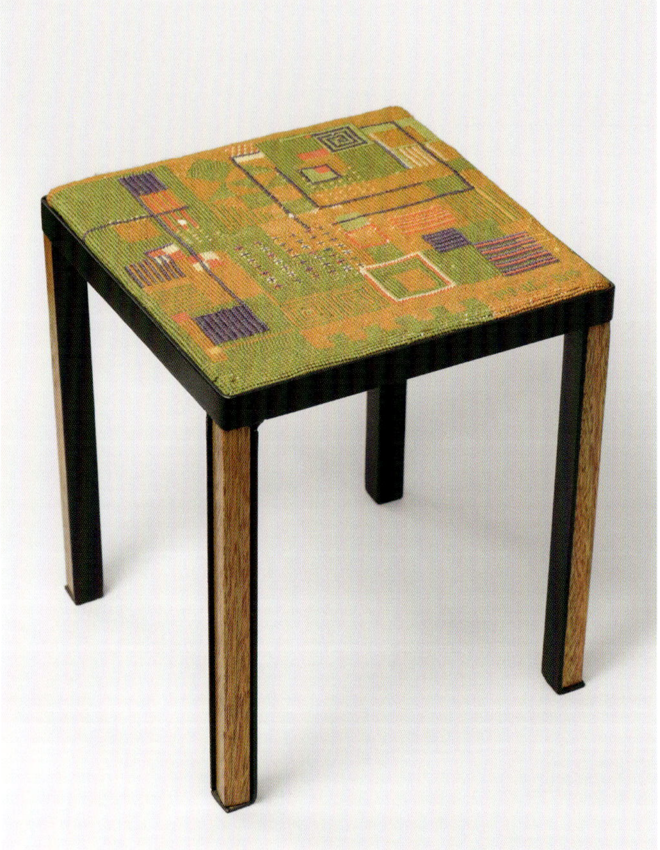

Peter Cotton 1918-1978, Canadian, left, *Spring-back dining chair*, 1951, plywood, steel rod
right, *Stool with abstract embroidery* (from *Delhaye Series*), c. 1953, embroidery: 1954, angle iron, plywood, solid wood, embroidery

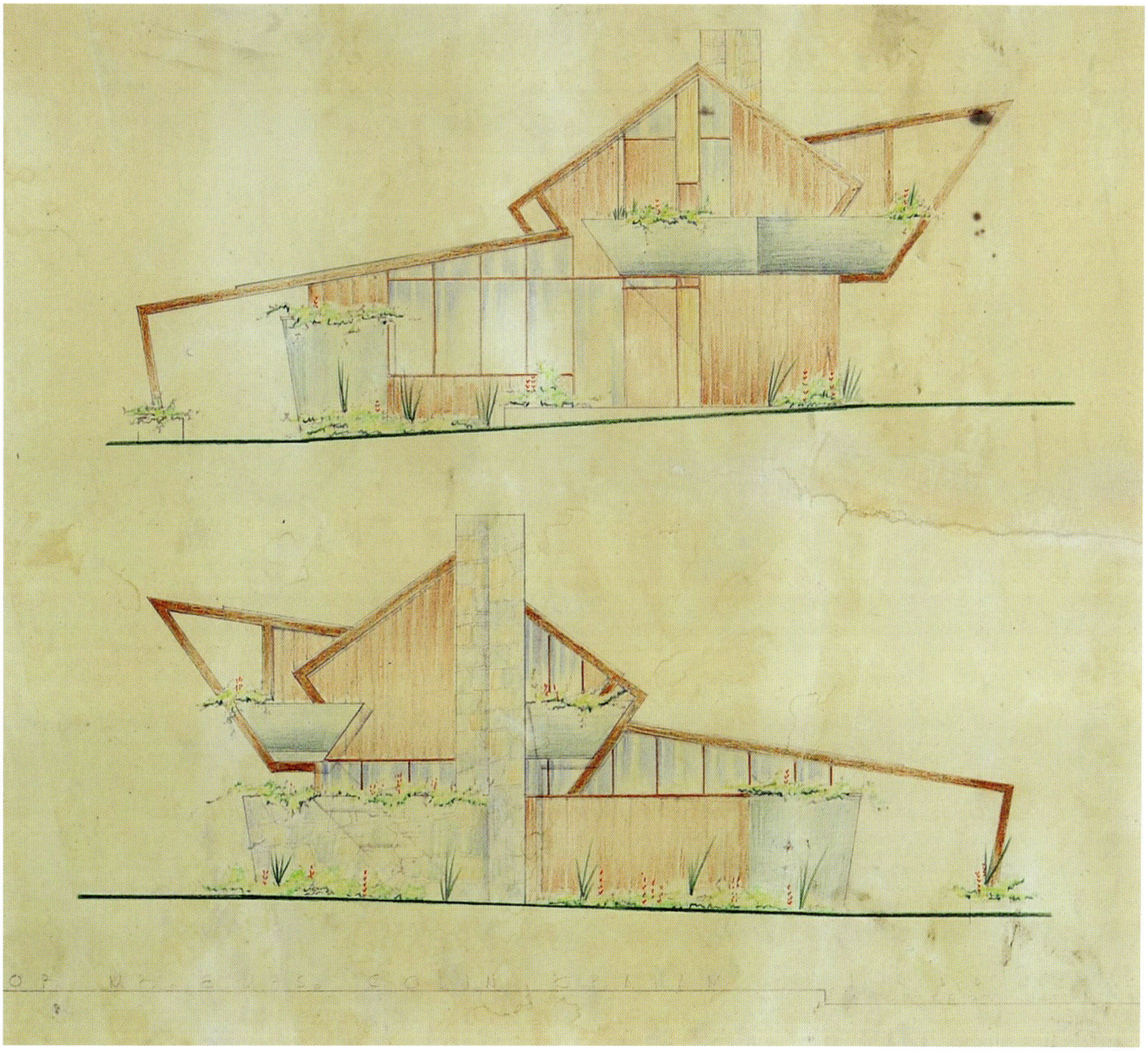

John Di Castri 1924-2005, *Elevation drawing of Colin and Sylvia Graham House*, c. 1953, watercolour on card

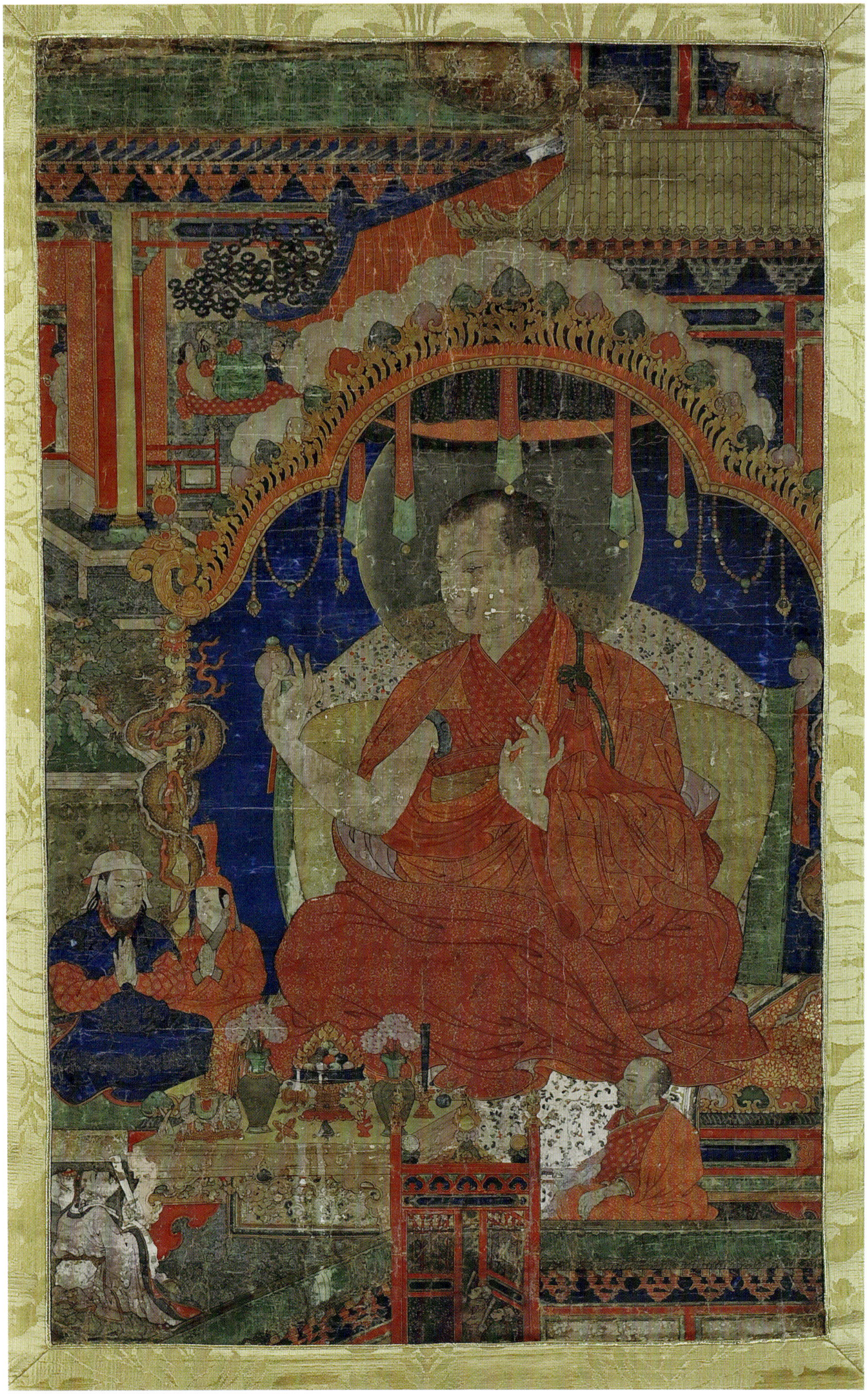

The Asian Collection Begins (1951–1973)

BARRY TILL

Victoria, a beautiful city located on the Pacific Rim, is Canada's closest city to the Far East. The city has played a pivotal role in early exchanges between Canada and Asia. It seems only fitting that Victoria's art museum, the Art Gallery of Greater Victoria (AGGV), would have one of the most distinguished Far Eastern art collections in Canada. This extensive collection encompasses all aspects and periods of Asian art and is extremely varied in its representation of the Near East, India, South and Southeast Asia, Central Asia, China, Japan, and Korea. The greatest strength of the AGGV's Asian collection lies in its holdings of Japanese and Chinese art. It has much of the finest and most outstanding Japanese art in Canada. It was Dr. Colin Graham, the first Director of the AGGV, who had the vision and daring to lay the foundations for the Asian collection, which would eventually develop a world renowned reputation.

The AGGV has been collecting Asian art since its inception. When he started his tenure, some of the first donations Colin received were Japanese prints. These were donated, along with European prints and drawings, by two American sisters, Catherine and Alexandra McEwen, who were stranded in Victoria during World War II. (Upon their deaths in 1957 they bequeathed $35,000 to the AGGV.) Colin related that until the AGGV took possession of the premises at 1040 Moss Street, there was no space in which to store these prints and the rest of the collection, other than a closet that was also used to store cleaning fluids and chairs.

It would be some time before the next Asian art works were added to the collection. In the 1950s there were a number of itinerant painters from the Hong Kong and Shanghai "schools of painting" who passed through Victoria on their way to New York and Paris. The AGGV welcomed them and often exhibited their work.

Phakspa with **Kublai Khan**
Tibetan, Thanka, 17th century, gouache on cotton

A few more Asian items were added to the collection in the late 1950s, such as Chinese textiles and a small but interesting collection of Tibetan thankas, sacred objects, and jewellery donated by Mrs. H.R. Gale, the widow of Major-General H.R. Gale, who accompanied a British trade/military mission to Tibet in 1905 where he purchased these items. In 1967 two fine ornate wooden Tibetan book covers were left to the AGGV in Mrs. Gale's bequest.

It was not until the 1960s that the AGGV's Asian collection started to take shape. The first significant purchases of Asian art were in the early 1960s through funds provided by Miss Kathleen Agnew and Mrs. Massy Goolden (Colin's aunt). With these funds Colin approached A.E. Newberry who owned an antique shop on Fort Street in Victoria. Mr. Newberry generously allowed Colin to select a number of good Asian antiques for a small fraction of their market value. When asked by Colin why he would do this, Mr. Newberry stated, "They are for the gallery and I'm a well-to-do man." Of the Chinese items purchased, the two most outstanding were a Song dynasty (960–1279) ceramic funerary pillow and a seventeenth century late Ming/early Qing ornate jade *bi* disc.

The big break for the Asian collection came in the summer of 1960, when Colin received a letter from Mrs. Isabel Pollard of San Francisco who wished to donate a work of art to the AGGV. When she visited Victoria the following year she expressed interest in building up a collection at the AGGV in memory of her late husband, Fred, as they had both lived in Victoria before Fred's death, and both had a connection to Japan. Fred Pollard's father had lived in Japan and had become one of its chief exporters of raw silk. Fred followed in his father's footsteps and achieved great financial success.

Colin established a very good rapport with Isabel and suggested that she might like to build up one or another of two collections: a Japanese art collection or a contemporary U.S. art collection. Isabel liked very much the idea of building a general Japanese art survey in Victoria. She had been interested in Japan from an early age and had spent a few weeks in Japan during her honeymoon with Fred in the late 1930s. They later settled in Victoria in a house on Gillespie Place, not far from where the AGGV would eventually take up permanent residence on Moss Street. After Fred's death, Isabel moved back to San Francisco, but she remained friends with many people in Victoria, including Miss Kathleen Agnew and later Hilda Hale. She did donate a few Asian items to the de Young Museum in San Francisco, but it was to the AGGV that she would donate nearly 1,000 Asian works of art.

In Victoria, Isabel was made to feel exceptionally special by Colin and succeeding directors, curators, and her Victoria friends, while if she had donated most of her pieces to the museum in San Francisco, she would simply have been just one of many major patrons of the arts. In Victoria, however, Premier David Barrett formally recognized Isabel Pollard in 1973 for her generous donations to the AGGV in the Legislative Assembly of British Columbia. That same year, the Mayor at the time, Peter Pollen, and Victoria's City Council, gave her a glowing tribute and an honorary citizenship certificate. It was at this time that it became quite obvious that the construction of an Asian Wing was necessary for the AGGV to properly showcase her wonderful gifts, and that a qualified Asian art curator be hired. The Fred and Isabel Pollard Gallery was completed by 1976 and Joan Stanley-Baker was hired as the AGGV's first Curator of Asian Art. Stanley-Baker was a gifted art historian, who would publish a number of important exhibition catalogues on the AGGV's Japanese collection.

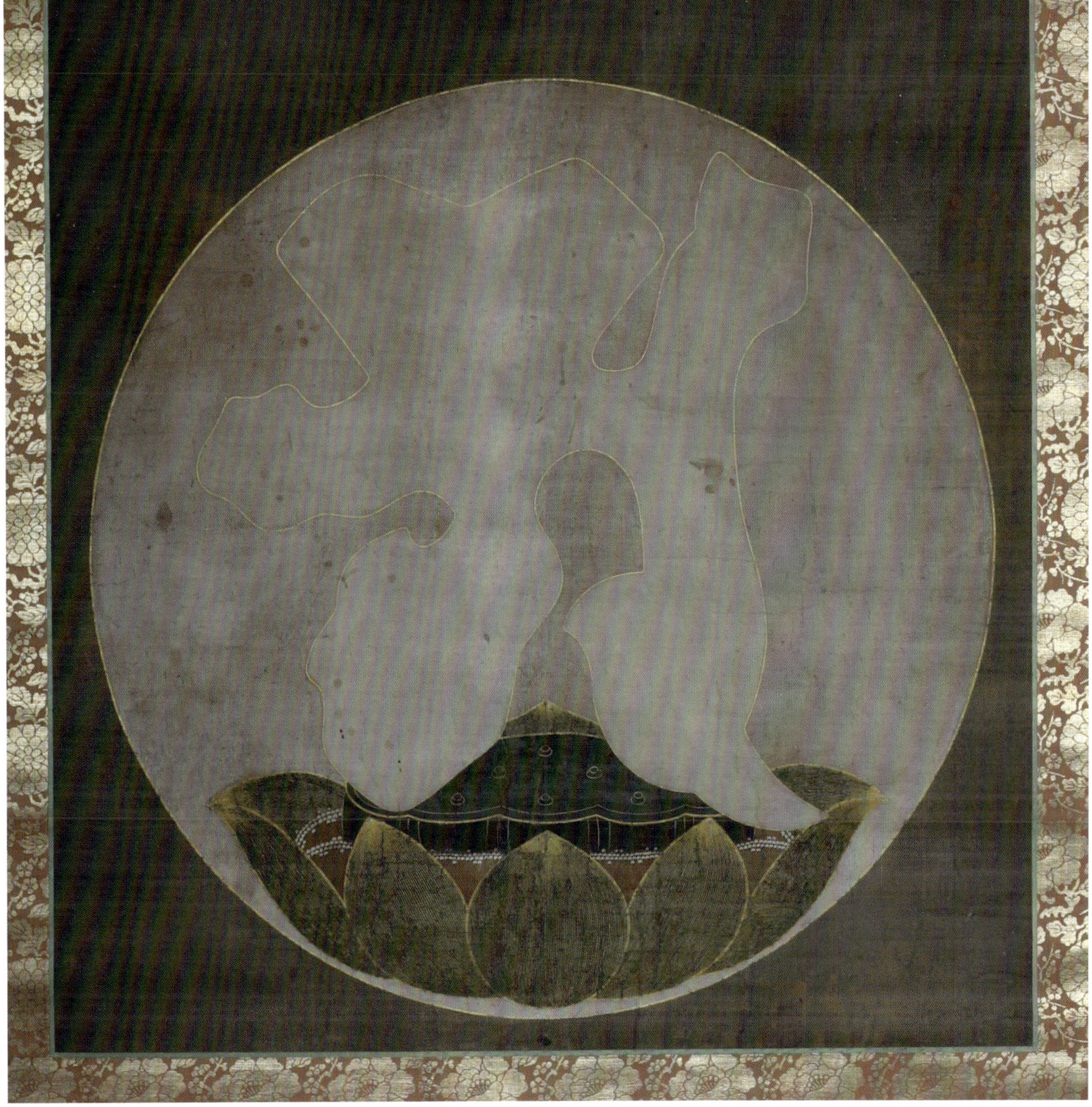

Unknown Artist Japanese, *A-ji-kan* (Meditational Painting on the letter "A"), Kamakura Period (14th century), hanging scroll, colour and cut gold leaf *(kirikane)* on silk

Isabel and Colin's collaboration at building up the AGGV's Asian collection started in earnest when Colin found some woodblock prints by leading Japanese masters in New York. He wrote to Isabel to see if she might be interested in purchasing them for the AGGV. She was, and these first Japanese pieces arrived in the summer of 1961. Over the next two decades Isabel was constantly on the lookout for Asian pieces for the AGGV. She often returned to Victoria, staying in budget hotels to save money for more acquisitions for the AGGV. In San Francisco she made an enormous number of purchases from the old established firm of T.Z Shiota. The art works included porcelains, lacquerware, miniature items like *netsuke* toggles, *inro* containers, and *tsuba* swordguards as well as a vast number of important prints by *sosaku hanga* masters like Kiyoshi Saito, Shiko Munakata, Sadao Watanabe, and Umetaro Azechi, and *shin hanga* master Hiroshi Yoshida. Isabel purchased a large number of early woodblock prints from R.E. Lewis and other works from a dealer called Shibata.

In 1963 Isabel enrolled at the University of California at Berkeley to work toward a BA, taking as many courses in Asian art as possible, graduating three years later. However, it was through the advice of important scholars and dealers that she was able to obtain some absolutely outstanding works of art. For example, in 1964 Dr. Hsio-yen Shih, Curator of Far Eastern Art at the Royal Ontario Museum (ROM), passed through Victoria and mentioned to Colin that she hoped to purchase some major works, but if she couldn't secure the necessary funding, the AGGV could try to acquire them. When Dr. Shih's plans fell through, Isabel purchased the pieces. One of the paintings was an exceptionally rare and important fourteenth century Kamakura painting of the Sanskrit letter "A" called the A-ji-kan (it appears to be the oldest extant major painting of this subject). It had been owned by a major Kyoto temple called Toji Temple (the painting was probably sold just after World War II during a period of poverty to help with the temple's finances) and was in the possession of Mr. Bunzo Nakanishi, a discreet and honourable art dealer-connoisseur-collector from Kyoto, who sold valuable Asian works of art to prestigious American and European art museums.

It was through Bunzo Nakanishi that the AGGV acquired a large number of major Japanese paintings and a fine collection of Japanese folk art (*mingei*). Bunzo would become a great friend of Colin's and the AGGV's, and would continue to come to Victoria (his favourite city) every year from then on until his death in 2004. His support for the AGGV was monumental. Not only did he identify important works for the AGGV to acquire, but freely offered good advice and boundless expertise as a mentor to the AGGV Asian art curators, donated a large number of paintings and textiles, and loaned his extensive personal collection of Asian art for exhibitions at the AGGV on a number of occasions. It was through Bunzo that the AGGV first became acquainted with one of Japan's most distinguished art historians, Dr. Toru Mori, the former Chairman of the Art History Department at the University of Osaka. He too became a constant visitor, enthusiastic supporter, and donor to the AGGV, and a trusted advisor to Isabel Pollard. It was he who recommended that she specialize in collecting eighteenth to early nineteenth century Japanese literati paintings called *nanga*. Isabel was able to acquire a number of exceptionally fine *nanga* paintings just before their prices began to skyrocket when large American museums began collecting them. Two of these, *Hawk in Snow* by Yamamoto Baiitsu and *Crows at Sunset* by Matsumura Goshun, are world renowned and rank amongst the finest paintings ever created by these two artists. Having built up a remarkable Japanese collection at the AGGV, Isabel Pollard would pass away in 1985—the same year that her dear friend and adviser, Dr. Toru Mori, died in Japan.

In the 1960s Colin organized two large-scale Asian exhibitions: *3,000 Years of Chinese Art* was on exhibit in 1963 and *Kamakura to Edo* in 1967. The former required loans from the Toronto's Royal Ontario Museum, Ottawa's National Gallery, Regina's Norman MacKenzie Art Gallery, and numerous private collectors in Victoria (mainly the D. Newell Smith Family Collection) and San Francisco. The latter Japanese exhibition required extensive loans from museums in Toronto and Seattle along with the Cleveland Museum of Art, the Los Angeles County Museum of Art, the Portland Art Museum, the Stanford University Museum, and the William Rockhill Nelson Gallery of Art as well as private collectors. Colin jokingly mentioned to me that to organize the Japanese exhibition he had to write letters on an old typewriter to request loans, to confirm arrival, and to thank everyone, adding up to some several hundred letters, all at a time when he was ill and propped up in his sick bed.

Colin also ventured beyond just China and Japan for his Asian exhibitions in the 1960s. In 1964 he struck up a friendly relationship with a leading American collector named Edwin Binney III by simply writing to compliment him on one of his exhibitions on Persian and Indian miniatures at the Portland Art Museum. Mr. Binney was so impressed with the letter that he hired a private plane to fly up to Victoria to meet Colin. From then on Mr. Binney allowed the AGGV to host exhibitions of his Indian, Persian, and Turkish miniatures, often shortly after they had been exhibited in major U.S. museums such as the Metropolitan Museum of Art in New York City. In 1967 he donated to the AGGV an eleventh century stone Indian sculpture of Brahma and a few years later a fine sculpture of Vishnu.

In 1961 Colin became friends with a Vancouver collector named Syd Hoare who had a collection of Chinese Song period (960–1279) ceramics. Mr. Hoare also collected an impressive collection of Korean Koryo celadons, which Colin displayed in 1966 and documented in a small brochure. Unfortunately, Mr. Hoare sold the celadons not long before their value greatly increased. He did donate a number of interesting Chinese works of art in the 1960s and a rather large group of Chinese ceramics in the mid-1990s, shortly before he passed away.

In the mid-1960s more important Asian works of art were added to the collection. Mrs. W.W. Ritchie gave three wonderful Tibetan thankas, one of which (with Phagspa and Kublai Khan) is exceedingly rare and extremely well rendered. This early seventeenth century painting is one of the most important Tibetan paintings in North America. Other important additions at this time came from a Frenchman named Etienne Sigaut who, while passing through Victoria, left behind some interesting items. Mrs. Phyllis Masters, an energetic board member of the AGGV, together with Colin were able to get him to donate Japanese samurai armour and helmets, old Chinese bronzes and textiles as well as an amazing Japanese palanquin (sedan chair) which once belonged to the Tokugawa shogun family.

In the late 1960s, through another board member, Madge (Molson) McElney, Colin struck up an acquaintance with her stepson, Brian S. McElney, a lawyer working in Hong Kong who was a major collector of Asian art. In 1968 Colin borrowed his Chinese ceramics for an exhibition which was very well received. Brian would come to store a number of his treasures for use at the AGGV in the 1970s and '80s. He would occasionally gift a piece or two in the 1970s and early 1980s, but by the late 1980s until the present he would bestow an astounding number of major Asian works of art (nearly 500 items) to the AGGV from archaeological Chinese jades, bronzes and ceramics, and gorgeous porcelains to a few hundred modern Chinese paintings by some of China's most famous twentieth century artists, as well as a large collection of Southeast Asian ceramics.

In 1972 about 100 pieces of Chinese works of art, mainly ceramics, were added to the AGGV collection by Mrs. King Foh Chen of Jakarta, Indonesia. About half a dozen pieces were quite rare and excellent additions to the collection, and the remainder made quite a nice study resource and formed an interesting nucleus from which to build on. As well, a monumental wooden twelve-fold screen with two side panels dating from the late eighteenth or early nineteenth century was brought out of Indonesia and presented to the AGGV. The screen, with its jade and precious stone relief sculptures on a burgundy lacquer ground, is quite spectacular and has wowed visitors to the AGGV whenever it is on display. Getting the collection out of Indonesia involved a great deal of diplomacy and cunning. Bertram Butler, a retired diplomat living in Victoria, was persuaded to help cut through the red tape, and with his help Colin was able to bring the collection to Victoria.

In 1973, during his final year as Director, Colin was able to help coordinate two Asian exhibitions of exceptional quality. Working with Dr. Hsio-yen Shih of the ROM, the two museums agreed to an exchange and to exhibit each other's Asian collections. Since the AGGV now had such a comprehensive Japanese collection, it was decided that the AGGV would loan the finest hundred pieces of its Japanese art to the ROM and in exchange the ROM would send about one hundred and fifty of its finer Chinese works of art to the AGGV. The Canada Council gave grants to produce two large handsome hardcover exhibition catalogues of the respective collections. After the AGGV's Japanese art collection was exhibited at the ROM, it was displayed at the Montreal Museum of Fine Arts, and then at the Vancouver City Museum before returning to the AGGV. It was a major feather in Colin's cap to have pulled off such an incredible and successful exchange, which drew in large audiences.

After Colin's retirement in 1973, he would continue working at the AGGV on a half-time basis for the next five years helping the next two directors, Richard Simmins and Roger Boulet. Before his retirement, Colin had met and established a good rapport with Mr. and Mrs. R.W. Finlayson of Toronto, who were exceptional collectors of Chinese and Japanese paintings. The Finlaysons were able to assemble a very sizable and significant collection of Chinese paintings of the Ming and Qing dynasties as well as a number of important Japanese *nanga* (literati) and *zenga* (Zen Buddhist) paintings. They consulted with dealers and scholar friends throughout the world and carefully chose a homogeneous representation of paintings. There were few fine private collections of Japanese paintings in North America, so when the Finlaysons decided to make the AGGV the repository for their Japanese paintings in the late 1970s, it had a tremendous impact on the AGGV collection and elevated it to one of the best Japanese painting collections in North America. After Mr. Finlayson's death in 1979, his widow, Marjorie, continued to donate to the AGGV Japanese paintings, Chinese paintings, Chinese tomb figurines, and Southeast Asian and Nepalese/Tibetan bronze Buddhist statues well into the twenty-first century. Before and after her death in 2006, her son, Fraser, carried on the family tradition by continuing to enhance the AGGV with wonderful Asian works of art.

Through the charisma of Colin Graham and the help and support of his charming wife, Sylvia, the AGGV was able to lay the groundwork for and set in motion the development of a truly distinguished world-class Asian art collection. Victoria's debt of gratitude to their hard work and dedication is immense. For the author of this essay, it is indeed a pleasure to know the Grahams and appreciate their great contributions and accomplishments towards the Asian collection of the AGGV.

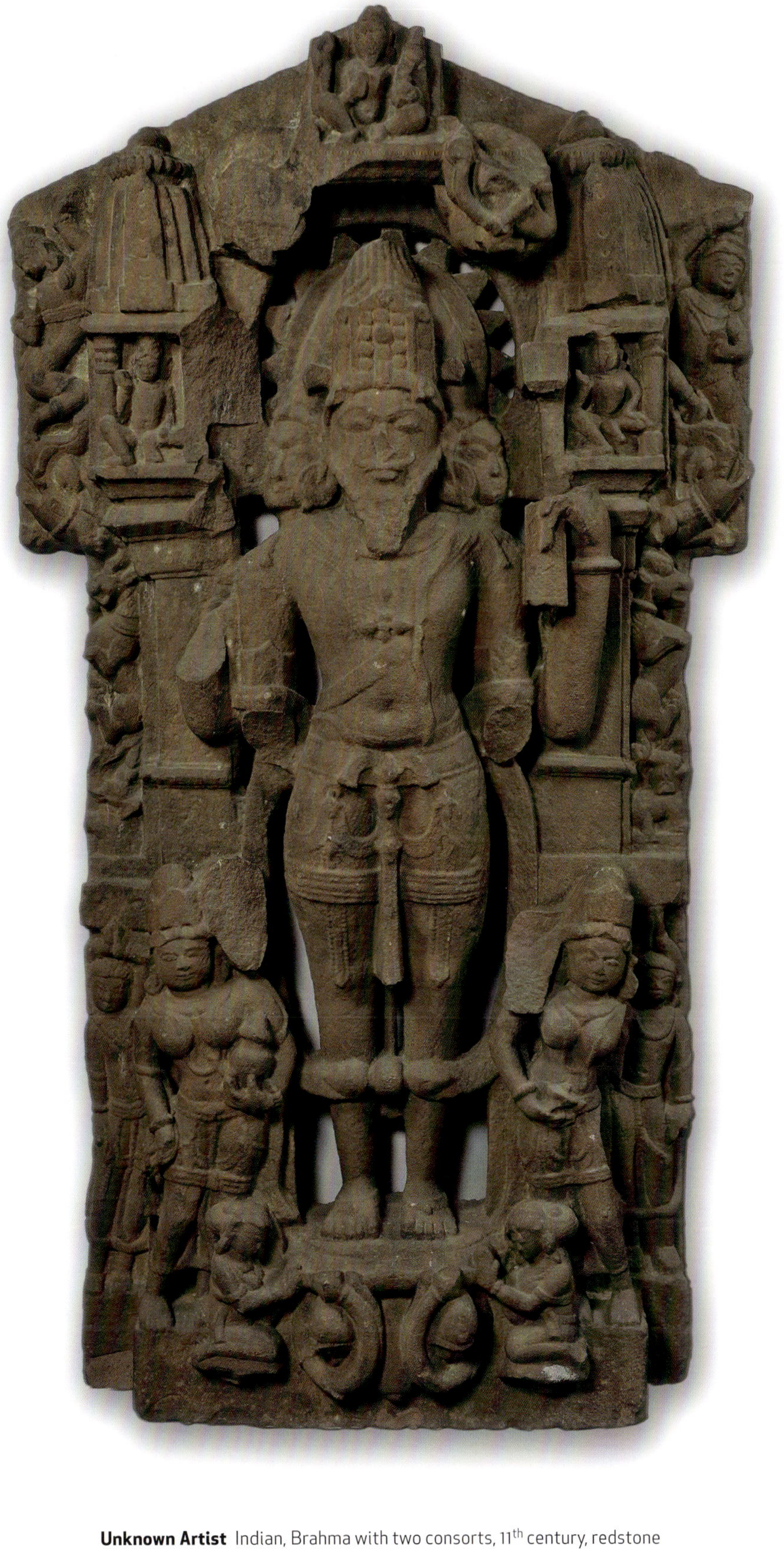

Unknown Artist Indian, Brahma with two consorts, 11th century, redstone

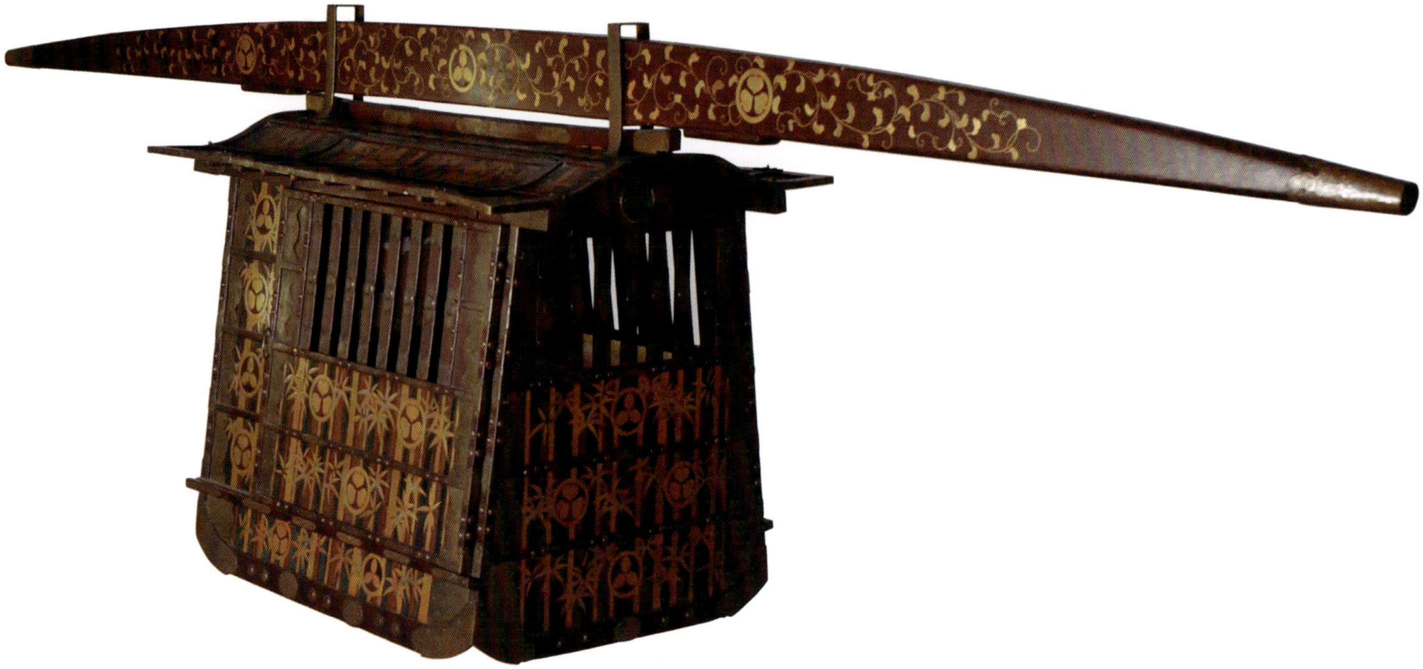

Unknown Artist Japanese, Sedan Chair (*norimono*) with Tokugawa family crest, Edo period, 18th century, wood with amber *nashiji* lacquer ground and gold, green, bronze and brown

Much of the information in this short essay has been gleaned from Colin D. Graham's *Moss Street Years: Three Decades of Controversial Hangings*, unpublished manuscript, 1981.

Colin Graham's Asian art catalogue publications

3000 Years of Chinese Art, March 1–March 31, 1963.

Early Korean Ceramics from the Syd Hoare Collection, February 15–March 6, 1966.

Kamakura to Edo, September 8 – October 1, 1967.

Japanese Sen Cha Ceremony Utensils from the Bruno Petzold Collection, April 8–June 30, 1981.

Selected Bibliography

Amos, Robert. "Bunzo Nakanishi," *Canadian artists and art resource directory*, 2005 at http://www.artistsincanada.co/php/article.php?id=682

_____. *An Introduction to Japanese Art,* Collections of the AGGV, No. 6, Victoria, 1980.

Hale, Hilda. *Indomitable Immigrant*, Victoria, 2000.

Henderson, Douglas. *The Arts of Tibet: Painting*, Collections of the AGGV, No. 6, Victoria, 1977.

Stanley-Baker, Joan. *Nanga, Idealist Painting of Japan*, Victoria, 1980.

Till, Barry. *The Land of the Rising Sun, Arts of Japan*, Victoria, 1998.

_____. *Mandate of Heaven, Treasures from China's Imperial Dynasties*, Victoria, 1996.

Tregear, Mary. *Chinese Ceramics Handbook*, Collections of the AGGV, No. 12. Victoria, 1978.

Vollmer, John, and Webb, Glenn T. *Japanese Art at the Art Gallery of Greater Victoria*, 1972.

The Asian Collection Begins (1951–1973)

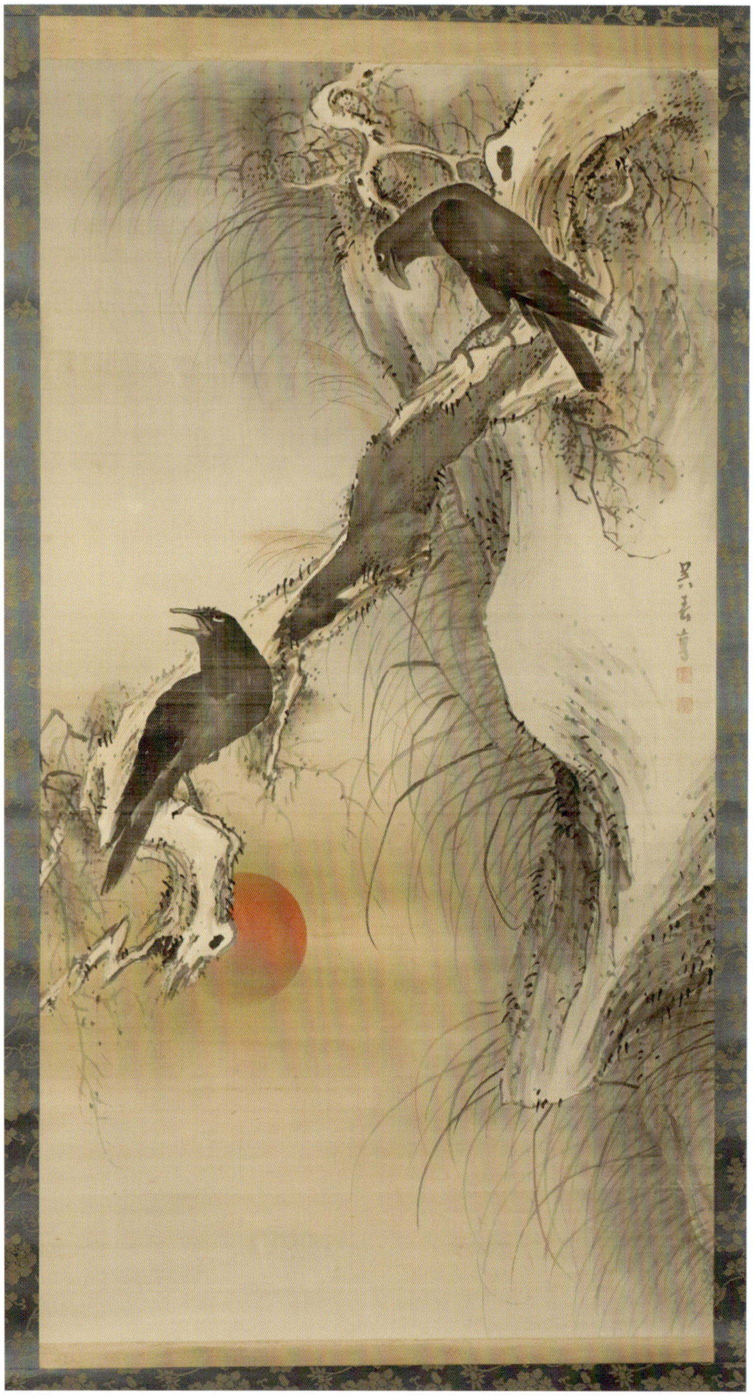

Matsumura Goshun 1752-1811, Japanese, *Two Crows In Sunset*, hanging scroll; ink and colours on silk

Tosa Mitsuoki 1617-1691, Japanese, *Jindo Fujoso-zu* (A Pictorial Description of the Defilement of Human Existence), hanging scroll; colour on silk

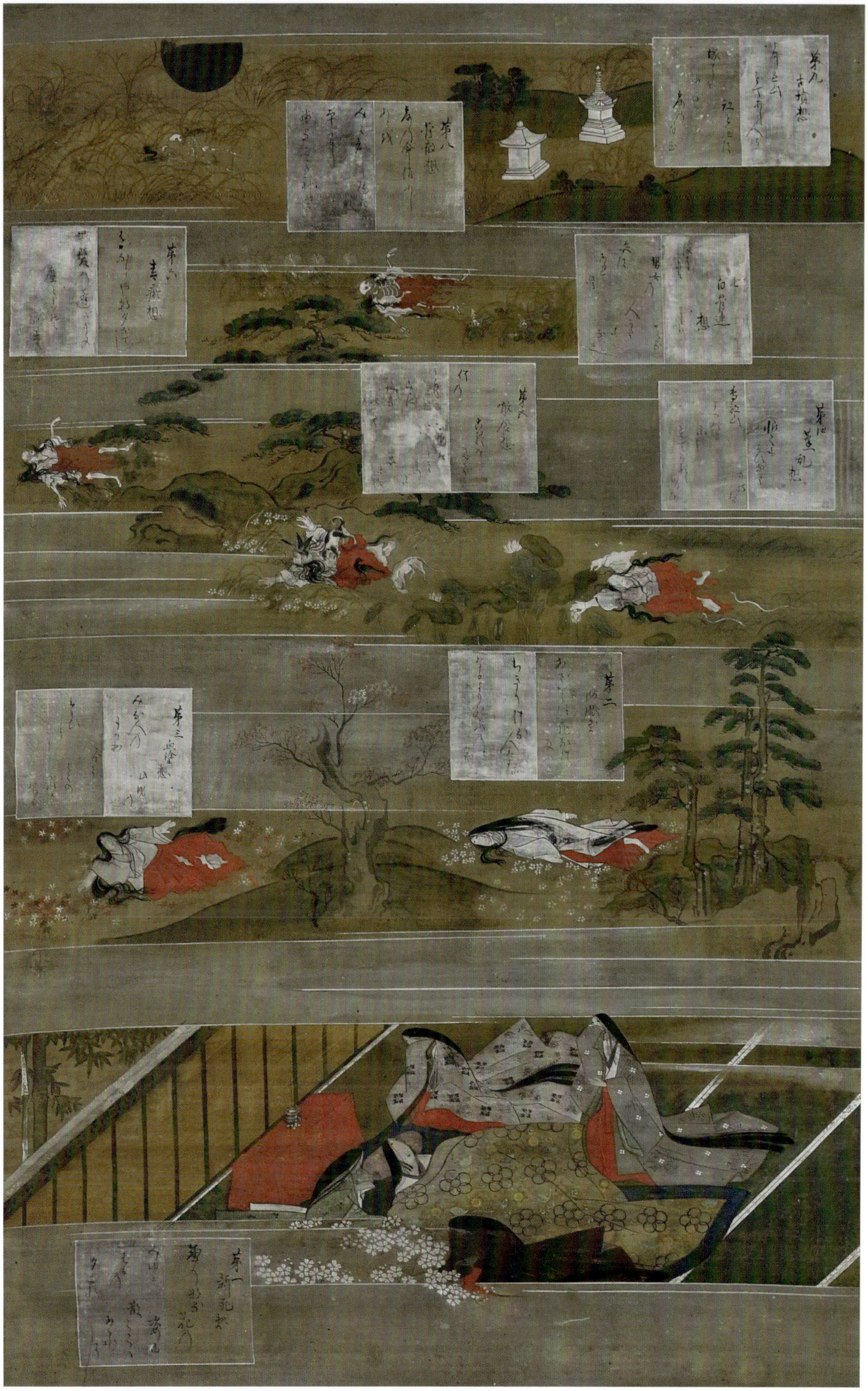

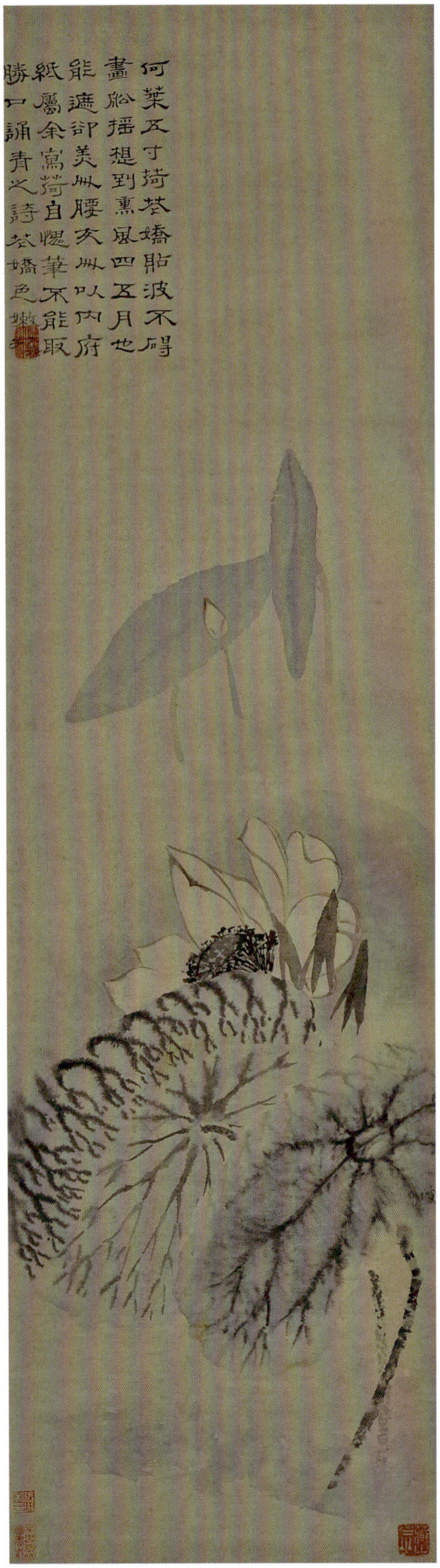

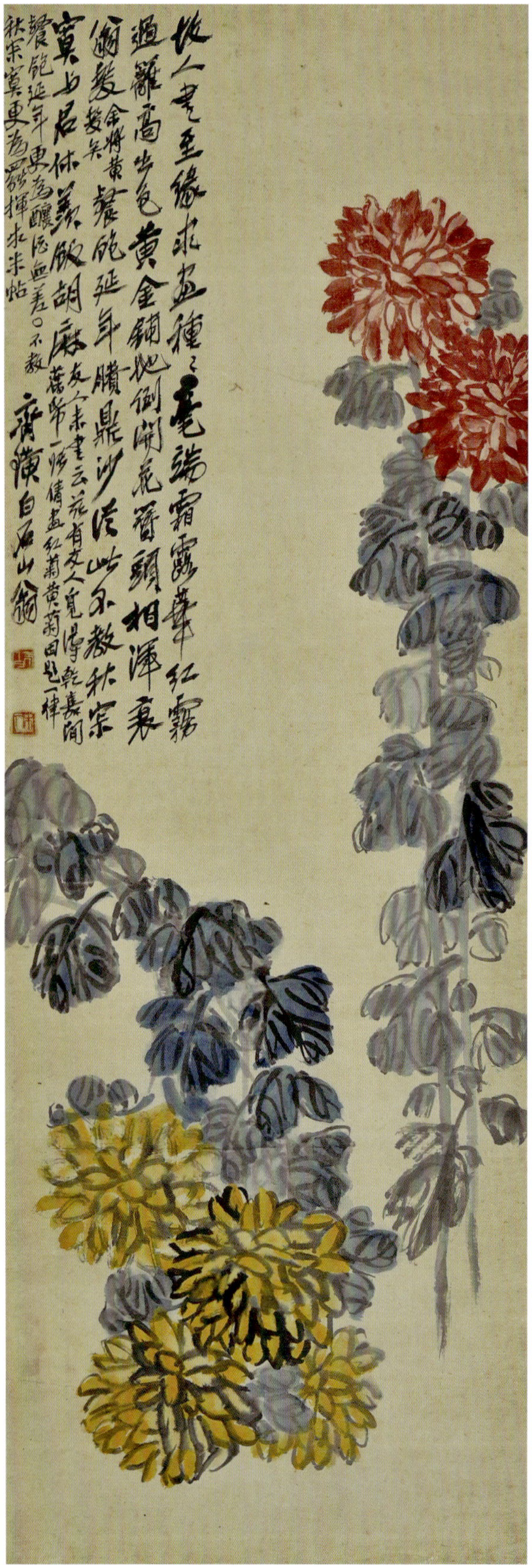

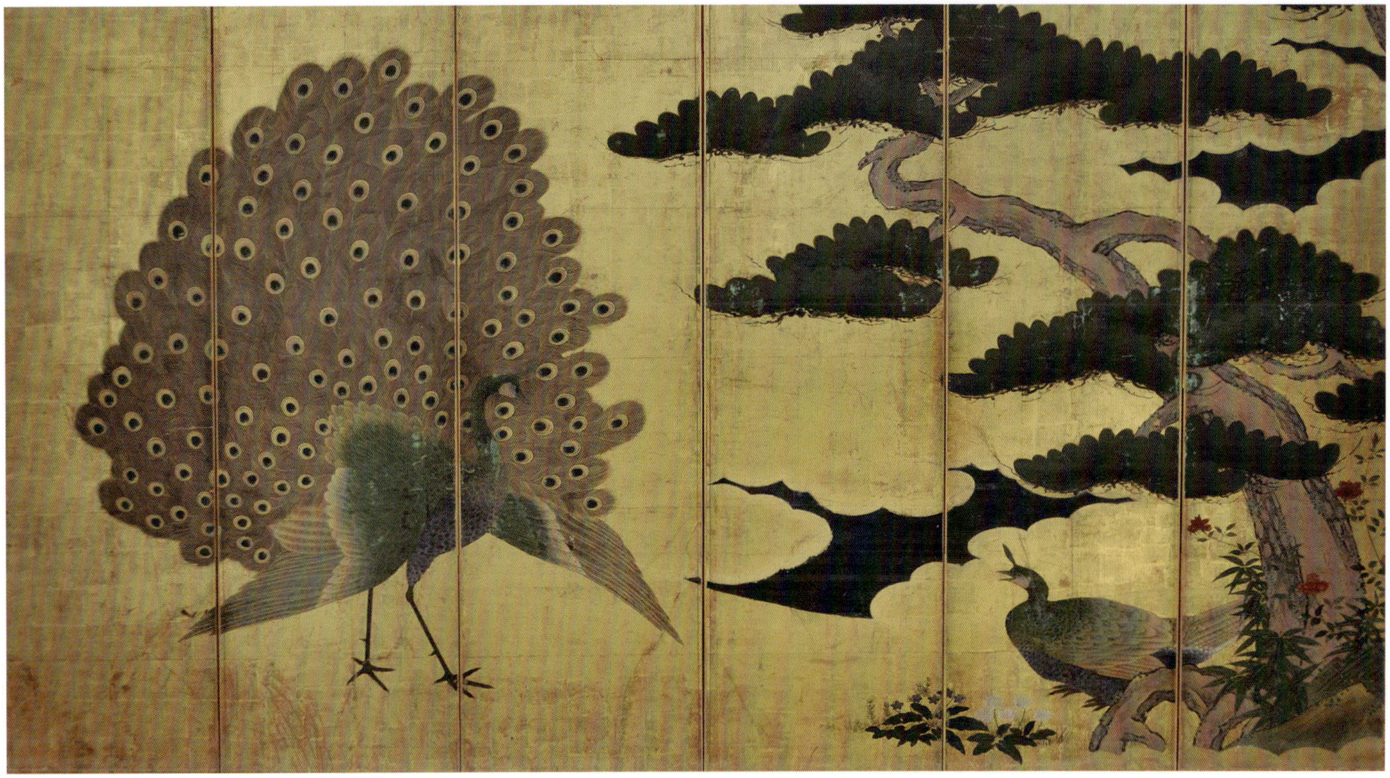

Dao Ji 1641-1714, Chinese, *Lotus*, nd, hanging scroll, ink and colour on paper

Qi Baishi 1863-1957, Chinese, *Chrysanthemums*, nd, hanging scroll, ink and colours on paper

Kano Sanraku 1559-1635, Japanese, *Peacocks and Pine Tree,* six fold screen, ink and colours on gold leaf

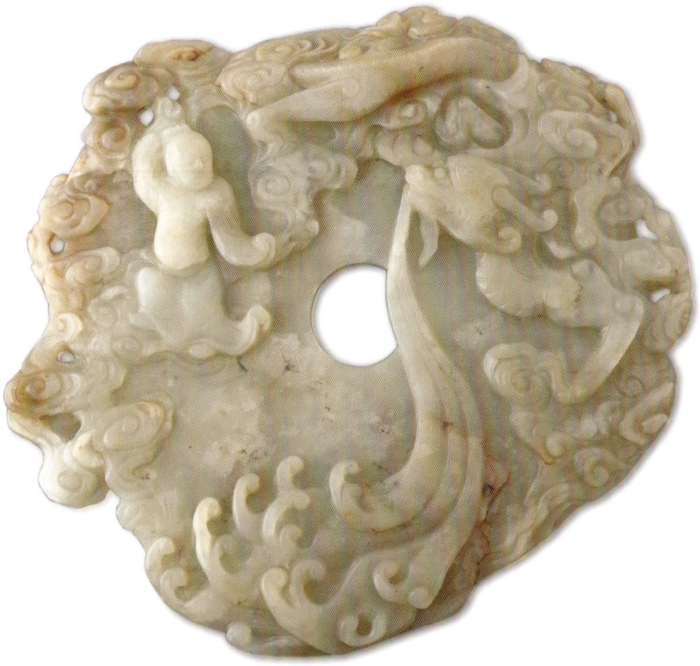

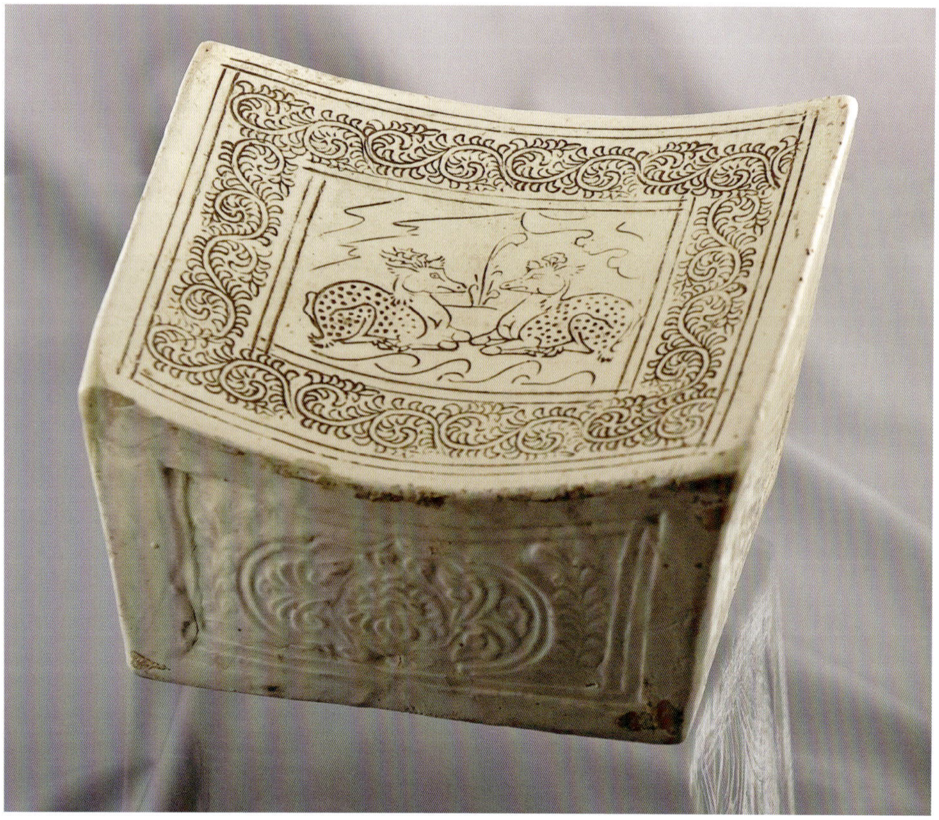

Unknown Chinese, Bi disc with human figure and dragon, Late Ming/early Qing period, 17th century, jade

Unknown Chinese, Rectangular Pillow with curved top, Northern Song Dynasty, late 11th/early 12th century, glazed stoneware, Cizhou ware

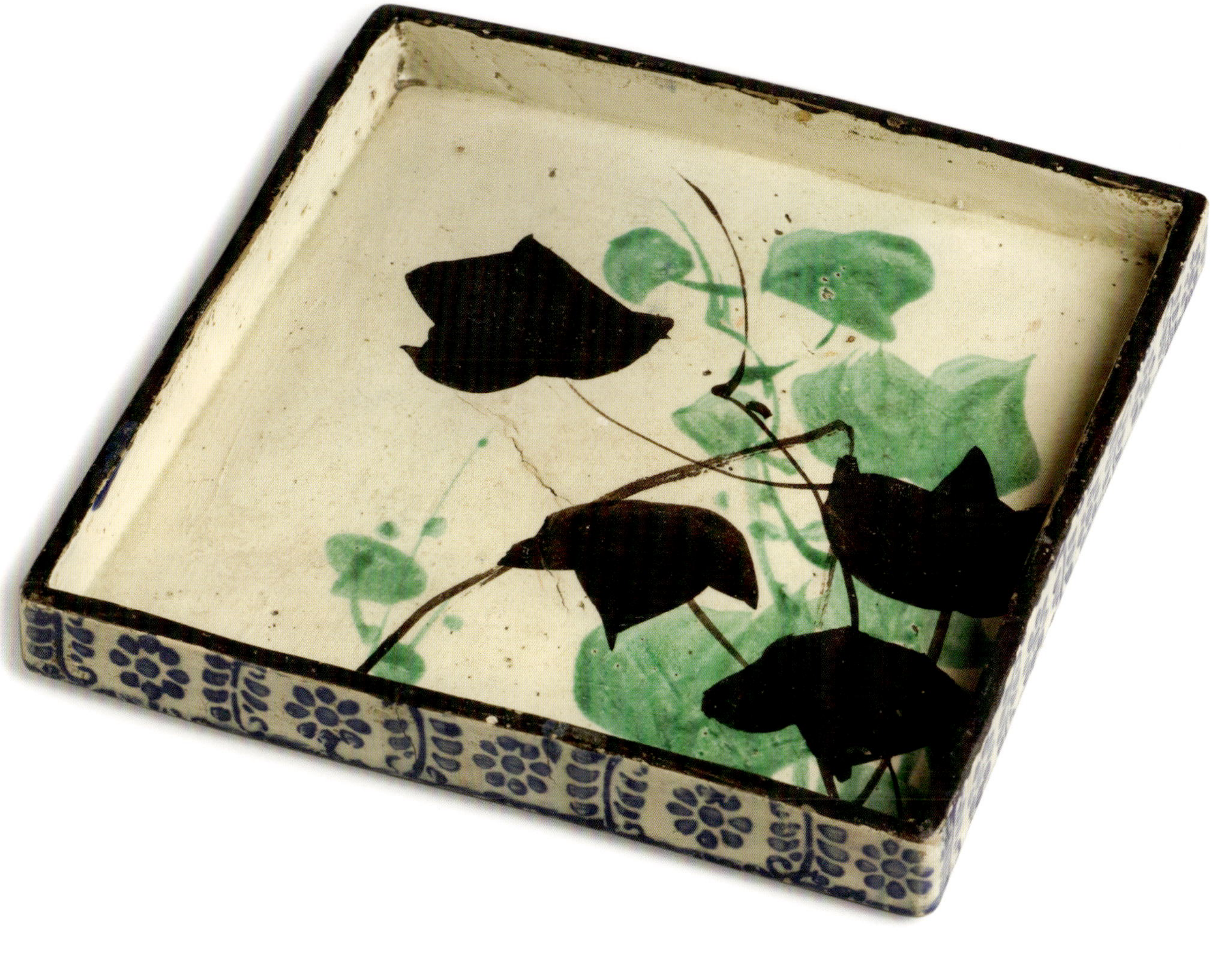

Ogata Kenzan 1663-1743, Japanese, Square plate, Kyoto ware, stoneware with overglaze enamels

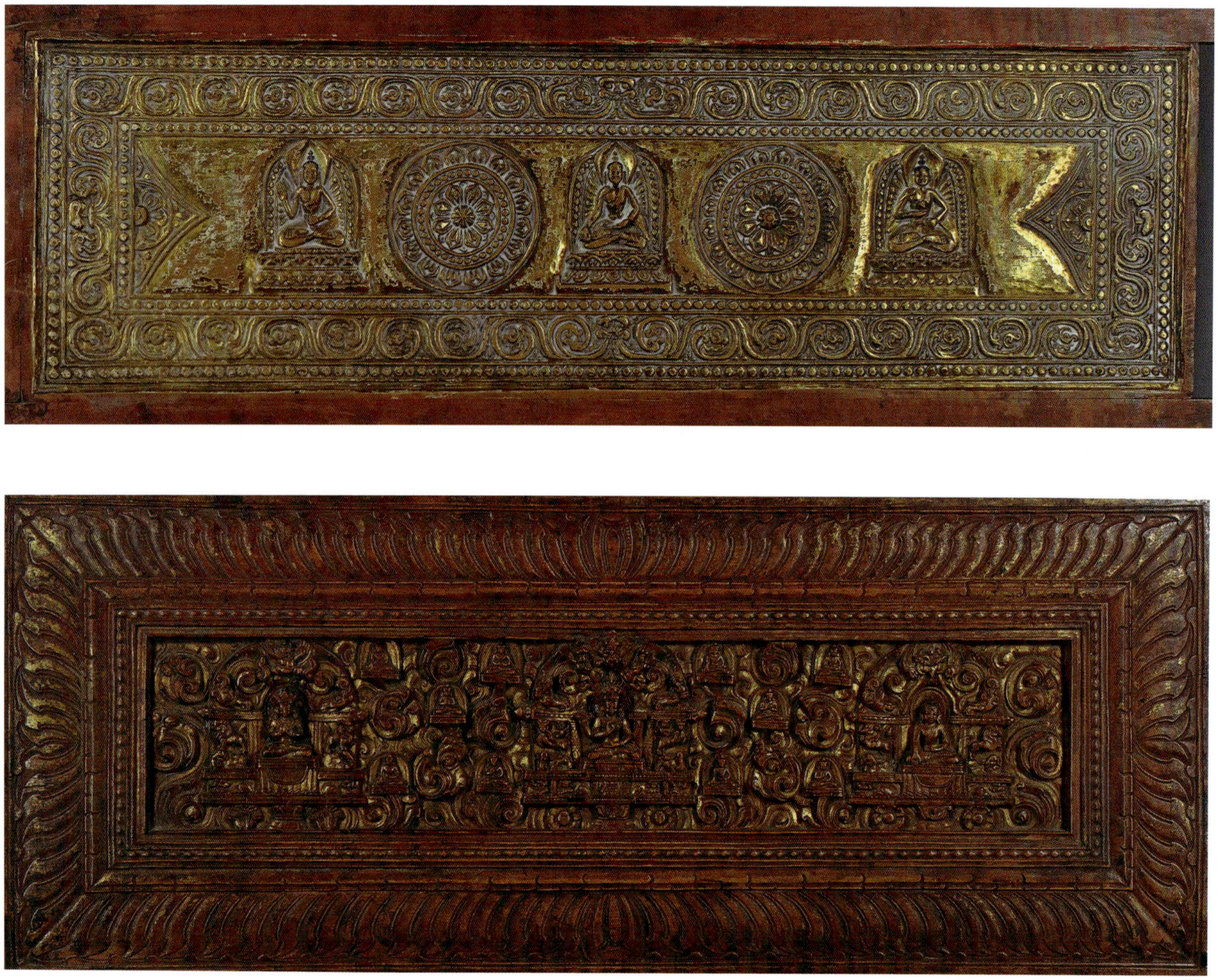

Unknown Artist Tibetan, Book Cover, 18th century, wood, gilt

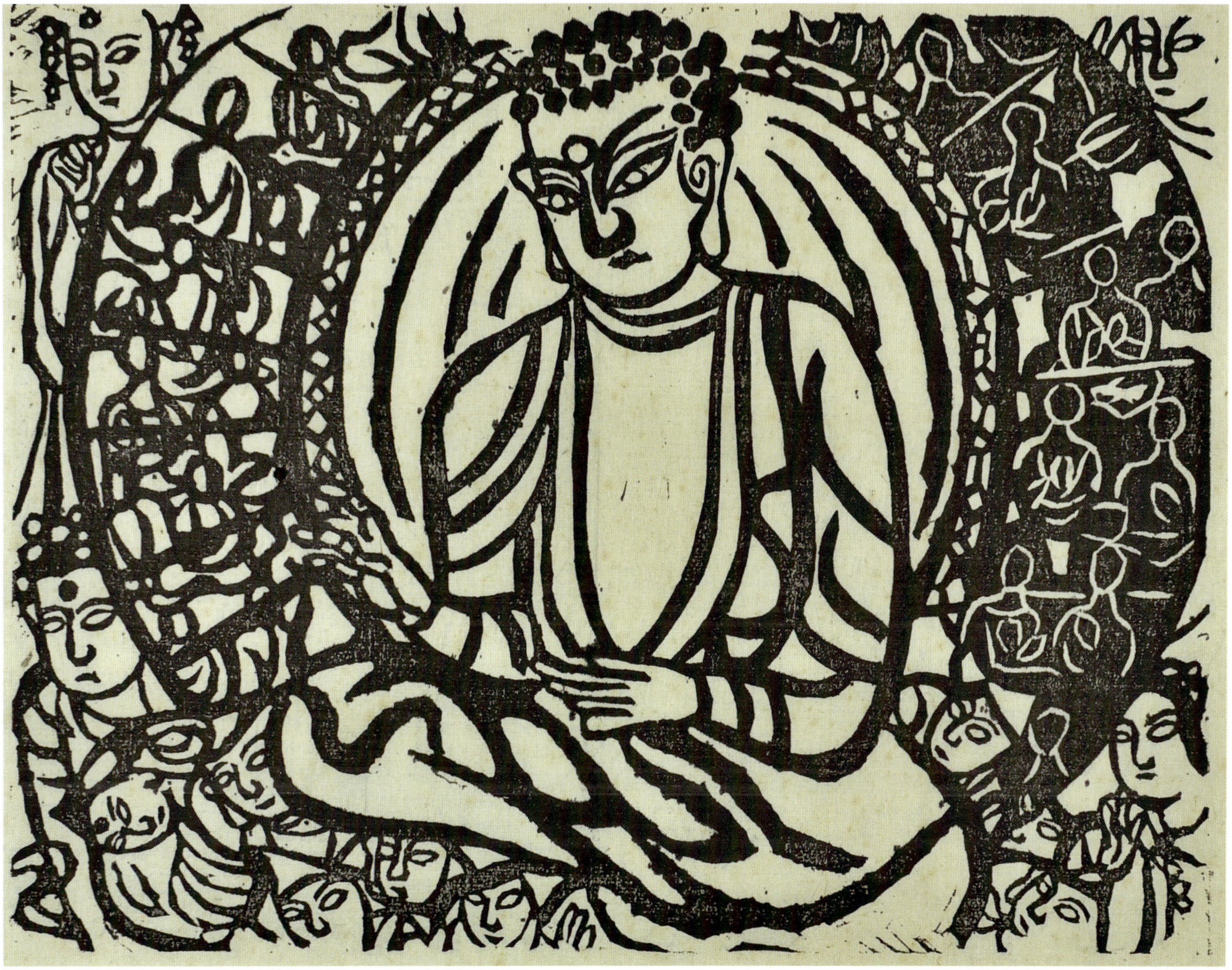

Munakata Shiko 1903-1975, Japanese, *Dainichi Nyorai,* nd, woodblock print

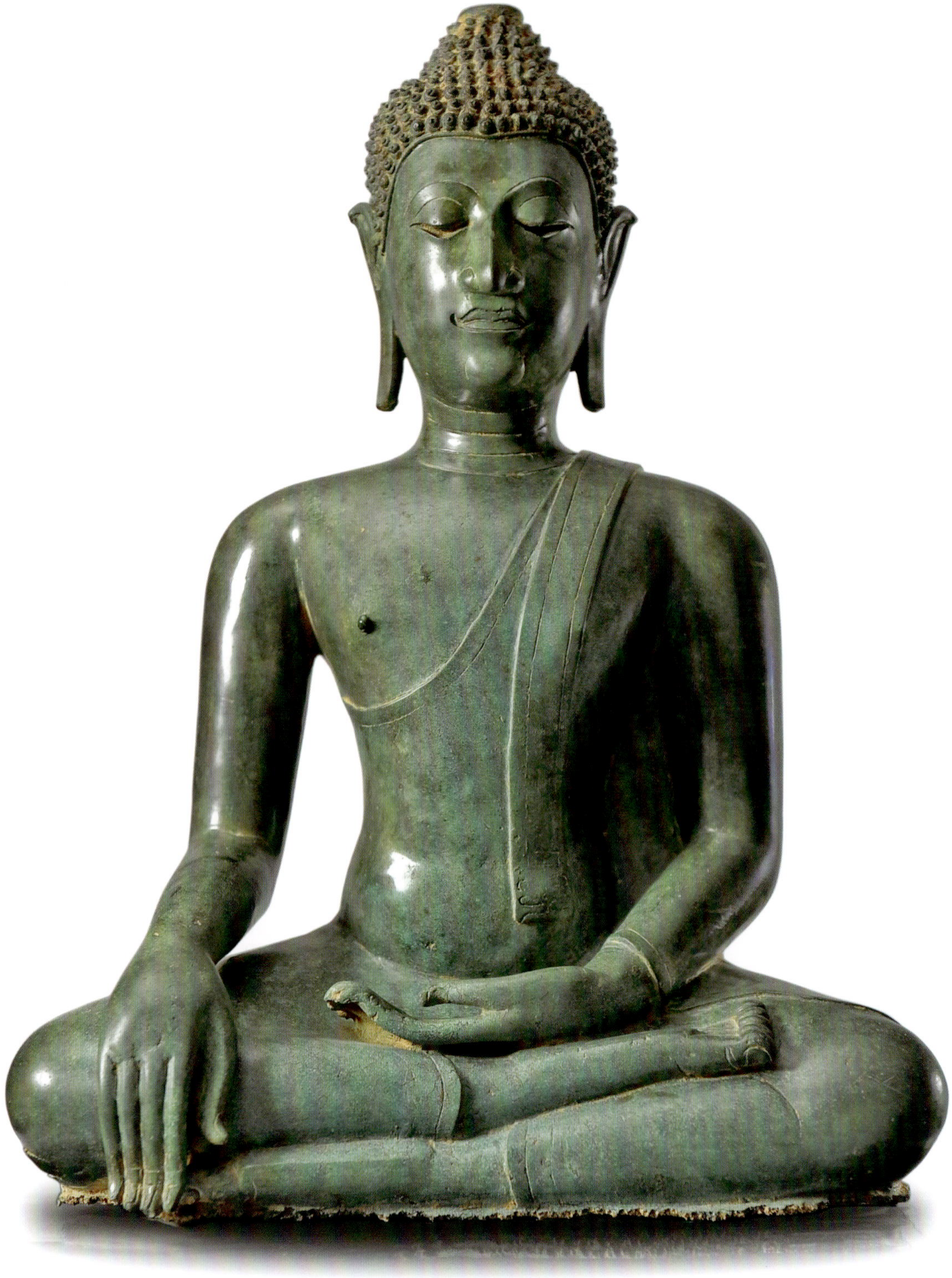

Unknown Artist Cambodian, *Seated Buddha Figure*, 13th century, leaded bronze

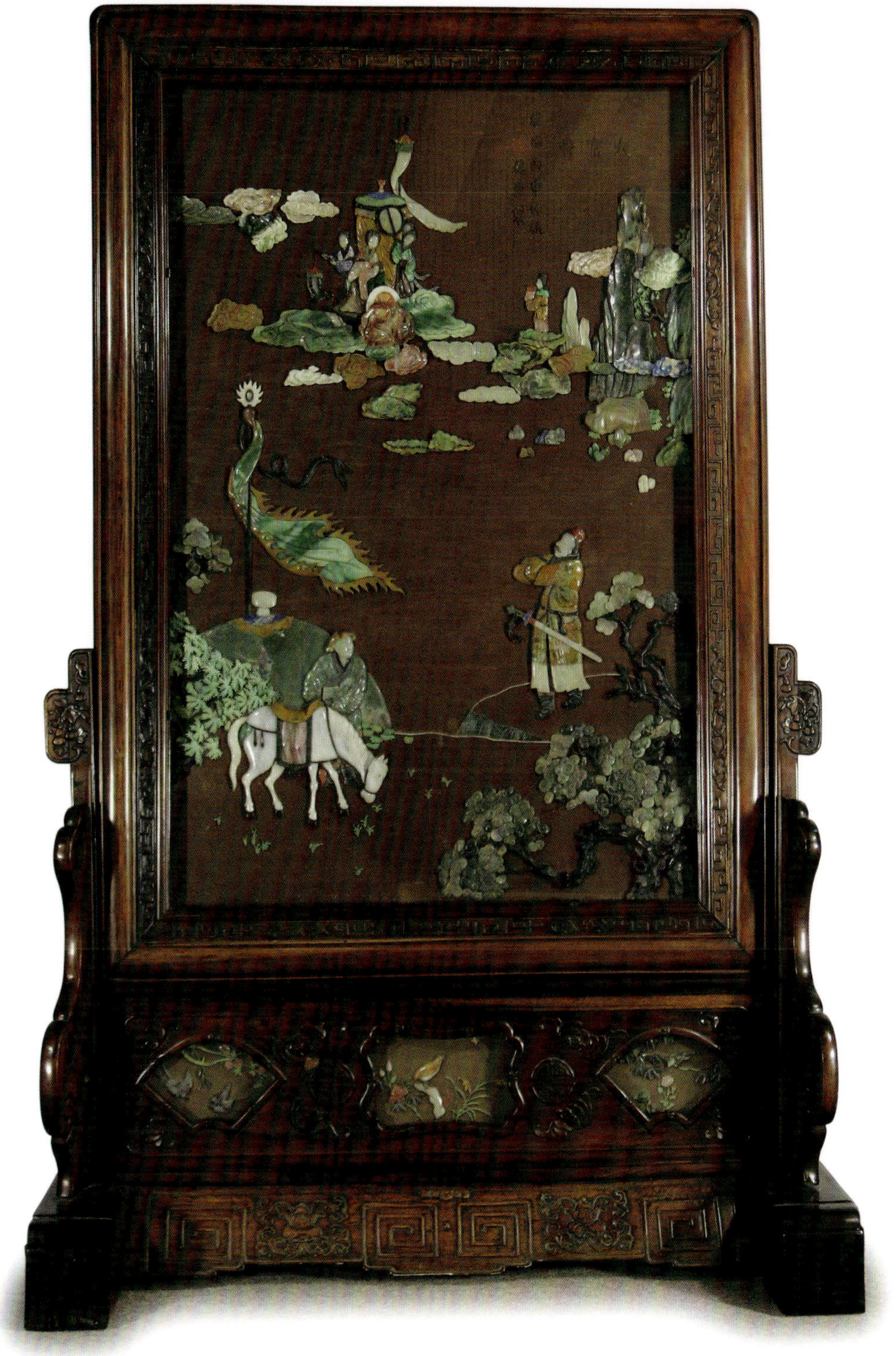

Unknown Artist Chinese, Twelve-Fold Screen with Side Panels, one side panel, (scenes from the Chinese novel – The Dream of the Red Chamber) late 18th /early 19th century, carved lacquer with inlay of jade and other precious stone

Exhibitions Lists

All dimensions are in centimetres with height followed by width by depth (where applicable).
All works are in the collection of the Art Gallery of Greater Victoria except where noted in *Colin Graham and West Coast Modernism* list.
* Indicates work is illustrated.

The Birth of the Collection

FINE ART

Barlach, Ernst Ludwig
1870-1938 German
Untitled (Der Tote Tag) 1912
lithograph on cream coloured wove paper
image: 27.5 x 36.4
Women's Committee Cultural Fund
1968.081.001

Bartolozzi, Francesco
1727-1815 British
*Joseph and Christ Child** nd
engraving on laid paper
40.8 x 29.0 plate
Dr. Gustav and Marie Schilder Collection
1964.206.001

Baxter, Iain
b. 1936 Canadian
*Still Life** 1965
plastic moulded relief
81 x 95.5 x 5
Gift of Colin Graham
1980.002.002

Bloore, Ronald L.
b. 1925 Canadian
Untitled-abstract circles 1960
ink on wove paper, wove
51.7 x 66.1
Anonymous Gift
1966.057.001

Bobak, Bruno
b. 1923 Canadian
Porcupine nd
conte on arches paper
47.4 x 62.7
Gift of Harold Mortimer Lamb
1964.151.000

Boudin, Eugene Louis
1824-1898 French
The Harbour of Fécamp nd
oil on panel
24.4 x 26.0 t
Gift of Harold Mortimer Lamb
1961.036.001

Brangwyn, Frank, Sir
1867-1956 British
Windmills, Bruges 1906
etching on cream laid Japan paper
image: 48.1 x 52.9
Gift of Mr. Guy Roberts, Sproat Lake
1960.021.001

Braque, Georges
1882-1963 French
Untitled: – Large White Bird
lithograph paper, laid
38.1 x 55.5
Gift of the French Government
1962.253.001

Breeze, Claude
b. 1938 Canadian
Island #5 after Rain 1968
acrylic on canvas
126.0 x 76.5
Elizabeth Marshall Bequest
1970.031.001

Bush, Jack
1909-1977 Canadian
Untitled 1965
lithograph on white wove paper
66.1 x 52.1
Women's Committee Cultural Fund
1971.108.001

Callot, Jacques
1592-1635 French
Les Miséres et les Malheurs de la Guerre (plate #11) nd
etching on ivory coloured laid paper
8.3 x 18.5
Gift of Col. N.J.W. Smith
1964.267.011

Carr, Emily
1871-1945 Canadian
*Dancing Tree** c.1938
oil on paper
61.1 x 91.6
Gift of the Hon. Mark Kearley in memory of Mabel Florence Kearley
1968.212.001

Van Ceulen, Cornelis Janssens
1593-1664 Dutch
*Portrait of a Lady in Black**
1658
oil on canvas
107.8 x 82.2
Gift of Capt. and Mrs. Massy Goolden
1962.027.001

Cézanne, Paul
1839-1906 French
*Artist's House at Anvers** nd
soft ground etching on white wove paper
image: 13.5 x 11.2
Women's Committee Cultural Fund
1968.068.001

Chambers, Jack
1931-1978 Canadian
Diego Drawing 1971
serigraph on reddish brown paper
image: 51.4 x 38.0
Anonymous Gift
1971.096.001

Daumier, Honoré
1808-1879 French
Epouvantée de l'Heritage 1871
lithograph on wove cream paper
image: 23.1 x 18.2
Fred & Isabel Pollard Collection
1964.018.001

Davis, Stuart
1894-1964 American
Untitled 1964
serigraph on white wove paper
image: 28.1 x 35.9
Fred & Isabel Pollard Collection
1968.190.001

Des Clayes, Berthe
1877-1968 Canadian
Village Road in Winter nd
pastel on paper
18.5 x 23.5
Henry Maurice Vaughan Weller Estate
1970.096.001

Duchamp, Marcel
1887-1968 French
*Coffee Mill**
(from *Du Cubisme*) nd
restrike etching on white wove paper
image: 23.1 x 14.0
Women's Committee Cultural Fund
1969.127.001

Durer, Albrecht
1471-1528 German
Agony in the Garden 1515
etching on cream coloured laid paper
22.6 x 15.9
Dr. Gustav and Marie Schilder Collection
1964.186.001

*Flight into Egypt** c.1504
woodcut on laid paper
30.0 x 21.2
Anonymous Gift
1965.138.001

Edell, Nancy
1942-2005 Canadian
Land Form 1968
etching, aquatint, softground with ink drawing on wove paper
60.5 x 46.0
Women's Committee Cultural Fund
1968.074.001

Feininger, Lyonel
1871-1956
German; American
*Storm** 1941
ink, watercolour on wove paper
27.9 x 38.4
Gift of Mark Tobey
1957.051.001

Goltzius, Hendrik
1515-1616 Dutch
The Betrayal of Christ 1598
engraving on ivory coloured laid paper
19.7 x 13.0
Dr. Gustav and Marie Schilder Collection
1968.038.001

Gow, Mary L.
1851-1929 British
*The Young Scholar** 1897
watercolour on wove paper
51.7 x 39.4
Gift of Mrs. Cyril Richards
1972.009.001

Goya, Francisco
1746-1828 Spanish
Disparate General nd
etching; aquatint on laid paper
image: 24.5 x 35.5
Myfanwy Pavelic Purchase Fund
1968.218.001

Greuze, Jean Baptiste
1725-1805 French
*Head of a Girl** c.1778
red chalk on laid paper
40.6 cm x 32.1
Mr. Rudolf Gutmann
1958.074.001

Hamilton, Mary Riter
1873-1954 Canadian
Mission of Charity nd
oil on canvas
59.7 x 48.5 sight
Gift of Rev. and Mrs. W.G. Wilson
1956.009.001

Harvey, Donald
b. 1930 Canadian
*Hot Spell** 1969
serigraph on paper
101.5 x 65.5
Gift of the Artist
1969.096.001

Heckel, Erich
1883-1970 German
Madehenkopf 1913
woodcut on cream coloured wove paper
image: 25.7 x 17.0
Library Purchase through the Mrs. Will Spencer Fund
1964.139.001

Hembroff-Schleicher, Edythe
1906-1994 Canadian
*Blue Girl in Boat** 1968
oil on board
71.2 x 61.0
Women's Committee Cultural Fund
1971.094.001

Holgate, Edwin
1892-1977 Canadian
The Lumberjack nd
woodcut on cream coloured laid paper
image: 12.4 x 9.8
Gift of Mr. Arthur Gresham
1964.029.001

Hughes, Edward John
1913-2007 Canadian
Trees on Savary Island 1936
drypoint on buff coloured wove paper
image: 20.0 x 25.0
Gift of Harold Mortimer Lamb
1957.006.001

Kandinsky, Wassily
1866-1944 Russian
*Stars** 1938
lithograph on ivory coloured wove paper
35.5 x 26.5 support
Gift of the Hon. Mark Kearley
1968.028.001

Kenojuak
c.1927-1990
Canadian; Inuit
Rabbit Eating Seaweed 1958
skin stencil on cream coloured wove Japan paper
image: 17.0 x 54.3
Gift of Mrs. P.S. Widdup
1964.159.001

Kiyooka, Roy
1926-1994 Canadian
*Menat** 1963
acrylic on canvas
106.0 x 106.0
Elizabeth Marshall Bequest
1970.041.001

Kollwitz, Käthe
1867-1945 German
*Sharpening the Scythe** 1921
etching on cream colour wove paper
image: 29.7 x 30.0
Women's Committee Cultural Fund
1964.044.001

Lievens, Jan
1607-1674 Dutch
St. Jerome in Penitence c.1631
etching; engraving on paper
image: 25.0 x 19.6
Dr. Gustav and Marie Schilder Collection
1968.162.001

Lismer, Arthur
1885-1969 Canadian
*Rock & Sumac, Georgian Bay** 1948
oil on canvas on board
40.7 x 50.8
Gift of the Artist
1957.028.001

Macdonald, Jock
1897-1960 Canadian
*Forms Evolved** 1951
watercolour, scraffito on wove paper
29.7 x 29.4
Anonymous Gift
1964.148.001

MacLeod, Pegi Nicol
1904-1949 Canadian
*Jane Asleep** 1944
watercolour on paper
48.0 x 57.6
Gift of Mrs. F. Maud Brown
1955.009.001

Maris, Matthijs
1839-1917 Dutch
*The Flower Arrangement** 1873
oil on canvas
60.0 x 37.2 sight
J.P.E. Klaverwyden Bequest
1967.068.001

Mason, Mary
1842-1924 English
The Sleeper nd
watercolour on paper
63.9 x 94.6
Gift of Mrs. P.D. Maunsell
1964.091.001

Massari, Lucio, attributed to
1569-1633 Italian
Noli me Tangere nd
brown ink, wash, black chalk, white highlights on laid paper
18.6 x 24.4
Bequest of Arthur S. Wyllie
1972.253.001

Milne, David Brown
1882-1953 Canadian
*Landscape (Boston Corners)** 1920
graphite, watercolour on paper
39.7 x 56.3
Gift of Mrs. F. Maud Brown
1955.017.001

Moore, Henry
1898-1986 English
*Pandora & the Imprisoned Statues** 1950
lithograph on wove paper
image: 31.5 x 21.
Myfanwy Pavelic Purchase Fund
1966.010.001
Reproduced by permission of the Henry Moore Foundation

Morris, Kathleen M.
1893-1986 Canadian
*Kiosk** nd
oil on board
25.7 x 35.4
Gift of Mrs. F. Maud Brown
1955.018.001

Morris, Michael
b. 1942 Canadian
*Screen Test** 1967
serigraph on paper
38.2 x 50.8
Gift of Simon Fraser University
1968.104.001

Napatchie Pootoogook
1938-2002 Canadian; Inuit
Bird Spirits 1960
stonecut on ivory coloured wove Japan paper
image: 41.7 x 51.0
Gift of Mrs. P.S. Widdup
1964.158.001

Onley, Toni
1928-2004 Canadian
Polar #30 1962
oil, collage on canvas
86.6 x 107.1
Elizabeth Marshall Bequest
1970.039.001

Ostade, Adriaen Van
1610-1684 Dutch
Three Men and a Jug nd
etching; engraving on buff laid paper
10.2 x 8.9
Dr. Gustav and Marie Schilder Collection
1968.030.001

Palmer, Samuel
1805-1881 British
Snowdon from Mount Siabod nd
charcoal, watercolour on paper
38.0 x 47.6
Gift of Mr. & Mrs. A. S. Wyllie
1963.101.001

Pavelic, Myfanwy
1916-2007 Canadian
Bob's Studio 1972
acrylic on canvas
106.9 x 76.2
Women's Committee Cultural Fund
1972.016.001

Pennell, Joseph
1860-1926 American
The "L" and Trinity Building 1911
etching on paper
39.3 x 26.0
Gift of Mr. Irving Dwinnell
1958.078.001

Rauschenberg, Robert
1925-2008 American
Untitled: figures; letters nd
transfer watercolour, pencil, gouache on paper
57.5 x 75.7
Gift of Mr. Syd Hoare
1968.232.001

Redon, Odilon
1840-1916 French
*Satan, From the Temptation of St. Anthony** nd
lithograph on toned laid paper
image: 31.3 x 25.4
Women's Committee Cultural Fund
1969.067.001

Rembrandt Van Rijn
1606-1669 Dutch
Adoration of the Shepherds 1654
etching on cream coloured laid paper
image: 10.5 x 12.8
Gift of Mrs. Isabel Lindsay
1968.062.001

*Descent from the Cross** 1633
etching on cream coloured laid paper
image: 52.1 x 40.6
Dr. Gustav and Marie Schilder Collection
1968.160.001

Renoir, Pierre Auguste
1841-1919 French
*Femme Nue Couchée** nd
restrike drypoint on cream coloured wove paper
plate: 12.8 x 19.9
Florence Scott Memorial Fund
1960.055.001

Rodin, Auguste
1840-1917 French
Mercury Emerging from a Cloud (Study for the Gates of Hell) nd
bronze
35.5 x 37.5 x 18.5
Anonymous Gift
1964.075.001

Rouault, Georges
1871-1958 French
Des Angles et du Bec 1926
aquatint on paper
image: 57.9 x 44.5
Women's Committee Cultural Fund
1962.001.001

Ruskin, John
1819-1900 English
Cockle Clams nd
watercolour, pencil on paper
image: 8.5 x 9.0
Gift of Mr. Arthur W. Wyllie
1970.003.001

Schmitt-Rottluff, Karl
1884-1976 German
Figure Reading "Brust" 1920
woodcut on cream coloured wove paper
image: 28.1 x 19.7
Anonymous Gift
1965.018.001

Shadbolt, Jack
1909-1998 Canadian
New Snow from My Window 1954
watercolour on paper
55.8 x 75.5
Women's Committee Cultural Fund and the Artist
1954.008.001

Sickert, Walter Richard
1860-1942 English
*L'Eglise du Poulet, Dieppe** c.1920
oil on canvas
45.5 x 54.2
Gift of Mrs. D Braide & Mrs. J.C. Hibbard in honour of the 100th Anniversary of their family settling in Victoria
1960.033.001

Siebner, Herbert
1925-2003 Canadian
*Houseboats, Canal, West Berlin** 1954
linocut on Gilbert Bond paper
image: 32.8 x 47.2
Gift of the Artist
1973.263.001

Tanabe, Takao
b. 1926 Canadian
Twilight 1960
sumi ink on paper
30.0 x 60.0 support
Women's Committee Cultural Fund
1971.088.001

Tobey, Mark
1890-1976 American
Christmas Night 1943
tempera on paper
37.6 x 51.5
Gift of Dr. Pierre R. Dow in Memory of Berthe Pouncy Jacobson
1980.093.006

Landscape 1957
tempera, gouache on paper
21.5 x 30.4
Women's Committee Cultural Fund
1957.027.001

*Woman in Hat** 1965
tempera on paper
32.9 x 20.5
Miss Margaret Smith, Tacoma
1970.024.001

Town, Harold
1924-1990 Canadian
*Cave** 1957
ink on hardboard
23.7 x 22.6
Canada Council Purchase Fund
1969.059.001

Traquair, Phoebe Anna
1852-1936 Irish
Paradise c.1907
watercolour, graphite, gouache on wove paper
image: 8.3 x 10.0
Anonymous Gift
1965.078.001

*The Saint's Hour** nd
watercolour, pencil on wove paper
12.0 x 19.7
Anonymous Gift
1965.081.001

Turner, Joseph Mallord William
1775-1851 British
The Bridge in Middle Distance 1808
etching, mezzotint on laid paper
26.5 x 39.8
1969.074.001

Unknown Artist
Italian? 18th C
*Pages from a Sketchbook** nd
sanguine crayon on laid paper
15.0 x 10.0
J. P. E. Klaverwyden Bequest
1967.093.001-.049

Varley, Frederick
1881-1969 Canadian
*Winter, Lynn Valley, B.C.** 1939
oil on card
30.3 x 35.7
Gift of Mrs. Vera Mortimer Lamb in memory of H. Mortimer-Lamb
1972.217.001
© Varley Art Gallery, Town of Markham

Vilallonga, Jesus Carlos de
b. 1927 Canadian
The Blind Man 1963
tempera on board
60.9 x 40.2
Gift of Dr. & Mrs. Max Stern, Dominion Gallery, Montreal
1963.169.001

Vlaminck, Maurice
1876-1958 French
House on a Hillside nd
woodcut on buff laid paper
image: 16.2 x 24.4
Women's Committee Cultural Fund
1968.153.001

Vliet, Jan Joris Van Der
c.1610-L.1635 Dutch
Beggar 1632
etching on ivory coloured laid paper
9.4 x 6.7
Dr. Gustav and Marie Schilder Collection
1962.240.002

Beggar 1632
etching on ivory coloured laid paper
9.4 x 6.8
Dr. Gustav and Marie Schilder Collection
1962.240.001

Beggar 1632
etching on ivory coloured laid paper
9.5 x 6.7
Dr. Gustav and Marie Schilder Collection
1962.240.003

Beggar 1632
etching on ivory coloured laid paper
9.2 x 6.2
Dr. Gustav and Marie Schilder Collection
1962.240.004

Vostre, Simon
1521- ? French
Page from a book with an Illuminated Illustration Showing the Delphic Sybil
1520
ink, tempera on parchment
plate: 14.0 x 9.1
Koerner Foundation Fund
1964.203.001

Watson, Homer
1855-1936 Canadian
*The Ploughman** nd
oil on card
16.6 x 23.5
Gift of Harold Mortimer Lamb
1957.041.000

Whistler, James MacNeill
1834-1903 American
*Vauxhall Bridge** 1861
etching on paper
19.8 x 23.7
Gift of Harold Mortimer Lamb
1963.154.001

Wise, Jack
1928-1996 Canadian
Cosmic Event 1966?
gouache, tempera on wove paper
19.8 x 28.5
Women's Committee Cultural Fund
1966.066.001

DECORATIVE ARTS

Bion, Nicolas French
Butterfield Pocket Sundial & Compass
17th – 18th C (1685-1715)
silver; glass; brass
7.0 x 6.1 x 1.9
Gift of Lady Stuart Taylor
1962.292.001

Castelli?; Venice? Italian
Drug Jar (Albarello)
c.1525
tin-glazed earthenware with enamel decoration
20.7 x 12.5 diameter
Given by friends in memory of Mr. J.J. Mero
1974.137.001

Delft Dutch
Posset Pot
c.1700
tin glazed earthenware
18.5 x 20 x 16.3
From the collection of J.E. Horvath with Financial Assistance from B.C. Lotteries and Mrs. Margaret B. McElney.
1980.014.009 a,b

Derby Factory English
Figure called King Lear
c.1760
soft-paste porcelain; glaze; enamel decoration
25.8 x 9.5
Ann & Joseph Pearson Collection
1979.229.001

Jan Grove b. 1930 and Helga Grove b. 1927 Canadian
Shallow Bowl with Radiating Design*
20th C
stoneware; glaze; enamel decoration
5.8 x 23.8 dia
Victoria Pottery Club Fund
1967.195.001

Madoura Pottery Studio Spanish
Plate Designed by Pablo Picasso*
20th C
earthenware; glaze; enamel decoration
23.0 dia
Gift of Mr. Joseph Egoyan
1964.052.001

Mel Munsen
b.1946 Canadian
Double Necked Glass Bottle or Vase
1972
glass; metallic lustre
16.5 x 13.6
Women's Committee Cultural Fund
1972.029.001

Unknown Maker English
Wine Glass
mid 18th C
glass; double white enamel twist
18.9 x 7.2 x 7.2
Gift of Thomas Watson
1967.110.001

Unknown Egyptian
Egyptian Amulet Necklace
Pre Common Era
faience; earthenware spacers; modern fibre stringing
106.0 circumference
Gift of Miss Kathleen Agnew
1961.002.001

Unknown Maker French
Miniature Cabinet early 19th C
tin-glazed earthenware; enamel decoration; gold
36 x 23 x 10.5
Gift of Princess Chikhmatoff
1963.106.001

Unknown Maker
Roman or Phoenician
Perfume or Unguent Bottle
1st -2nd C
glass
5.2 x 3.5
Gift of Miss Ethel Bruce
1960.032.001

Unknown Maker
Roman or Phoenician
Perfume or Unguent Bottle
1st -2nd C
glass
14.0 x 3.0
Gift of Miss Ethel Bruce
1960.031.001

Unknown Maker
Roman or Phoenician
Perfume or Unguent Bottle
1st -2nd C
glass
13.0 x 7.2
Gift of Miss Ethel Bruce
1960.030.001

Unknown Maker Mexican
Colima-Style Dog Vessel
100 BC – 400 AD
earthenware; slip
24.0 x 37.0
Anonymous Purchase Fund
1969.062.001

Unknown Maker
American; Amerindian; Pueblo
Amerindian Pot early 20th C
earthenware; mineral-based paint or slip
10.0 x 14.0
Women's Committee Cultural Fund
1954.014.003

Unknown Maker Peruvian
Male Figure Jug
19th century
earthenware; glaze
21.0 x 12.0
Gift of Mrs. A.H. Gordon
1952.009.001

Unknown Maker
Necklace of Moulded Enamel
late 19th – 20th C
enamel, moulded and glued
28.0 x 20.0 x 4.0
Gift of Mrs. Thos. G. Knox
1962.243.001

Unknown Maker
Russian; Balkan
Portable Icon Depicting Christ, the Virgin, John the Baptist, Archangel Michael & Saints
19th C
brass; enamel
6.4 x 17.1
Fred & Isabel Pollard Collection
1961.023.001

Unknown Maker
Bohemian or English
Amber Glass Vase
early - mid 19th C
glass; cased or flash-glass method with engraving
17.7 x 9.0
Gift of Mrs. P.S. Widdup
1962.075.001

Unknown Maker Anglo-Irish
Creamer or Jug c.1830
cut lead glass
12.7 x 18.7 x 11.1
Gift of Mrs. C.W. Graham
1962.195.001

Unknown Maker
Spanish (Valencia)
Fan with Painted Scenes of Figures in Forest
late 19th – 20th C
ivory; woven fabric; metal; shell; paint
26.7 x 45.0
Mrs. J.H. McElney Fund
1962.041.001

Unknown Maker
Continental
Diadem Comb with Inset Cameos
late 18th – early 19th C?
shell; gold; silver?
15.1 x 17.5 x 5.3
Given by Friends in memory of Princess Jennie Chikhmatoff
1971.055.001

Unknown Maker Greek
Krater or Wine Cup
5th C BCE ?
earthenware; slip decoration
10.0 x 24.8
Anonymous Gift
1965.003.001

Unknown Maker Persian
Gurgan Vase with Iridescent Blue Glaze
12th – 13th C
earthenware; glaze
23.5 x 14.6
Fred & Isabel Pollard Collection
1969.097.001

Welder, Sam. English
Caster*
1720-21
Britannia (standard) silver
17.0 x 6.7
Fred & Isabel Pollard Collection
1962.093.001 a,b

Worcester English
Dish with Imari/Kakiemon-Style Decoration*
c.1775
soft paste/steatite porcelain; enamel decoration; gold
4.9 x 29.0
Fred and Isabel Pollard Collection
1962.107.001

Unknown Maker Continental
Silk Shawl with Gold Embroidery Design and Tassels
late 19th – early 20th C
silk; metallic thread; vegetable and/or aniline dyes
190.0 x 160.0
Gift of Mrs. T. A. Walters
1968.258.00

Colin Graham and West Coast Modernism

Bates, Maxwell
1906-1980 Canadian
Emily Carr Painting a Landscape 1964-1965
watercolour on paper
35.6 x 45.7
Private Collection, Victoria

*Kindergarten** 1965
oil on canvas
91.2 x 121.8
Art Gallery of Greater Victoria, Purchased with funds from the Mortimer-Lamb Bequest, Women's Committee and Private Donors
1982.007.001

*Beautiful B.C.** 1966
Oil on canvas
93.0 x 124.0
Collection of the Vancouver Art Gallery, Siwash Auction Funds
Photo: Vancouver Art Gallery

Cocktail Party 1977
Oil on canvas
106.5 x 91.3
Collection of the Vancouver Art Gallery, Vancouver Art Gallery Acquisition Fund

Binning, B.C.
1909-1976 Canadian
Ships at Quiet Anchor 1948
Oil and graphite on hardboard
128.5 x 68
Collection of the Vancouver Art Gallery, Gift of the Vancouver Art Gallery Women's Auxillary

*Convoy Under Way** 1948
oil on board
79.5 x 109.0 sight
Art Gallery of Greater Victoria, Gift of Mrs. B.C. Binning
1985.042.001

Ship Chandlery c.1953
oil, graphite on card
75.8 x 51.0
Art Gallery of Greater Victoria, Gift of Mrs. B.C. Binning
1983.075.001

Triptych for Aesthetic Idolatry 1953
oil on burlap, board
48.9 x 68.5 x 5.6
Art Gallery of Greater Victoria, Gift of Mrs. B.C. Binning
1983.075.002

*View of Fisherman's Cove** 1944
ink on paper
49.8 x 61.0
Art Gallery of Greater Victoria, Gift of the Estate of Jessie Binning
2008.033.001

*Boat Rental** nd
graphite on paper
30.3 x 45.4 cm
Collection of the Morris and Helen Belkin Art Gallery, University of British Columbia. Gift of the estate of Jessie Binning, 2008
BG3054
Photo: Howard Ursuliak, Vancouver

Carr, Emily
1871-1945 Canadian
Forest Interior, 1932
Oil on canvas
110.0 x 80.0
Collection of the Morris and Helen Belkin Art Gallery
Gift of Associate Prof. Emeritus John A. McDonald, 1988 (BG117)

Deep Woods 1936
oil on paper
89.6 x 59.6
Art Gallery of Greater Victoria, Gift of Flora Hamilton Burns and Patricia Keir in memory of their parents, Mr and Mrs Gavin Hamilton Burns
1994.055.005

*Light Swooping Through** 1938-39
oil on canvas
111.0 x 68.5
Art Gallery of Greater Victoria, Gift of the Hon. Mark Kearley
1964.229.001

*Odds and Ends** 1939
oil on canvas
67.4 x 109.5
Formerly in the collection of the Greater Victoria Public Library. Transferred to the Art Gallery of Greater Victoria.
1998.001.001

*Happiness** 1939
Oil on paper
84.8 x 54 cm
The Maltwood Museum, Gift of Nikolai and Myfanwy Pavelic
Photo: Courtesy of the Maltwood Museum.

Ciccimarra, Richard
1924-1973 Canadian
*Laughing Woman** 1956
chalk, charcoal, wash, tempera, varnish on ochre coloured wove paper
61.3 x 45.8 support
Art Gallery of Greater Victoria, Women's Committee Cultural Fund
1962.030.001

Untitled (3 Figures) c. 1956-1958
gouache on paper
61.0 x 43.2
Private Collection, Vancouver, BC

Descent c. 1966-1968
oil on masonite
58.8 x 121.9
Private Collection, Vancouver, BC

Woman with Hummingbird 1956-1957
gouache and vanish on board
45.0 x 60.0
Private Collection, Victoria, BC

*Woman with Oranges** 1956-1957
Gouache and varnish on board
60.0 x 45.0
Private Collection, Victoria, BC
Photo: Bob Matheson, Victoria

Regretted Evening 1961
Goauche and vanish on board
54.6 x 61.0
Private Collection, Victoria, BC

Cotton, Peter
1918-1978 Canadian
*Spring-back dining chair** 1951
plywood, steel rod
37.0 x 50.0 x 75.0
Collection Allan Collier
Photo: Bob Matheson, Victoria

*Stool with abstract embroidery (from Delhaye Series)** c. 1953, embroidery: 1954
angle iron, plywood, solid wood, embroidery
30.0 x 30.0 x 34.0
Collection Allan Collier
Photo: Bob Matheson, Victoria

A3MKII armchair 1953
plywood, steel rod, upholstery
69 x 56 x 76.5
Collection Allan Collier

Glass-topped coffee table design: 1950; manufactured: 1951
steel rod, angle iron, glass
95.0 x 49.0 x 44.0
Collection Allan Collier

Lowback armchair 1953
angle iron, steel rod, upholstery
72.0 x 80.0 x 75.0
Collection Allan Collier

Di Castri, John
1924-2005 Canadian
*Elevation drawing of Colin and Sylvia Graham House** c. 1953
watercolour on card
43.4 x 90.6
Collection of Colin and Sylvia Graham

(Model for the) *Colin and Sylvia Graham House* 1953
(converted barn into modern home - destroyed)
Model created by Jordan Beggs, Victoria, 2009

De Castro, Robert
1923-1986 Canadian
Untitled (Black Wood Shape with Six Holes Along Bottom) nd
wood; paint
26.5 x 28.5 x 10.0
Art Gallery of Greater Victoria, Collection of Robin and Sylvia Skelton
1998.035.004

Untitled (Black Wood Shape with Six Holes along Mid Line) nd
wood; paint
21.0 x 40.0 x 10.5
Art Gallery of Greater Victoria, Collection of Robin and Sylvia Skelton
1998.035.005

*Untitled (Ten Wood Sections with Holes)** nd
wood; paint
66.0 x 70.0 x 10.0
Art Gallery of Greater Victoria, Women's Committee Cultural Fund
1983.005.001

*Bingo** nd
Wood
71.1 x 41.9 x 27.9
Anne Mayhew Collection
Photo: Bob Matheson, Victoria

Hughes, Edward John
1913-2007 Canadian
Coastal Steamer, Sidney 1948
Pencil on paper
24.8 x 35.6
A. William Everett Family

Edge of the Wood, Gabriola Island 1953
Oil on canvas
79.0 x 96.9
Collection of the Vancouver Art Gallery, Gift of J. Ron Longstaffe

*Bastion, Nanaimo** 1954
Oil on canvas
88.9 x 71.1
Collection of Eric and Shirley Charman
Photo: Bob Matheson, Victoria

*Steamer at the Old Wharf, Nanaimo** 1958
oil on canvas
61.0 x 94.0 support, sight: 59.7 x 93.2
Art Gallery of Greater Victoria, Gift of Mary Alice Segal, Miles Keenleyside, Anne Katherine McCullum and Sara Lynn Jackson
1992.056.001

Nanaimo Harbour nd
watercolour on paper
44.5 x 59.7
Courtesty of Winchester Galleries, Victoria, BC

Bates, Pat Martin
b. 1927 Canadian
*Silent Round for the Gravel Gardens of the Mind** 1968
perforated pressing with paint, plexi, and collage
118.0 x 122.6 x 10.8
Artist's Collection
Photo: Bob Matheson, Victoria

Mandorlas of the Veils that Lift 1969
drawing with white, black and silver inks on handmade Arches paper with grommets in a lightbox
76.3 x 107.0 cm
Artist's Collection

Black Star mandorla (for Rumi in an Arctic Night) c. 1966
drawing with white and black inks, paint, and grommets
77.2 x 56.0
Artist's Collection
Photo: Bob Matheson, Victoria

*Silent Mandala for Gravel Star Garden** 1968
silver foil, grommets, ink, silver threads, silver leaf, perforated relief and bas-relief pressing with chine collé in screenprinted lightbox
118.3 x 125.7 x 11.8
Artist's Collection

*Flight Window of the Alchemy Letter from the Sun to the Moon** 1968
lacquer paint silkscreen on plexiglas
42.0 x 42.0 x 29.5
Artist's Collection
Photo: Bob Matheson, Victoria

*Letter Through the Window from the Sun to the Moon** 1967
lacquer paint silkscreen on plexiglas
49.0 x 67.1 x 20.5
Artist's Collection
Photo: Bob Matheson, Victoria

Mayhew, Elza
1916-2004 Canadian
*Procession** 1960
bronze
38.1 x 38.1 x 109.2
Courtesy of Winchester Galleries, Victoria, BC
Photo: Bob Matheson, Victoria

*Priestess** 1961
bronze
76.2 x 101.6 x 40.0
Courtesy of Winchester Galleries, Victoria, BC
Photo: Bob Matheson, Victoria

*Princess** 1963
aluminum; wood, paint
127.0 x 26.0 x 13.0
Art Gallery of Greater Victoria, Gift of George & Lola Kidd
2008.003.010

*The Supplicant** 1963
bronze
134.6 x 27.9 x 20.3
Private Collection, Victoria, BC

Demeter 1971
aluminum
158.8 x 49.5 x 21.6
Mayhew Family Collection

Persephone 1971
aluminum
158.8 x 50.8 x 25.4
Mayhew Family Collection

Passageway 1976
bronze
55.2 x 30.5 x 17.8
Mayhew Family Collection

Peterson, Margaret
1902-1997 Canadian
*The splitting of Tiamat** nd
watercolour, tempera on Japanese paper
46.2 x 30.5 support
Art Gallery of Greater Victoria, Mrs. C.W. Graham Fund
1962.202.001

*The Zodiac Keepers** nd
egg tempera on gesso on board
64.7 x 95.6 support
Art Gallery of Greater Victoria, Canada Council Funds
1960.038.001

Song of Solomon – our hearts seasonless joy 1959-1962
oil on tempera
48.3 x 38.1
Anne Mayhew Collection
Untitled 1959-1962
egg tempera on board
50 x 66
Anne Mayhew Collection

Untitled nd
egg tempera on board
37 x 48
Anne Mayhew Collection

*Gods Rising from the Abyss** 1961
egg tempera on board
86. 5 x 210.5
Private Collection, Vancouver, BC
Photo: Ted Clarke, image this Photography of Art, Vancouver

Pullan, Selwyn
b. 1922 Canadian
Interior of a John Di Castri designed home, Victoria
c. late 1950s, early 1960s
black and white photograph
53.3 x 45.7
Collection of Bombast Furniture Ltd., Vancouver, BC

Interior of the Shadbolt Home, Burnaby, B.C.
c. late 1950s early 1960s
black and white photograph
53.3 x 45.7
Collection of Bombast Furniture Ltd., Vancouver, BC

Shadbolt, Jack
1909-1998 Canadian
*Winter Pods** 1951
watercolour on paper
67.0 x 93.0 sight
Art Gallery of Greater Victoria, Women's Committee Cultural Fund
1954.016.001

Autumn Tokens 1958
oil on canvas
126 x 141
Collection of the Vancouver Art Gallery, Gift of Dr. John L. Parnell

*Masks & Fetishes** 1966-70
watercolour and ink on paper
76.3 x 101.5
Collection of the Morris and Helen Belkin Art Gallery, University of British Columbia. Gift of Rosalie May Benton, 1997
Photo: Howard Ursuliak, Vancouver

*Adjustable Venus** 1969-70
Watercolour, ink, colour chalk, acrylic and gouache on board
76.0 x 101.2
Collection of the Morris and Helen Belkin Art Gallery, University of British Columbia. Gift of the Faculty Club, UBC, 1973
Photo: Howard Ursuliak, Vancouver

After Fire (Salmon Barbecue) 1956-58
Gouache, watercolour, ink, and casein on paper
56.6 x 77.5
Collection of the Morris and Helen Belkin Art Gallery
Gift of the Faculty Club, University of British Columbia, 1994 (BG705)

Siebner, Herbert
1925-2003 Canadian
*Afternoon, Lake Como** 1953
oil on canvas
120 x 180
Private Collection, Victoria
Photo: Bob Matheson, Victoria

Dream of a Soldier 1956
Oil on panel
40.6 x 46.5
Art Gallery of Greater Victoria, Michael Dane Memorial Collection
1971.077.001

*Crowd Looking for a Friend** 1973
acrylic on canvas
127.0 x 88.9
Collection of Michael and Donna Kanovsky, Victoria, BC

Smith, Gordon
b. 1919 Canadian
*Coast Range** nd
oil on canvas
86.8 x 121.7 support
Art Gallery of Greater Victoria, Leon and Thea Koerner Foundation Funds
1960.040.001

Red Painting 1957
oil on canvas
86 x 166.5
Collection of the Vancouver Art Gallery, Gift of the Vancouver Art Gallery Women's Auxilliary

*Wet Night** 1953
oil on canvas
79.5 x 90
Collection of the Vancouver Art Gallery, T. Eaton Co. Picture Purchase Fund
Photo: Courtesy of Vancouver Art Gallery

The Asian Collection Begins 1951–1973

JAPAN

Baiitsu Yamamoto
1783-1856 Japanese
*Hawk in Snow**
hanging scroll; ink on silk
149.7 x 72.8
Fred and Isabel Pollard Collection
AGGV 1967.143.001

Goshun Matsumura
1752-1811 Japanese
*Two Crows In Sunset**
hanging scroll; ink and colours on silk
137 x 75
Fred and Isabel Pollard Collection
AGGV 1967.144.001

Hanko Okada
1782-1846 Japanese
Sailboat on an Inky River
album leaf mounted as a hanging scroll, ink on paper
30.4 x 42.1
Gift of Mr. and Mrs. R.W. Finlayson
AGGV 1978.266.001

Hiroshi Yoshida
1876-1950 Japanese
Taj Mahal 1932
woodblock print, 35 x 49.5
Fred and Isabel Pollard Collection
AGGV 1968.211.001

Mount Rainie 1939
woodblock print, 35 x 49.5
Fred and Isabel Pollard Collection
AGGV 1968.210.001

Kenzan Ogata
1663-1743 Japanese
Square plate*
Kyoto ware, stoneware with overglaze enamels, side 18 cm
Fred and Isabel Pollard Collection
AGGV 1971.123.001

Mitsuoki Tosa
1617-1691 Japanese
Jindo Fujoso-zu (A Pictorial Description of the Defilement of Human Existence)*
hanging scroll; colour on silk
91.9 x 58.2
Women's Committee Cultural Fund
AGGV 1966.002.000
Provenance: Formerly belonged to the Tokugawa shogun family

Naonobu Kano
1607-1650 Japanese
Triptych of *Three Winter Friends: Bamboo, Pine and Plum*
hanging scrolls, ink and colours on paper
each 90.6 x 46.1
Gift of Mrs. E. Gotz in memory of Percy Gotz
AGGV 1970.104.001 a-c

Sanraku Kano
1559-1635 Japanese
*Peacocks and Pine Tree**
six fold screen, ink and colours on gold leaf
Gift of Uno and Diane Langmann, AGGV 1995.019.001
Screen from the Nijo Castle in Kyoto sold by Bunzo Nakanishi's father of the Yamanaka & Company to the famous American architect Frank Lloyd Wright in the early 20th century). Bunzo rediscovered it at Uno Langmann Limited in Vancouver. It was recently restored by the National Research Institute for Cultural Properties in Tokyo.

Shiko Munakata
1903-1975 Japanese
*Dainichi Nyorai** nd
woodblock print
30.2 x 39.4
Fred and Isabel Pollard Collection. AGGV 1971.028.001

Unknown Artist Japanese
A-ji-kan (Meditational Painting on the letter "A")*
Kamakura Period (14th century)
hanging scroll, colour and cut gold leaf *(kirikane)* on silk
100.8 x 98.5
Fred and Isabel Pollard Collection.
AGGV 65.128

Unknown Artist Japanese
Stem Bowl Early 19th century
stoneware with overglaze enamels
ht. 14.5
Fred and Isabel Pollard Collection
AGGV 1962.116.001
.
Unknown Artist Japanese
Sedan Chair (*norimono*) with Tokugawa family crest*
Edo period, 18th century
wood with amber *nashiji* lacquer ground and gold, green, bronze and brown
ht. 150
Gift of Mr. S. Etienne Sigaut, AGGV 1964.230.001

Unknown Artist Japanese
Buddha Edo period, 18th century
wood, lacquer, gilt
55.2
Irving Dwinnell Bequest
AGGV 67.80

Utamaro Kitagawa
1754–1806 Japanese
*Mother with children** nd
woodblock print
38 x 24.3
Gift of Miss Katherine McEwen, AGGV1950.008.001
This print was one of the first two Asian acquisitions of the Art Gallery of Greater Victoria

Yoshitaka Nakao
1911-? Japanese
Washing Hair nd
woodblock print
79 x 48.5
Fred and Isabel Pollard Collection
AGGV 1967.016.001

CHINA

Dao Ji
1641-1714 Chinese
*Lotus** nd
hanging scroll; ink and colour on paper
119.2 x 35
Gift of Mrs. Marjorie Finlayson
AGGV 1989.040.001

Gong Xian
active 1656-82 Chinese
Landscape nd
album leaf mounted as hanging scroll, ink on paper
22.9 x 52.1
Fred and Isabel Pollard Collection
AGGV 1965.002.001

Huang Daozhou
1585-1646 Chinese
Landscape nd
fan mounted as hanging scroll, ink on gold paper
16 x 50.4
Given Anonymously
AGGV 1965.001.001

Hua Yan
1682-1765 Chinese
Butterfly and Orchids nd
album leaf, ink and colours on paper
32 x 37
Gift of Mrs. Marjorie Finlayson
AGGV 1993.071.001

Cricket and Spider on Grass nd
album leaf, ink and colours on paper, 32 x 37 cm
Gift of Mrs. Marjorie Finlayson
AGGV 1993.071.001

Lan Ying
1585-1657/8 Chinese
Enlightened Conversation amid Cloudy Peaks
fan mounted as hanging scroll, ink and colours on gold paper
16.7 x 55.6
Fred and Isabel Pollard Collection
AGGV 1968.013.001

Lu Zhi
1496-1576 Chinese
Magnolias nd
hanging scroll, ink and colours on paper
143.5 x 57.1
Gift of Mr. and Mrs. R.W. Finlayson
AGGV 1977.120.001

Ma Quan
active late 17th/early 18th century Chinese
Autumn Flowers nd
hanging scroll, ink and colours on silk
90 x 41
Gift of Sydney Hoare, Vancouver
AGGV 1964.071.001

Pan Gongshou
1741-1794 Chinese
River and Sky Clearing After Snows nd
hanging scroll, ink and colours on paper
70.6 x 29.9
Gift of Mrs. Marjorie Finlayson
AGGV 1988.026.002
.

Qi Baishi
1863-1957 Chinese
*Chrysanthemums** nd
hanging scroll, ink and colours on paper
160 x 76.5
Gift of Mr. Brian S. McElney
AGGV 1995.050.012

Unknown Chinese
Funerary Jars Five Dynasties/ Northern Song period, 10th/11th century
glazed stoneware
hts. 27.9 and 25.5
Gift of the Chen King Foh Family
AGGV 1972.077.001 & 1972.062.001

Unknown Chinese
Rectangular Pillow with curved top Northern Song Dynasty*
late 11th/early 12th century
glazed stoneware, Cizhou ware
ht. 15.2 cm
Mrs. Massy Goolden Fund,
AGGV 1963.115.001

Unknown Chinese
Bi disc with human figure and dragon* Late Ming/early Qing period, 17th century
jade
d. 20.0
Mrs. Massy Goolden Purchase Fund
AGGV 1963.111.001

Unknown Artist Chinese
Two Boys (he he er xian) Qing dynasty, 18th century
greenish white jade
7.1
Fred and Isabel Pollard Collection
AGGV 1968.227.001

Unknown Artist Chinese
Bowl in Shape of a Lotus Leaf Qing Dynasty, 18th century
Bamboo
length 16.2
Gift of Mr. Brian S. McElney
AGGV 1975.042.001

Unknown Artist Chinese
Buddha Head Ming dynasty (1368-1644)
limestone
66.0
Given in memory of R.W. Finlayson by the Finlayson family
AGGV 1984.034.001

Unknown Artist Chinese
Twelve-Fold Screen with Side Panels (scenes from the Chinese novel – The Dream of the Red Chamber)*
late 18th /early 19th century
carved lacquer with inlay of jade and other precious stone
Gift of Mrs. K.F. Chen and Family
AGGV 9999.328

Yuan Jiang
active c. 1690-1724 Chinese
Wonderful View of Penglai in Autumn nd
hanging scroll, ink and colours on silk
152.5 x 159
Fred and Isabel Pollard Collection
AGGV 1964.038.001

OTHER ASIAN CULTURES

Phakspa with **Kublai Khan**
Tibetan
Thanka*
17th century
gouache on cotton
82.0 x 50.8
Gift of Mrs. W.W. Ritchie
AGGV 1965.068.001

Unknown Artist Tibetan
Book Covers* 18th century
wood, gilt
28.6 x 74.4
Bequest of Mrs. H.R. Gale
AGGV 1967.219.001 and .002

Unknown Artist Indian
Lunette with Buddha and Followers Gandharan, 2nd/3rd century
grey schist, ht. 24.7 cm
Fred and Isabel Pollard Collection
AGGV 1967.180.001

Unknown Artist Indian
Pilasters Gandharan, 2nd/3rd century
grey schist
ht. 33.1
Fred and Isabel Pollard Collection
AGGV 1967.181.001

Unknown Artist Indian
Vishnu 11th century
sandstone
ht. 57.0
Gift of Mr. Edwin Binney III
AGGV 1971.102.001

Unknown Artist Indian
Brahma with two consorts*
11th century
redstone
Gift of Mr. Edwin Binney III
AGGV 1967.043.001

Unknown Artist Nepalese
Carved Panel with Ganesha
18th century
wood
ht. 33.8
Gift of Colin and Sylvia Graham
AGGV 2008.010.001

Unknown Artist Cambodian
*Seated Buddha Figure**
13th century
leaded bronze
ht. 40.0
Gift of Fraser Finlayson
AGGV 2003.009.002

Unknown Artist Burmese
Praying Monk 19th century
wood, lacquer, gilt, pigment, glass, ht. 33.2
Harold and Vera Mortimer Lamb Bequest
AGGV 1980.054.001

Credits

Curators: Mary Jo Hughes, Michael Morris, and Barry Till

Publication Project Manager: Mary Jo Hughes

Editor: Joan Padgett

Publication Design: Frank Reimer

Printer: Friesens Corp.

Photography: All photos by Stephen Topfer, Art Gallery of Greater Victoria except where noted in Exhibition Lists.

Printed in Canada

The Volunteer Committee Art Gallery of Greater Victoria

British Columbia Arts Council
Supported by the Province of British Columbia

Canada Council for the Arts
Conseil des Arts du Canada

CRD
Making a difference...together

Art Gallery of Greater Victoria
1040 Moss Street
Victoria, British Columbia
Canada V8V 4P1
1.250.384.4101 aggv.bc.ca